The Architectura
of Thomas Hard

Revised Edition

Designed by Lottie Crumbleholme
for Alacrify www.alacrify.co.uk

ISBN 978-0-900341-50-2

Contents

Foreword

Now that architectural scholarship has begun to concern itself strongly with the problems of High Victorian change it would be possible to welcome the publication of Thomas Hardy's architectural notebook with no more than a passing reflection that its author became one of the literary giants of his age. We have here a kind of study-book already familiar in the 18th century but made, in this instance, by a young man confronted with the stylistic and technical innovations of the 1860s. As Dr Beatty observes in his wonderfully exhaustive commentary, this was a challenging time.

Today, its monuments are already begrimed and decayed but through the young Hardy's sketches and memoranda we can feel the excitement of the new things – of 'early French' detailing, of Ruskinian naturalism in ornament and of the possibilities of construction in iron. This would be an instructive document if its author were un-named. That it is from the hand of Thomas Hardy gives it a startling aura. The sensibility to architectural forms and devices shown on some of these pages is a thing which, once acquired, can never be lost. Hardy had it and no study of him as man, novelist and poet can be complete without recognition of this fact.

John Summerson

Preface

This notebook belongs to the F.E. Hardy Memorial Collection, now preserved in the Dorset County Museum, Dorchester. As far as is known, it is the only architectural notebook of Hardy's to have survived. Certainly no other has yet come to light. It is a pocket book of worn and faded dark maroon leather, with marbled edges and end-papers. The drawings are for the most part in pencil, the writing in ink. It relates mainly to the decade 1862–1872, which was a most active one in Victorian architecture and engineering. Sir George Gilbert Scott (1811–1878) was the doyen of the architectural profession; the Great Exhibition in 1851 had changed the attitude of many architects to the use of iron and glass and inaugurated the exhibition habit now familiar all over the world. Mid-Victorian prosperity was reflected architecturally not only in the huge size of some of the mansions constructed but also in their boldness of design, the Battle of the Styles often being resolved by an unhesitating mixture. High Victorian architects such as William Butterfield (1814–1900) and G.E. Street (1824–1881) were at the height of their powers, their work differing principally from their 19th-century predecessors who imitated medieval Gothic, in that they set out to design churches in an original Gothic style of their own time which could never be taken for a copy of the medieval. Up and down the country church restoration was proceeding with unabated enthusiasm, and with what many people considered disastrous results. These feelings eventually crystallised, for example, in the foundation by William Morris (1834–1896) of the Society for the Protection of Ancient Buildings in 1877. For a young architect it was a challenging time.

Many people think of Thomas Hardy first and foremost as a novelist and poet; but in fact he began life as an architect, not abandoning the profession, as a source of income at any rate, until he was in his early thirties. One of the chief interests of this Notebook, as I hope to show, is that it gives us a better idea of the sort of thing he did as an architect, thereby also affording us a clearer insight into the influence his first profession undoubtedly had on his development as a writer.

C.J.P. Beatty

Post script

Since Sir John Summerson wrote the above Foreword in the mid-1960s there has been a great upsurge of interest in everything Victorian. This is in large part due to the foundation of the Victorian Society in 1958 and to its subsequent activities and publications, together with the work of its prime mover, Nikolaus Pevsner. With regard specifically to Thomas Hardy, my own further research has led me to examine more closely *Specimens of Mediaeval Architecture...*by Eden Nesfield (1862) and E.L. Garbett's *Rudimentary Treatise on the Principles of Design in Architecture...* (1850). This latter book remained in Hardy's possession all his life.

CB
2005

Acknowledgements

In the preparation of the 1966 edition I gratefully acknowledged help and advice from the following

Dr H.F. Brooks, Birkbeck College, London University.
Hugh Crickmay, Architect of Weymouth.
Francis Dalton, Curator of the Dorset County Museum, Dorchester.
John B. Dwight, Fellow of Magdalene College, Cambridge.
Dr Royston Lambert, Fellow of King's College, Cambridge.
Roger Peers, Curator of the Dorset County Museum.
Dr John Stevens, Fellow of Magdalene College, Cambridge.
Sir John Summerson, Curator of Sir John Soane's Museum, London.
The Royal Commission on Historical Monuments.

Now, in 2005, only Roger Peers survives of the individuals in this list, but my gratitude remains to them all.

I also wish to express my warmest thanks to the following for their assistance in the preparation of the revised Introduction

James Ayres.
Richard de Peyer, Curator of the Dorset County Museum until 2001.
Dorset County Library, Dorchester (Reference Dept.).
Peter Howells, former Chairman of the Victorian Society.
List continues.

Mr and Mrs T.W. Jesty, formerly of Max Gate, Dorchester.
Judy Lindsay, Director of the Dorset County Museum from 2003.
Prof. Emeritus Michael Millgate, University of Toronto.
Jane Preston, Plush Publishing, Dorset.
Mrs Margaret Richardson and the library staff of the RIBA, London.
The Society for the Protection of Ancient Buildings, London, represented by the Secretary, Philip Venning and the Archivist, Miss Cecily Greenhill.

Subcribers

John Charles Allen
Gordon Ashdown
James Ayers FSA
Revd David Ayton MA
Chris Beales
Angela Bell & Billy Beck
Jean Brooks MA
Richard Burleigh
Dr Alan Chedzoy
Peter W Coxon
Susan Crawford
V Crutchley
Tony & Pat Daniels
Philip M de Paris
Alan & Margaret Dodge
Felicity Gardner
Robert Goddard
William Greenslade
M A Hansford
Dr Paul E Hatcher
John Hatton
Dr M A Hill
Mr R P F Hughes
Professor Robert Knecht
Bruce Lewington
Henry E Lock
Malcolm Lofts
M D Miller
Michael Millgate
Rosemary Moore
Vincent Morris
Ian Moss
Stephen Mottram
Dr Michael Murphy
Dr Birgit Plietzsch
Dr Sue Powell
John & Jane Preston
Fred Reid
Mary Rimmer
Elizabeth Rokkan
Caroline Sandwich
Donald & Miriam Scott
Mr & Mrs C M Searle
Helen A Sill
Anne & Kristian Smidt
Furse Swann
Lilian Swindall
W Taylor
Patrick Tolfree
Paul Tomlinson
Lee Walton
Dr P C Whitwell Machen
Peter Williams
R A Yates

Bibliography

Bibliographical Note

The place of publication is London throughout, unless otherwise stated.

All quotations from Thomas Hardy's novels have been taken from the Macmillan Wessex Edition, 1912–31. The following references occur frequently in the Introduction:

1 Purdy denotes: *Thomas Hardy. A Bibliographical Study* by R.L. Purdy, 1954
2 *The Life* denotes: *The Life of Thomas Hardy 1840–1928*, 1962. This is the re-publication by Macmillan in one volume of Florence Hardy's two books: *The Early Life of Thomas Hardy 1840–1891*, 1928, and *The Later Years of Thomas Hardy 1892–1928*, 1930. The 1962 text is identical with the two earlier volumes but not all the illustrations have been reproduced.

Books and Pamphlets

Armstrong, W.J.C., *A Rambler's Guide to Boscastle with St. Juliot*, Launceston, 1931.

Beatty, Claudius J.P., *Thomas Hardy Conservation Architect*, Dorchester, 1995.
– *The Part Played by Architecture in the Life and Work of Thomas Hardy* (PhD Thesis, London University, 1963), published as one volume with: *A Biography of Thomas Hardy as Architect* (1980), Dorchester, 2004.
Blunden, Edmund, *Thomas Hardy*, 1941.
Brandon, Raphael, *Analysis of Gothick Architecture*, 1847.

Clarke, Basil F.L., *Church Builders of the Nineteenth Century*, 1938.

Dickens, Charles, *Dombey and Son,* 1847–8.

Eastlake, Charles, *A History of the Gothic Revival,* 1872.

Fergusson, James, *A History of Architecture.* 3 vols, 1865–7.

Garbett, Edward Lacy, *Rudimentary Treatise on the Principles of Design in Architecture,* 1850.

Goodhart-Rendel, H.S., *English Architecture since the Regency; an Interpretation,* 1953.

Hitchcock, Henry-Russell, *Architecture: Nineteenth and Twentieth Centuries,* 1958.

Hutchins, John, *The History and Antiquities of the County of Dorset.* Third Edition ed. William Shipp and James Whitworth Hodson, 1861–73.

Jones, Owen, *The Grammar of Ornament,* 1856.

Kerr, Robert, *The Gentleman's House; or how to plan English Residences from the Parsonage to the Palace*, 1864.

Lea, Hermann, *Thomas Hardy's Wessex,* 1913.

Moule, G.H., *Stinsford Church and Parish*, Dorchester, 1949.

Nesfield, W. Eden, *Specimens of Mediaeval Architecture Chiefly Selected from Examples of the 12th and 13th Centuries in France and Italy,* 1862.

Perkins, Thomas, *The Churches of Rouen.* (Bell's Handbooks to Continental Churches), 1900.

Pevsner, Nikolaus, *Pioneers of Modern Design*, 1960.

– *Some Architectural Writers of the 19th Century,* 1972.

Phelps, William Lyon, *Autobiography with Letters*, 1939.

Quiney, Anthony, *John Loughborough Pearson*, 1979.

Rodin, Auguste, *Cathedrals of France* (English translation and notes by Elisabeth C. Geissbuhler, 1965), 1914.

Ruskin, John, *The Seven Lamps of Architecture*, 1849.

Rutland, William R., *Thomas Hardy. A Study of his Writings and their Background,* Oxford, 1938.

– *Thomas Hardy*. Glasgow, 1938.

Shaw, Richard Norman, *Architectural Sketches from the Continent*, 1858.
Summerson, John, *The Unromantic Castle*, 1990.
Swann, Furse, *Thomas Hardy and West Knighton Church* [leaflet], 1994.

Thomas, D. St John, *A Regional History of the Railways of Great Britain* Vol. I *The West Country*, 1960.

Viollet-le-Duc, *Lectures on Architecture*, 1972.

Journals, Periodicals and Series

The Architectural Review Feb. 1962 and April 1967
The Builder 1860–63, 1886, 1894 and 1928
The Building News 1864, 1871
*Buildings of England Series edited by N. Pevsner et a*l.
Colby Library Quarterly Nov. 1954
Harper's New Monthly Magazine 1880–1
Journal of the Royal Society of Arts 1927
The L.C.C. Survey of London Vol. 18, 1937
The Royal Commission on Historical Monuments, Vol. I West Dorset
The Thomas Hardy Year Book No. 4, 1974

Introduction to the Notebook

Thomas Hardy, 2 June 1840 – 11 January 1928

Hardy's Early Years

In a letter to Kegan Paul the publisher in 1881, Hardy revealed that for at least four generations his direct ancestors had been master-masons with a set of journeymen-masons under them. Thomas Hardy himself was born in a small thatched cottage, which he liked to style the homestead, built by his great-grandfather in 1801 on the edge of the heath in the hamlet of Higher Bockhampton, in the parish of Stinsford, Dorset. He was a frail child and did not attend the village school until he was eight. Two years later he was sent to a Dorchester day-school where he could benefit from the teaching of a certain school-master, Isaac Glandfield Last, who had acquired a high reputation in the district. He remained under this excellent teacher for the rest of his school days.

Hardy's Career in Architecture up to 1872

Hardy's connection with architecture as a means of livelihood began in 1856 when he was apprenticed to John Hicks (1815–69), architect and church-restorer of Dorchester, a kindly man who allowed Hardy some leisure for studies other than architecture. Hicks's link with the Notebook is only incidental: see p. 88, where 'Mr. H' stands for Mr Hicks, and also p. 46. In the early days of my researches into Hardy's architectural career I visited the offices of Messrs Crickmay and Sons, Architects, Weymouth, and came upon some drawings for Hawkchurch Rectory which were marked 'Hicks September

1855'. In 1862 Hardy went to London 'to pursue the art and science of architecture on more advanced lines' and almost at once found employment as an assistant under A.W. Blomfield, ARA (1829–99) with whom he remained until 1867. A son of the Bishop of London, Blomfield had been articled to Philip Charles Hardwick (1822–92) and had opened his office in 1856. A few months after Hardy had joined him, Blomfield moved to 8 Adelphi Terrace, an address that appears on the inside of the front cover of the Notebook, together with 16 Westbourne Park Villas W., Hardy's private address at that time.

Hardy could not have happened on a more satisfactory employer. Jovial and energetic, with plenty of work on hand especially in the way of church-building, Blomfield quickly realised Hardy's exceptional abilities and promoted his well-being in every way possible. Indeed Hardy remained on very friendly terms with his old employer until the end of Blomfield's life, yet the latter's name does not once appear in the Notebook. In November 1862, proposed by Blomfield, Hardy became a member of the Architectural Association, the first of its kind in Britain, founded by Robert Kerr (1823–1904) and Charles Gray (1828–81) in 1847 to promote the training of would-be architects and, incidentally, to put the grasping Pecksniffs of the profession out of business. During Hardy's active years of membership – his name was struck off the list in 1872 when it was discovered that he had not paid his subscription for two years – organised architectural education had hardly got into its stride. The members learnt from each other. Papers were read and discussed and in the design classes students criticised each other's work. In 1863 Hardy won a prize offered by William Tite (1798–1873) for the design of a country mansion and in the same year was awarded the silver medal of the RIBA for his essay 'On the Application of Coloured Bricks and Terra Cotta to Modern Architecture' – a significant choice for the 1860s, a decade in which an increasing interest was shown in materials and craftsmanship. The officers of the AA were young men of many different interests and calibres and gave their services free. They included, apart from A.W. Blomfield himself, one of the most successful church architects of the day, R. Kerr, the co-founder of the AA, whose buildings certainly had 'plenty of go' to use the current Victorian vernacular, and, of course, Thomas Roger Smith (1830–1903). Smith was born in Sheffield, and after a private education entered the office of Philip Hardwick (1792–1870), spending a year and a half in travel before beginning independent practice in 1855. He was President of the AA in 1860–61 and 1863–64 and was elected a fellow of the RIBA in 1863. He designed many buildings in India, including the European General Hospital in Bombay in 1864. Hardy gave the young architect in *A Pair of Blue Eyes* T. Roger Smith's surname. Moreover Hardy makes him travel to Bombay in a professional capacity. Visits of architectural interest were also organised by the AA, one of which Hardy alludes to in his 'Memories of Church Restoration' (1906), namely, a tour of Westminster Abbey with George Gilbert Scott as cicerone.

By the summer of 1867 Hardy was in poor health and Blomfield agreed that he should go back to the country to regain vigour. He was therefore very pleased to accept work with his first employer, John Hicks, who at that time was in need of an assistant. His second spell with Hicks lasted intermittently from July 1867 till the winter of 1868–69. Hicks died on 12 February 1869, and G.R. Crickmay (1830–1907), a developer and architect of Weymouth, took over the practice. At the end of April Crickmay wrote to Hardy to ask if he would help him in carrying out certain church restorations that Hicks had begun or undertaken. Hardy agreed and in the first instance stayed in Weymouth – his lodgings were at 3 Wooperton Street – until towards the end of 1869. On 11 February 1870 Crickmay again wrote to Hardy to ask him if he could go to Cornwall to take a plan and particulars of a church that he was about to rebuild there. Hardy left for St Juliot, Boscastle, on 7 March, returning to Weymouth on 12 March. Perhaps it is as well to answer at this point the question why the Revd Cadell Holder (1803–82), Rector of St Juliot, should have chosen a Dorset architect to do the work rather than a local man. Why did Holder not consult St Aubyn, for example, who had restored Lesnewth Church nearby in 1865? (Had he done so Hardy's life would have taken a very different turn.) Did a personal connection mean a lot to Holder? The architect he chose was John Hicks of Dorchester, whose father, James Champion Hicks, was Perpetual Curate of Rangeworthy, Gloucestershire, from 1834 to 1855, the very parish where Holder himself had been curate from 1827 to 1830, his first appointment on going down from Oxford. From Rangeworthy, he moved only about four miles to Alveston where he was curate for twelve years and no doubt often in touch with the Revd Hicks in the neighbouring parish. In fact, with the exception of the living of Avenbury, Herefordshire, which preceded his move to Cornwall, Holder's working life was spent mostly in Gloucestershire and the Bristol area. We find in addition that James Hicks, elder brother of John, and Coulthurst Holder, younger brother of Cadell, were contemporaries at Oxford. In all the Hicks and Holder families were acquainted with each other from the 1830s onwards.

The restoration of St Juliot was to occupy Hardy on and off for about two years. It was at St Juliot that he met the Rector's sister-in-law, Emma Lavinia Gifford, who became his first wife. Pages 38, 39, 43 and 74 or 75 – the pagination is misleading here – refer to this period in his life.

By 5 April 1870, Hardy had resumed lodgings in Weymouth and by 2 May he had completed most of the detailed drawings for the restoration of St Juliot church. About the second week in May Hardy left Crickmay and started for London, where he helped Blomfield again for a short time and also assisted Raphael Brandon for a few weeks, though not continuously. As an architectural pupil Hardy had studied the Brandons' *Analysis of Gothick Architecture* (1847). As we read in *The Life*, Raphael Brandon was a man who interested Hardy much. He was convinced that modern English architecture should be based on English Gothic and not on French, as was shown in his well-known design for the Catholic Apostolic Church in Gordon Square, 1854, now the University Church. It was this book, I suggest, that first taught Hardy to appreciate the art of metal work in Gothic architecture: see particularly pp. 177–8 for the design of a wrought iron hinge and closing ring, reminiscent of the 13th-century wrought iron work on the south door of Eaton Bray Church, Bedfordshire, illustrated in Brandon.

Hardy visited St Juliot in August 1870 and again in May 1871. During April, June and July 1871 he was once more assisting Crickmay, returning to St Juliot in October. He appears to have gone back to Crickmay's after his visit to Cornwall, for as late as 3 January 1872, he was still using a Weymouth address. Crickmay is mentioned in the Notebook no fewer than five times: as G.R.C. on pp. 16, 91 and 161 and as Mr. C. on pp. 63 and 88. Weymouth is mentioned on the inside of the front cover and on p. 6, Radipole on p. 33 and Broadway on p. 21. 'M. St.', on p. 20 is in all probability Maiden Street, Weymouth. We now know, thanks to the Notebook, that Hardy also did a great deal of other architectural work for Crickmay besides church restoration, as I shall show later on.

In the spring of 1872 Hardy again set out for London and chose once more to live in Westbourne Park, but this time at 4 Celbridge Place, an address that appears on the inside of the front cover of the Notebook. It was during this period that Hardy assisted T. Roger Smith in designing schools for the London

School Board, which had then lately come into existence, public competition between architects for such designs being arranged by the Board from time to time. In August 1872 he went to St Juliot on holiday and at about that time heard from Professor Smith that another of the six Board-school competitions for which Hardy had helped to prepare designs had been successful, and that he would be welcomed back on more liberal terms, if he felt dissatisfied. Hardy declined this offer and with this refusal appeared to end his career as a professional architect – or that is what he would have us believe. In fact, after an interval of about eight or nine years, he continued, in an advisory capacity at least, to make use of his professional skills for the rest of his life.

Dating of the Notebook

The very few dates that appear are as follows: p. 22, 1866; p. 38, 1870; pp. 74–5, 1871–72; p. 91, Ap. 28 71; p. 116, Aug. 14 1920; p. 163, 1861; p. 172, Jan. 27 & Feb 3 1871; p. 190, Mar 31–65. The date 1842 occurs on the ground plan of Stinsford Church inserted between pp. 115 and 116, thereby highlighting the history of the church whose font greatly interested Hardy. He was to design the plinth of the restored font in 1920. One other sketch, though undated, should be mentioned here: that on p. 25 of the respond to the south arcade in Stinsford Church which Hardy sketched from the original. A similar drawing on a single sheet of paper dated 1861 is preserved in the Dorset County Museum. In the absence of photocopying or later modern techniques an architect's assistant was expected to be able to reproduce sketches of details or of ground plans at will, but these two sketches were probably done for Hardy's own pleasure and satisfaction. Two sketches of Glastonbury Abbey and Denchworth Church, which were pasted in later on p. 113, bear the dates March/61 and Apl. 1863 respectively. The West Knighton sketches on pp. 109–12 were probably done in 1893.

Max Gate Dorchester, the most recent address that appears on the inside of the front cover of the Notebook, was Hardy's home from 1885 until his death. For the most part, as far as one can judge, the matter in this Notebook was produced between 1862 and 1872 with the definite exception of only eleven pages, i.e. pp. 109, 110, 113 (half only), 114–15, 116–17, 119–20. The lettering on pp. 187–8 suggests that Hardy might have begun the Notebook at the other end during his time with Hicks. Page 186 and part of 185 are also reminiscent of *A Manual of Gothic Mouldings* by F.A. Paley (1845), which Hardy studied during that early period.

Domestic and Functional Architecture

Although this Architectural Notebook is very small it might reasonably be called a microcosm of the Victorian age. Not only does it deal, as one would expect, with almost every aspect of Gothic church architecture and the plans of large houses (pp. 57, 159 and 190), but in fact also contains many pages that have a direct bearing on industry and commerce and the day-to-day living of ordinary people in town and country. On p. 2 shipbuilding is mentioned in a passage on Pine Timber, which Hardy probably copied from a trade journal. Similar passages can be found on pp. 85, 160 and 162. Pine was a relatively new wood in Victorian England and much used (alas!) in church work. To judge from this Notebook the building of church schools was still going strong when Hardy was working for Crickmay, for Hardy seems to have supervised or carried out the building of several schools in and around Weymouth: see Trinity Schools, p. 6, Radipole Schools, p. 33 – (the use of the plural here makes us think of the school as a collection of different classrooms) – and Broadway School, p. 21. Problems of drainage, cesspools and water-closets are thoroughly explored on pp. 6, 9, 46, 68–70, 88, 91, 165 and 169. On p. 169 Hardy advises: 'Stop rat holes with cement mixed with broken glass'. Page 9 is particularly interesting: here practical details of drainage vie for the reader's attention with sketches that show Hardy's appreciation of Gothic art. Notes on the housemaids' sink and closet, which have been allowed partially to obliterate other architectural details, were surely added during his time with Crickmay. It is perhaps worth noting here that in his standard work of over 450 pages, *The Gentleman's House* (1864), R. Kerr, who characteristically suggests that a lavatory be placed near the entrance-hall principally for the use of gentlemen visitors, as they 'can always find their way to the Entrance-Hall, if nowhere else', cannot spare a line to describe the housemaids' sanitary arrangements!

Sectional drawings of windows of all kinds take up a lot of space. See pp. 14–21 for practical and workmanlike details of shutters, bay windows, casements, etc. Similar technical drawings of windows or their details also appear, for example, on pp. 42, 49–50, 56, 58, 63, 70, 73 and following, and p. 90. Roofs are dealt with on some twenty different pages: see pp. 3, 8, 21, 22–3, 28,

30–2, 36, 51, 53–5, 56, 59, 60 (ridge plates), 77, 80–5, 90, 162 and 166, where in the original some blue wash or ink shading appears in the diagram. The roof of a common street house is carefully drawn into the bottom of pp. 22 and 23, while, more interestingly, as early as on p. 3 details of cast-iron construction are clearly shown. According to John Summerson's essay 'Charting the Victorian Building World' from his book *The Unromantic Castle* (1990):

> Both wrought and cast iron have a long history. Cast iron was in every-day structural use by 1837,...Then came rolled iron, extensively used in the Crystal Palace, 1851. Rolled iron, i.e. rolled out of the lump into sheets, plates, girders and joists of various sections, swept the board. (p. 168)

Hence the details and specifications of iron girders which Hardy presumably copied from a trade journal 'The same amount of metal in the form of a rolled beam would do the work, and dispense with the wood altogether.' assuredly words anathema to most Gothicists. Yet it was only a year or two later that no less a medievalist than Viollet-le-Duc wrote in his *Lectures on Architecture*, 1872:

> Architecture is the sister of Science:
> ...if [architects]...persist in...refusing that aid which science would gladly give them, the function of the architect is obsolete; while that of the engineer is commencing...
> (As reproduced in *The Architectural Review*, June 1947, p. 229)

And how many other Gothicists have been concerned, even in a minor capacity, with railway engineering of any kind? Work on some aspect of railway construction is definitely recorded on pp. 4, 30, and 61.

Then there are intimations of a housing estate and the plans of several houses. Hardy was probably responsible for supervising the construction of at least some of the G.H. houses (see pp. 42, 56, 86 and 190). These initials refer to the Greenhill district of Weymouth where Crickmay built various houses in 1871. Page 56 is particularly informative, with its neat functional drawings showing Hardy's careful attention to detail. His concern with the siting and convenience of larger houses is clearly manifested in the ground plans on pp. 43, 44 and 46. We know, for example, that he stayed at the St Juliot Rectory

(p. 43). Hardy notes that Syward Lodge, Dorchester, also on p. 43, is 'on a very difficult site – a steep slope to S.W.' All the more interesting, then, that Lady Michel should have said – as carefully noted by Hardy on p. 43 – that 'it was the most convenient house she had ever lived in'. Lady Michel was the wife of General Sir John Michel, later Field Marshall (1804–86), of Dewlish and Kingston Russell. Presumably Syward Lodge was the town house Lady Michel occupied when her husband was on military expeditions abroad. It was a commodious house and was later converted into flats. When I viewed the ground-floor flat I verified to my own satisfaction that the rooms corresponded by-and-large to those on the plan, but of course few of them were being used as originally intended. Syward Lodge was pulled down in the early 1960s. Mr R. Smith's house on p. 44 corresponds to West Stafford Old Rectory (now called Glebe Court). Hardy refers to Canon Smith, presumably Canon R. Smith in *The Life* on pp. 249–50. Stinsford House, the plan of which Hardy sketched at the bottom of p. 44, has had a very chequered history. In Hardy's time it was a private residence, and later became a school. Subsequently it was abandoned and much vandalised. Now at last it has recovered much of its former glory through painstaking internal reconstruction, comprising nine commodious units and a restoration of the formal garden to the south. The sketch of the third house on the page is still unidentified, but it is a neater version of the rough sketch on p. 190.

There are ground plans of five other dwellings. As recorded on p. 394 of *The Gentleman's House*, R. Kerr's cheapest house could have been built for £850–£1,200 in the country or £1,250 in London, the villa on p. 59 of the Notebook being priced at £1,350. Was this plan copied from a trade journal or is this Hardy's own design? Surely it was not deliberately sited so that the principal bedrooms, drawing- and sitting-rooms face north?

On p. 57 there is the ground plan of Hemstead House, Kent, designed by David Brandon – no relation of Raphael Brandon – in 1862. Hardy probably copied this plan from *The Builder*, 1862, p. 260. In *The Gentleman's House*, Hemstead is one of the houses especially selected for critical notes. See plate XXX which also shows the ground-floor plan of the house, and p. 444, which begins as follows:

> This is an exceedingly good example of freely modified Classical plan, – we may indeed call it mediaevalized Classical. To begin with the Entrance, this is perfect.

> The combined Hall and Staircase within thus assume very much of the character of a Gothic Hall,... The Saloon, taking it in the Palladian sense, as a Public-Apartment,... is a charmingly skilful feature.

Hemsted (sic) does not appear in the Index to *West Kent and the Weald* in the *Buildings of England* series. It is now in fact Benenden School. Hardy was interested in large country houses. The ground plan of an even bigger country mansion on p. 159, which I have been unable to identify, not even with the help of *Country Life*, may also be explained in this way.

The largest house Hardy actually seems to have been concerned with as a working architect is Slape House, Netherbury, near Beaminster, Dorset (see pp. 77–8 and possibly 79), where Crickmay was responsible for making considerable alterations in 1871–72. The house has been described as follows in *An Inventory of the Historical Monuments in Dorset* Vol. I West, pp. 173–4:

> The property formerly belonged to the Strode family and remains of a 17th-century house are incorporated in the E. end of the present building which was erected early in the 18th century...The N. front has a projecting central bay...; the porch is a modern addition...The S. front has projecting side wings...The E. end is largely of the 17th century and retains some three-light windows with labels...

The two smallest designs in this section are for labourers' cottages on pp. 160 and 163–4. The housing conditions of the rural poor were a problem near to Hardy's heart. In almost every novel he condemns selfish and unscrupulous landlords and draws attention to the plight of the agricultural labourer obliged to leave his family cottage owing to the iniquities of the laws of land tenure then in force. Almost the last thing Hardy ever wrote was an article in support of an appeal to preserve the ancient cottages of England. This appeared in the *Journal of the Royal Society of Arts* on 18 March 1927.

The design shown on p. 163 is interesting. From 141 plans submitted – 149 according to Hardy – the prize for a double cottage to cost not more than £220 the pair was awarded to Messrs Richardson and Ross of Darlington, according to *The Builder*, 16 March 1861. But the award appears to have gone to the wrong persons. A correspondent in *The Builder* of 3 August in the same year wrote:

If you will refer to your paper of July 7, 1860, you will find the *prize* design...nearly an exact copy of Mr. Strickland's plan, as published by you.

The great objection I see to the prize plan is –

1. The direct draught from back to front doors.
2. The manner in which the entrance door is cribbed:...
3. The small size of the pantry, there being no cellar.
4. Only one door to scullery, and that opening in entrance...
5. The sinks are badly situate for light...

Some of these faults are even visible on Hardy's tiny drawing.

Public buildings also figure prominently in the Notebook. We know that Crickmay was responsible for erecting the Weymouth and Dorset Eye Infirmary, King Street, Weymouth, in 1871 (see pp. 80 and 88) and for carrying out extensive alterations to the Weymouth Royal Infirmary, School Street in 1870 (also on p. 80). It was known as the Royal Hospital and Dispensary. Altogether this would account for Hardy's great interest in the newly completed St Thomas's Hospital, London. The facts he noted down about the hospital on pp. 170–2 were taken from a description of St Thomas's by its architect, Henry Currey (1820–1900), which was published in *The Building News* (1871). On p. 164 Hardy considers how many cubic feet of air should be allowed per inmate in the dormitories of hospitals, barracks, prisons and lodging houses. Lower on the same page he lists the dimensions of eight public buildings. The sketch of ground-floor windows W.T. Hall at the bottom of p. 49 refers to Wareham Town Hall, for which Crickmay was responsible 1869–70.

During the years Hardy spent with Blomfield, London was undergoing great changes. Hardy tells us that, from 8 Adelphi Terrace, he saw the Embankment and Charing Cross Bridge built. When he first arrived in London, Hungerford Market was still in being where Charing Cross Station now stands. Hardy also recalls a journey on the new Underground Railway where, he thought, everything was excellently arranged. But Victorian assurance did not only express itself in new engineering wonders. Some nine months after the opening of Charing Cross Station in January 1864 the Strand Music Hall (see p. 162) was completed on the site of the old Exeter 'Change. The obituary of its architect, E. Bassett Keeling (1836–86) states that at the time of its erection it was much criticised and that it certainly exhibited many eccentricities of design. Nevertheless, it had the merit of originality and effectiveness and was not only something novel in its way but had even some influence on the style of other buildings erected soon after it. Its roof was constructed entirely from wrought iron and zinc (see p. 69 for a note on zinc which Hardy copied from *The Builder*, March 26, 1864). Its cast-iron columns with copper foliations to their capitals bring to mind the University Museum, Oxford, opened in 1860. Even to the layman the short extract which Hardy copied from *The Building News* reveals striking ingenuity. He must have known the building well, at least from the outside, though I can find no mention of it in *The Life*. The S.M.H. was subsequently converted into the Gaiety Theatre. In complete contrast to S.M.H. and also in the Strand stood Exeter Hall (see p. 164), it too no longer in existence. Built to the designs of J.T. Deering-Gandy (1787–1850), who was distinguished for his purity of taste and knowledge of Greek architecture, its massive stone entrance porch was a fine example of the Corinthian order. See *The L.C.C. Survey of London*...Vol. 18 (1937), p. 126. According to *The Life* Hardy attended oratorios there.

A variety of details and accessories is scattered throughout the Notebook. On p. 49 alone a handsome Ruskinian knocker shares the top of the page with details of stables and the floor of a church or chapel, while the rest of the page is taken up with 'Cesspool to school W.C.'s', a simple plan for a double architrave, rafters and other details. For a school seat and gutter outlets, see p. 6, for rain water pipes p. 28, for wine bins p. 37 – (Wine Bins at Knighton must refer to Lewell Lodge) – for gates pp. 62 and 168, for flues p. 63, for French drains p. 70 and French fireproof flooring p. 86 – no narrow chauvinism here – for glazing see p. 71 (the second page so numbered), for skylight p. 80, for 'Inner strap of hinge' p. 70, for treads and risers of stairs p. 89, for staircases p. 161, for cellars p. 167 and for 'Bath Room' p. 91. (The information for this last item was copied almost verbatim from 'Water Service of Dwellings', published in *The Building News*, April 28, 1871, pp. 320–1.) On how to sink a well, see pp. 78–9. No feature is too insignificant for Hardy's whole-hearted attention, and one feels too that he could have made many of these features himself. Take for example the light and strong gate on p. 168; there is enough information here for any self-respecting do-it-yourself enthusiast. For Hardy, then, an architect should be conversant with such subsidiary crafts as carpentry and joinery, even if he is not a practising craftsman himself.

The technical vocabulary too can be fascinating. In alterations of houses we learn that girders are invaluable: used as shoring and *needles* they occupy little space (p. 53). A dormer with glazed *cheeks* (p. 50), an *elbow* in a pipe (p. 46) and a *shoulder* in the *heel* post of a gate (p. 168) strike fresh on my layman's ear. I wonder, also, whether 'common pugging' (p. 52) is still practised today. Later, Hardy made appropriate use in the novels of some of the technical vocabulary that appears in the Notebook: for example, 'bradded' on p. 42 is used in *Under the Greenwood Tree* (p. 18) and 'cramps' on p. 47 in *The Hand of Ethelberta* (p. 330).

Gothic Work

I should like to begin this section with a quotation from *A Pair of Blue Eyes.*

> XXXVII
>
> **'After many days.'**
>
> KNIGHT roamed south, under colour of studying Continental antiquities.
>
> He paced the lofty aisles of Amiens, loitered by Ardennes Abbey, climbed into the strange towers of Laon, analyzed Noyon and Rheims. Then he went to Chartres, and examined its scaly spires and quaint carvings: then he idled about Coutances. He rowed beneath the base of Mont St. Michel, and caught the varied skyline of the crumbling edifices encrusting it. St. Ouen's, Rouen, knew him for days; so did Vezelay, Sens, and many a hallowed monument besides. Abandoning the inspection of early French art with the same purposeless haste as he had shown in undertaking it, he went further, and lingered about Ferrara, Padua, and Pisa. Satiated with mediaevalism, he tried the Roman Forum.

We must now turn our attention to Knight's statement a few pages later in chapter 37. I quote:

> ...it may perhaps interest you to know that I have been attempting the serious study of Continental art of the Middle Ages... (p. 401)

We read further in Purdy:

> Sir Arthur Blomfield, with whom I was working, first set me on the track of early French Gothic, of which he was a great admirer, and I won as an architectural prize the books of Nesfield and Norman Shaw on the same subject. (p. 159)

When Hardy won the William Tite prize in 1863 he received the sum of £3, and it would appear that he spent the money on two books; *Architectural Sketches from the Continent* by Richard Norman Shaw, 1858, and *Specimens of Mediaeval Architecture Chiefly Selected from Examples of the 12th and 13th Centuries in France and Italy and Drawn* by W. Eden Nesfield, 1862. Presumably Hardy bought these books at the instigation of his employer, A.W. Blomfield, and it is easy to imagine his enthusiasm on first handling these beautiful folio volumes – a young man not yet 23 who must have wondered whether *he* would ever make the traditional architectural tour of France and Italy to see these masterpieces for himself. In the meantime he was, I suggest, totally captivated by the finely executed measured drawings therein and must have felt, as he gazed at them, as Keats did on first looking into Chapman's Homer. And thus, through the pages of Nesfield, Hardy journeyed vicariously in France and Italy and made the character, Henry Knight, in *A Pair of Blue Eyes* take the same route, visiting the places in alphabetical order, according to Nesfield, that is, with one or two deviations. (Strictly speaking, the plates in Nesfield are not in alphabetical order all the way through.) Norman Shaw does not seem to have interested Hardy so much.

That Hardy looked very closely at Nesfield can be deduced from his having copied a considerable number of details from it into his Notebook. One can understand why Hardy was immediately struck with the Ardennes Abbey drawing (plate 5 in Nesfield). He would have noticed the homely touch of the peasant woman with the child in her arms and the piles of ?hay visible through the half-open door, showing that the abbey – or part of it at least – had been converted into a great barn for the local community. After all, he was a countryman himself. Wooden doors, especially if decorated with geometric patterns, fascinated him and he added this one to his collection on p. 13 of the Notebook. (It is not an exact copy.) As a Gothic craftsman too he was interested by the trefoil arch that seems to form part of the tympanum, and recorded its shape, accurately this time, on p. 35, though in reverse.

What made Hardy pick on this particular detail from Coutances (plate 11) – a tiny flower-shaped corbel, or rather, decorative terminal to a shaft (reproduced on p. 26 of the Notebook) – we shall never know. But I suggest that it comprises within itself, for Hardy at least, the whole of the cathedral, just as the smallest insect, according to Rodin in his book *Cathedrals of France*, offers a representation, abridged yet total, of the entire universe.

Next, the carved shapes of oxen on the tower of Laon Cathedral took his fancy (plate 37). I expect he knew why they had been placed there; it was by way of commemorating their contribution to the building of the church, as it was they who dragged up the hill the heavy stones that were used in its construction. And is it not appropriate that these head-and-shoulder sketches of humble beasts should share p. 27 of the Notebook with figures of angels and saints and Christ bearing his cross?

At Noyon he found much to admire in a particularly fine chapter house. First he copied from plate 93 the window tracery from the west side of the building on p. 12 of the Notebook, together with one example of the crocketed buttresses, both seen from the front. From plate 64 he carefully reproduced a chimney on a slightly bigger scale (p. 33 in the Notebook). Several of the same type can be seen on the Mont St Michel drawings by Nesfield. Did Hardy then copy this functional detail as being the best example of its kind? Perhaps, but he may also have been surprised to note its resemblance to one of the chimneys at Athelhampton Hall, a Tudor manor house near Dorchester, which he knew well, having painted a watercolour of it in c. 1858. Then from plate 66, again from the chapter house, he copies mouldings of the base of the shaft and a section of the rose window (p. 106 in the Notebook) both in reverse.

From plate 78 he made a neat drawing (front view) of a round arch divided into two smaller arches supported by a central pillar. It was perhaps the stark simplicity of this Romanesque design – a rather common motif, one imagines – that fascinated him, the stone work between the sweep of the bigger arch covering the two smaller ones being left blank. This detail was taken from the abbey of St Rémi at Rheims (p. 48 in the Notebook).

Then, from plate 83 the section of the base of the large column round the apse of Sens Cathedral took his eye. This he reproduced, again back to front as it were, on p. 107 of the Notebook.

Hardy's drawing at the top of p. 48 in the Notebook of a pointed arch with a quatrefoil tracery just below the apex, the arch itself being divided by a single shaft creating two equal trefoil openings, was taken from the west porch of the duomo at Ferrara, plate 92 in Nesfield and the only Italian example in this group. This feature would have been chosen, I suggest, as a contrast to the triforium arch at St Rémi and perhaps to show the development in style from the Romanesque to the later Gothic.

What conclusion can be drawn from these details that Hardy copied from Nesfield? Are the same principles at work in the Wessex novels? Omitting the purely technical examples – the sections of mouldings and the like – these sketches often show Hardy's ability to select one detail to represent the whole. To gaze at the west porch of Ferrara is an overwhelming experience. How can one take it all in? But pick one distinctive detail – as Hardy did – and the camera of the brain will bring the rest into focus in later years. Similarly, in *Jude the Obscure* Hardy writes of the church 'with the Italian porch' and 'helical columns', the latter detail identifying it at once as being based on the University Church of St Mary in Oxford. Other examples will readily occur to Hardy readers: the gargoyle on Weatherbury Church in *Far from the Madding Crowd* and the stone mask at the back of High Place Hall in *The Mayor of Casterbridge*.

Why do Beauvais, Le Mans – and Paris for that matter – not appear in this paragraph from *A Pair of Blue Eyes*? This is where it is relevant to mention Norman Shaw. It would appear that Nesfield carefully consulted Shaw's work before selecting plates for his own so that there would be no duplication. Shaw does in fact provide sketches of Beauvais, Le Mans and Notre Dame de Paris, but the Abbey Church of St Ouen in Rouen still eludes me. It may simply be that Hardy wishes to draw our attention to a building that is every bit as imposing as the cathedral and altogether even more worthy of our close inspection and admiration. In his book *The Churches of Rouen* (1900, p. 61), the Revd Thomas Perkins – incidentally, a close friend of Hardy's – writes:

> The aged verger tells all English visitors that the greatest of all Englishmen whom he has known, Mr John Ruskin, often declared it in his hearing to be the most perfect monument of pure Gothic in the world;

and Fergusson, in his *History of Architecture*, writes of it as follows: 'The church of St. Ouen at Rouen is beyond comparison the most beautiful and perfect of the abbey edifices of France...'

The Hardys visited Rouen on their honeymoon in 1874 and 'the two spires and lantern of St Ouen's are mentioned in chapter XXXIV of *The Hand of Ethelberta*.

Other Gothic Work

Most of the sketches of Gothic details in the Notebook were probably done during the time Hardy was working for Blomfield, that is to say between 1862 and 1867. They are as varied as any details previously described in this Introduction and prove Hardy to be a true High Victorian in his eclecticism. On p. 7 mouldings from Alkham Church, Kent, contrast with a Victorian design incorporating a vesica, with Verona partially rubbed out in the centre. Alkham is not far from Dover which Hardy visited in September 1862. French influence appears again on p. 10 with mouldings from Notre Dame, Etampes. The two designs, presumably by Hardy, for fonts on pp. 18 and 23 respectively, are chunky and typically High Victorian. See also p. 100 for Hardy's interest in the ornamentation of a font with marble inlay in two colours, and on p. 72 (the first so numbered), Hardy copied out the specification of another font.

One Gothic church which I cannot fail to mention appears on p. 22. It was first identified for me as Findon Church, Sussex, by Canon Basil F.L. Clarke, author of *Church Builders of the Nineteenth Century* (1938), and subsequently his opinion was confirmed by the vicar of Findon. Hardy's sketch represents Findon Church in 1866 and is thus an interesting record of what the building looked like before the extensive restorations carried out by Scott from September 1866 to July 1867.

The sketches on pp. 24 and 25 show Hardy studying 13th-century stiff leaf sculpture and the one on p. 25 of the respond to the S arcade in Stinsford Church is especially felicitous. Page 26 is particularly varied. Hardy's interest in woodwork construction is evident in the sketch pasted in on yellow tracing paper. His obvious fascination with the geometric patterns in the creation of wooden doors is clear from the eight sketches which occupy almost the whole of p. 13. Likewise he devotes an entire two pages, namely 182 and 183, to the door of the S transept of Notre Dame de l'Epine near Chalons sur Marne. Presumably, p. 182 shows the full-page drawing of the interior of the door while 183 shows the exterior of the same. Also on p. 26 the Gothic mouldings, pinnacle and corbel from Coutances (plate 5 in Nesfield) are finely drawn. The identity of the church band, so vividly portrayed at the bottom of the page, still eludes me. Hardy has marked it 'copied', but the authorities I have consulted, including the British Museum and the Victoria and Albert Museum, agree that it is early Victorian, possibly from the 1840s. It was *not* copied from T. Webster's famous picture: *A Village Choir*!

Hardy was an admirer of Pugin (1812–52) and that 'honesty and truthfulness in design and manufacturing' (to quote N. Pevsner in his *Pioneers of Modern Design*, p. 23), which Pugin stood for and which made him a precursor of the Arts and Crafts Movement, is exemplified by the Notebook as a whole. Hardy certainly eschewed all sham in architecture and he is careful to point out anything specious:

> Columns (deceptive) – 'brick core, & cemented with Parian, on which can paint & marble – ' (p. 59)

In Enckworth Court, with its free-stone facings and its dark green columns, brick at the core, Hardy deliberately created a house in which Pugin would have torn his hair. See the description of Enkworth Court (strictly speaking its more modern wing) in *The Hand of Ethelberta*, p. 329.

On p. 32 notice the half-sketch of a window, c. 1200; on p. 34 the fine drawing of a capital, and below, a commanding angel, delicately drawn, with a spare wing nearby! Gabriel, perhaps, as his attitude suggests the Annunciation. On p. 35 two tiny angels confabulate, quite unmoved by the welter of Gothic sketches on the rest of the page. Could the superimposed sketch on yellow tracing paper on p. 36 be a copy of French domestic architecture? On pp. 38 and 39 Hardy's fine sketches of highly carved 15th-century bench-ends (St Juliot Church, Cornwall 1870) give little idea of the dilapidated state of the originals. 'The old oak seats, with their original carved ends, remain for the most part, but miserably mouldy and wormeaten' says a letter dated 1854. W.J.C. Armstrong's *A Rambler's Guide to Boscastle* is the source of my information here. And Hardy did not sketch these bench-ends until some 16 years later. Regrettably they were removed before expert knowledge could save them and are said to have been bought by a local farmer and turned into household furniture.

Page 40 shows a study of the springing of an early Gothic vault. On p. 41 there are shouldered Gothic arches and a large cross designed to adorn the apex of a church roof. The face of Christ with an elaborate halo may be Hardy's design.

The identity of those natural shapes not named by Hardy on pp. 65 and 67 must remain problematical. The 'white trumpet-shaped mosses' in *The Return of the Native* (p. 400) resemble the mosses on p. 65; both these have been identified botanically not as mosses but as lichens of the species *Cladonia*. The plant drawn just above the word 'Lichen' on the same page is not unlike some of the bedstraw family while the spiral forms at the bottom could be ferns not yet unfurled (reminding us of 'fern-sprouts like bishops' croziers' in *Far from the Madding Crowd* p. 163) or even ammonites! The motifs on pp. 64, 66 and 101, some of which are both tiny and curious enough to delight a Paul Klee, appear to have been inspired by *The Grammar of Ornament*, by Owen Jones (1856), a standard work which all Neo-Gothic architects consulted. Pages 177–8 are on yellow tracing paper pasted in and are wholly taken up with the design of a wrought-iron hinge and closing-ring based on brake and hart's tongue fern, the latter being mentioned on p. 5 of *Jude the Obscure.*

The sketch of one of the massive pillars of Fontevrault on p. 94 shows Hardy's interest in early Romanesque architecture. Were the Gothic details on p. 95 copied from a book? Laon (Window Sill Drip, page 95) is mentioned on p. 398 of *A Pair of Blue Eyes*.

The only sketch on p. 96 was copied from *Rudimentary Treatise on the Principles of Design in Architecture* by Edward Lacy Garbett, Architect (1850). This is the only book of architectural interest which Hardy kept in his library. It now rests in the Beinecke Rare Book and Manuscript Library, New Haven, Connecticut. I have not seen the original but Alfred W. Mueller, Public Services Assistant, who has looked through the original, assures me that there are no significant notes therein. He did send me a copy of the title page, however, with Hardy's signature in the top right-hand corner. The letter 'H' is neatly looped twice, bottom left and upper right, which makes it, I think, a very early signature. Hardy may have acquired the book before leaving for London in 1862. The drawing in the Notebook, which is about the same size as Garbett, was copied from p. 159, chapter VI, described as 'the Cross-Vault' at the top. The drawing is in fact the top of a 'Square cross-vault, resting *upon* and *against* the angles only of its base'.

If Hicks introduced this book to Hardy, as seems likely, he certainly did him a service. This humble text-book, one of a series on divers subjects, provides the student with a history of architecture with particular stress on the comparison between Greek and Gothic architecture. Ruskin may have published *The Seven Lamps of Architecture* in 1849 – and Garbett quotes from it showing that he is up to date – but more importantly Garbett quotes Hogarth's 'line of Beauty' and several passages from the *Discourses* of Sir Joshua Reynolds.

These quotations reveal a breadth of vision in Garbett far more useful to the student than Ruskin's insistence on the primacy of Venetian Gothic to the relative detriment of almost everything else. In his book *Some Architectural Writers of the Nineteenth Century* (1972), chapter XIX, entitled 'Greenhough and Garbett', Pevsner writes:

> [Garbett's treatise] is a small, unassuming book, but...the only one of its date in England to face fully what architectural theory ought to involve. It is in its setting of problems much more like textbooks on architectural design today than like any of the writings so far examined. We do not know who Edward Lacy Garbett was, perhaps the son of William, surveyor of Winchester Cathedral, or of Edward Garbett, designer of the remarkable church of 1819 at Theale which took Salisbury Cathedral as its model...The 'Higher Beauties' of chapter four are Imitation of Nature and, firmly based on Reynolds, the Imitation of Masters, Honesty as against Deception, and especially Constructive Truth. These side by side with Constructive Unity, 'are the two most important principles to be borne in mind, in tracing the history of architecture' and in understanding 'the two standard systems which the world has hitherto seen' – the Greek and the Gothic.

This battle of the styles is clearly foreshadowed by the two manor houses on the Kingston Maurward estate near Dorchester, which Hardy knew very well. The Old Manor House is Elizabethan, probably built for Christopher Grey, and Kingston Maurward House was built by George Pitt in 1717–20 and is distinctly classical in design. 'The two houses are linked by an avenue that lays proper emphasis on their relationship' (Newman's and Pevsner's *Dorset*). It is also worth mentioning that the church at Theale, which appears as Gaymead in Hardy's Wessex, was designed by the second Garbett in Pevsner's article. Extraordinary! Was it Hardy's love of Salisbury Cathedral that made him choose this village as his Gaymead in *Jude the Obscure* and in 'The Son's Veto'?

The sketches on pp. 97 and 98 look like Victorian Gothic designs. Indeed it is worth quoting Nicolas Taylor in his review of the Notebook in *The Architectural Review* April 1967 on this very page 98: '[there] is a small sketch of a vaulted clerestory which suggests a startlingly modern approach to the free arrangement of abstract stained glass'. I did not realise the importance of this feature until I discovered the unexecuted church design by Thomas

Hardy where the windows were to be 'glazed with Cathedral glass Colours & Shapes at random'. Hardy's breaking up of the window space, I wrote, is not only striking and original but may also be intended as a deterrent to zealous parishioners who hope to immortalise themselves in glass of often indifferent quality and design (*The Thomas Hardy Year Book*, No. 4, p. 66, 1974).

The harmonious colour contrasts on p. 100 were taken from a paper by J.G. Crace entitled 'On the Decoration of the International Exhibition Building' which appeared in *The Builder*, 1862, p. 258. Pages 102 to 107 deal with various aspects of Gothic construction, such as blank arcading and ribs on p. 103, mouldings of the base of a column on p. 104, jamb mouldings to a panel (stone) on p. 105, string courses, section of a rose window and section for a cusp on p. 106, and various mouldings on p. 107, representative, presumably, of the sophisticated draughtsmanship Hardy was required to execute for Blomfield.

The two sketches on p. 113 were both pasted in later, the Glastonbury sketch dated March 1861, taking us back indeed to his time under Hicks at Dorchester. This probably marks the first visit to a place he revisited on at least two occasions, in August 1904 on a bicycling tour and on 28 August 1924 when he went with his wife to hear Rutland Boughton's musical version of *The Queen of Cornwall*. The lower sketch of Denchworth Church, Berkshire, and the village school is dated April 26 1863. It is worth noting that G.E. Street designed the school and restored the church, but I doubt whether this was Hardy's reason for making the sketch. His favourite sister, Mary, had left Salisbury Training College in 1862 to take up her first post as schoolmistress at Denchworth.

The folded drawing on thin brown paper of Stinsford Church before the alteration about the year 1842 was inserted later between pp. 115 and 116 and is not numbered. It depicts a ground plan of the church as it was when the gallery was still in position and the entrance to the church was through a door in the north wall. In other words it was the church of *Under the Greenwood Tree*. In his 'Notes on Stinsford Church', April 1909, addressed to the Restoration Committee, Hardy wrote:

> If an organ be really required I should say, speaking for myself alone, that the old west gallery should be re-erected for it. Such west galleries, which were unadvisedly destroyed in the last century are now getting replaced in some churches, there being

no point in the edifice which so completely controls the singing of the congregation as a west gallery.

These words proved to be prophetic when, during the autumn of 1996, just such a gallery and organ were installed in the church. These were dedicated by the Bishop of Sherborne at a special Choral Evensong on 2 December 1996. The instrument was built by Brian Daniels of Chard, and the gallery, designed by Roy Fewtrell of the Crickmay Partnership – a firm which was originally founded by G.R. Crickmay for whom Hardy worked between 1869 and 1872 – was erected by C.G. Fry and Son of Litton Cheney. The front panel of the old organ in the chancel was retained as this instrument was given to the church in June 1931 by Miss Katharine Hardy (1856–1940) in memory of her parents, her sister Mary, and her brothers Thomas and Henry.

To return to the Notebook, on pp. 114–17 we have a glimpse of Hardy at work, now an old man of 80. It is 1920 and he is repairing the old Norman font, discovered in seven pieces in the churchyard, to make it fit for re-use after a lapse of some 200 years. First, there is a rough ground plan of Stinsford Church to remind himself of its proportions and size, including many measurements (p. 114); then a careful drawing of the cracked font itself, whose shape and ornamentation resemble that of another Norman font in the district. A visit to the village church of Martinstown, about 2 miles west of Dorchester on 14 August 1920 is recorded on p. 116. In his 'Notes on Stinsford Church' mentioned above, he had already suggested that the old font be re-erected 'on a plain square base'. This is in fact what was done.

On pp. 157–8 is a detailed description of a church which I can now confidently assert is St Peter's Vauxhall, having compared it with the discussion and illustrations of this particular church in Anthony Quiney's biography (1978) of J.L. Pearson. Among its striking features is the vaulting, unusual at the time. Hardy may have copied this account from a trade journal; but he could even have seen the building under construction c. 1863, and indeed been influenced by it when designing his own unexecuted church (1870) which I have examined elsewhere (*The Thomas Hardy Yearbook*). St Peter's is visible to railway passengers approaching Waterloo Station.

A great deal of this section on Gothic architecture is pervaded by Ruskinian influence. Ruskin's ideas had helped to form the artistic climate of the age and we know that Hardy was familiar with at least some of his writings at this early date. Yet Hardy never had a good word to say about Ruskin as art critic that I can discover. In this Notebook there is enough interest in Gothic ornamentation generally to show that Ruskin was very much in the air, but this was not the only influence in such matters. Hardy clearly read the current trade journals on every aspect of his profession and examined *The Grammar of Ornament* very thoroughly. He must have known that its author, Owen Jones (1809–1874), was not only a notable interior designer but also the architect of the Egyptian, Greek – incidentally, Paula Power wishes to make a Greek court of the quadrangle of Stancy Castle in *A Laodicean* (pp. 90–1) – Roman and Alhambra courts for the Crystal Palace in 1851. Readers are referred to the Appendix below, where I identify many motifs from Owen Jones.

When Hardy first arrived in London he obviously found the architectural scene stimulating and carried off two prizes within two years. This initial enthusiasm did not last. In *The Life* Hardy wrote:

> Having somewhat settled down with Blomfield, but feeling that architectural drawing in which the actual designing had no great part was monotonous and mechanical; having besides little inclination for pushing his way into influential sets which would help him to start a practice of his own, Hardy's tastes reverted to the literary pursuits that he had been compelled to abandon in 1861... (pp. 46–7)

He felt frustrated. He had not been to the University. He was not well connected. If his potential as an architect is to be gauged from this Notebook alone it is evident that, while few draughtsmen could be more sensitive and precise, Hardy's fertile imagination was largely engaged elsewhere.

Craftsmanship and Engineering

For Hardy craftsmanship was innate, something inherited from his master-mason father and forebears who could think and work in no other way. This does not mean that he was unaware of what William Morris and others were trying to do in the 1860s and 70s. In his *English Architecture since the Regency*, Goodhart-Rendell has described Morris's concept as follows:

> The craftsman foreseeing his labour as he made his pattern, the artist adapting his pattern as he did his work; these were to be *one*.

Hardy, in fact, tried to apply these standards to architecture as a whole, his idea of a 'technicist', which I discuss below, corresponding closely to Morris's ideal. One of the main features of the Notebook is the obvious craftsmanship of the draughtsman. Hardy's love and admiration for the craftsman, especially the country craftsman, find ample expression in the Wessex novels. Old James, the stone-mason in *Under the Greenwood Tree,* is the first such character to be fully rounded out. In *A Pair of Blue Eyes* Stephen Smith's father is also a stone-mason and in describing him Hardy stresses the versatility of the country craftsman as opposed to his urban counterpart (pp. 95–6).

It is clear from the Notebook that Hardy himself was no narrow specialist either. The same point is made about the brothers Sol and Dan Chickerel in *The Hand of Ethelberta* (p. 110) a carpenter and joiner, and house painter respectively.

> ...I am a very good staircase hand; and I have been called neat at sash-frames; and I can do a little at the cabinet-making. I don't mind framing a roof, neither...and I am always ready to fill up my time at planing floor boards by the foot.

> And I can mix and lay flat tints,' said Dan,... 'and pick out mouldings, and grain in every kind of wood you can mention – oak, walnut, satinwood, cherry-tree –

It is almost as if these two were working from the Notebook itself. Furthermore they are country workmen:

> Sol and Dan...had quickly obtained good places of work under a Pimlico builder; for though the brothers scarcely showed as yet the light-fingered deftness of London artizans, the want was in a measure compensated by their painstaking, and employers are far from despising country hands who bring with them strength, industry, and a desire to please. (*idem*, p. 225)

No wonder Sol and Dan Chickerel rise to the status of builders and sign a contract to build a hospital for £20,000 (*idem*, p. 457). Significantly, too, a stone-mason and not an architect is the hero of *Jude the Obscure* which I shall discuss further below. But this Notebook is the work of an architect, not of a single craftsman. In *A Laodicean* we get a glimpse of just such an architect at work. Hardy told W. Lyon Phelps that *A Laodicean* 'contained more of the facts of his own life than anything else he had ever written', a statement which the Notebook certainly corroborates as far as architecture is concerned. See particularly *A Laodicean*, p. 4 for a description of the technique Somerset employed to record the mouldings of old churches; pp. 63 and 67 for Somerset's interest in fonts; pp. 393–4, 443–5, 448–51 for his interest in Northern French Gothic.

In *A Laodicean* Hardy wrote:

> At [Somerset's] suggestion Paula had agreed to have the works executed as such operations were carried out in old times, before the advent of contractors. Each trade required in the building was to be represented by a master-tradesman of that denomination, who should stand responsible for his own section of labour, and for no other, Somerset himself as chief technicist working out his designs on the spot. By this means *the thoroughness of the workmanship* would be greatly increased in comparison with the modern arrangement, whereby a nominal builder, seldom present, who can certainly know no more than one trade intimately and well, and who often does not know that, undertakes the whole.
>
> But notwithstanding its manifest advantages to the proprietor, *the plan added largely to the responsibilities of the architect*, who, with his master-mason, master-carpenter, master-plumber, and what not, had scarcely a moment to call his own. Still, the method being on the face of it the true one, Somerset supervised with a will. (p. 282) (my italics)

These two paragraphs speak for themselves, but without the Notebook we could only have guessed at the full significance of the phrases in my italics above. There are numerous pages in the Notebook that testify to Hardy's efforts to learn about, and if possible to perfect himself in, the technique of carpentry. The same is true of plumbing as exemplified in rain-water pipes, drains and the like. Hardy sometimes notes two ways of overcoming the same structural difficulty (see p. 88) and it is clear that for him each building presents its own special problem. On pp. 90–1, for example, the future author of *Tess of the d'Urbervilles* includes the following suggestion among notes on the construction of a dairy for 90 cows.

> A verandah round outside would be desirable for shade…, & convenient for drying & airing the utensils. (cf. *Tess of the d'Urbervilles*, pp. 216–17)

But what does all this preliminary work lead up to? Here, I suggest, a phrase from the same passage in *A Laodicean* gives us the answer:

> Somerset himself as chief technicist working out his designs on the spot. (p. 282)

'Technicist' is virtually Hardy's own coinage. The earliest example of the use of the word in the OED has been taken precisely from this quotation in *A Laodicean*. It implies something more than what we associate with the word 'technician'. The technicist is a creative artist. The building grows organically, moulded, as it were, by the hands of the technicist in charge. The word allows for that on-the-spot inspiration which Hardy would call spontaneity. Indeed, as his final comment in his review of the Notebook in *The Architectural Review* (April 1967) Nicholas Taylor wrote:

> It will be difficult to omit from future books on nineteenth-century architectural theory the passage from *A Laodicean* quoted above beginning 'At his suggestion...'

But where *A Laodicean* is most unexpectedly autobiographical is in the part played by engineering. It was a great pity that Hardy fell ill when only the first thirteen chapters were completed but was nevertheless compelled from his sick-bed to keep the publishers supplied with parts for the novel's appearance in Harper's New Monthly Magazine from December 1880 to December 1881 (see Purdy, p. 37). Hardy classed *A Laodicean* as a 'novel of ingenuity' and I only surmise that, had he not been so ill at the time of writing, he might well have used his ingenuity to give greater emphasis to the challenge of engineering in the 19th century rather than involve his readers in a plot progressively more intricate and melodramatic. We now know, thanks to the Notebook, that Hardy did have some first-hand experience of engineering, however small. It is unusual for a Gothicist to take much interest in railway engineering, to say the least of it. Scott may have designed St Pancras Station but it was left to Barlow to roof over the actual lines and platforms with what was at the time the widest single span in the world.

Hardy's experience at Crickmay's, working with rolled iron and helping in the construction of railway buildings and the like, gave him a practical insight into the problems of engineering that he would otherwise never have had. Although the firm of Crickmay could not confirm this from their records at the time of the first publication of the Notebook, I still think it unlikely that Hardy would have been concerned with railway work for any other employer. And from then on, it is only one step to the creation of Somerset, the young Gothic architect, who in a deftly contrived situation is brought round to a serious appraisal of railway engineering. Here is Somerset in conversation with Paula Power whose castle he hopes to restore:

> 'You represent science rather than art, perhaps.'
> 'How?' she asked, glancing up under her hat.
> 'I mean,' replied Somerset, 'that you represent the march of mind – the steamship, and the railway, and the thoughts that shake mankind.'
> She weighed his words, and said: 'Ah, yes: you allude to my father. My father was a great man;...'
> 'Did you know that my father made half the railways in Europe, including that one over there?' she said...
> ...'Have you seen the tunnel my father made? The curves are said to be a triumph of science. There is nothing else like it in this part of England.'
> (*A Laodicean*, pp. 101–2)

The railway does not play a conspicuous role in Hardy's other novels. In *Desperate Remedies*, Hardy's first published novel (1871) it does, however, serve as an example of the powerful forces of change. Upon the advent of the steam age, road traffic declined even more sharply in Dorset than elsewhere according to D. St John Thomas in *A Regional History of the Railways of Great Britain*, Vol. I, *The West Country* (1960, p. 136), and with it many a famous coaching inn, like the Three Tranters in *Desperate Remedies*, suddenly deprived of its main source of trade, was left to fall into decay. Significantly, *The Mayor of Casterbridge* is set in the pre-railway age. It is all the more disappointing, therefore, that for reasons of ill health Hardy failed to maintain the promise of the early chapters of *A Laodicean*, as there is certainly room in Victorian fiction for a serious novel inspired by the rival claims of science and art, or in other words by those of Archimedes, Newcomen, Watt, Telford, and Stephenson on the one hand and Pheidias, Ictinus, Callicrates, Chersiphron, Vitruvius, Wilars de Combray, and William of Wykeham on the other – to use Hardy's own selection of great engineers and architects (*A Laodicean*, pp. 124 and 241 respectively). That he had probably once intended to do so seems evident from the following words:

> When he had conscientiously admired the construction of the massive archivault, and the majesty of its nude ungarnished walls, he looked up the slope...
> Somerset still remained where he had placed himself, mentally balancing science against art, the grandeur of this fine piece of construction against that of the castle, and thinking whether Paula's father had not, after all, the best of it,...(p. 106)

Somerset's first reaction to the tunnel may have been a little trite for the 1880s:

> The popular commonplace that science, steam, and travel must always be unromantic and hideous, was not proven at this spot,
> (*A Laodicean*, p. 104).

but his later appreciation of it as an impressive example of functional skill (quoted above) provides a firm basis for further debate. This novel was published in 1881 and many years had passed since Mr Dombey and Major Bagstock made their dramatic journey to Leamington (*Dombey and Son* was published in 1847–48), and even more years since Turner painted his almost visionary picture *Rain, Steam and Speed* in 1844, which incidentally Hardy much admired as he recorded in *The Life*, p. 216. There is, alas, precious little engineering in the rest of the book and the debate is not settled, as it were, until *Jude the Obscure* (1896) where one or two cursory though important references make it clear that Hardy acknowledges the inevitable triumph of the iron road and modernity generally:

> 'Shall we go and sit in the Cathedral?' [Jude] asked, when their meal was finished.
> 'Cathedral? Yes. Though I think I'd rather sit in the railway station.' [Sue] answered,...
> 'That's the centre of the town life now. The Cathedral has had its day!'
> (*Jude the Obscure*, p. 160)

Hardy and Restoration

The Notebook throws much fresh light on the importance of church restoration in Hardy's life and work. Three churches come into the picture here, those of Stinsford, St Juliot and West Knighton in that order. The first concerns the restoration of about 1842, some two years after Hardy's birth; the second the restoration of 1870–2 for which Crickmay was ultimately responsible, or in Hardy's own words for which he 'Made' . drawings . in . March . 1870...in . its . ancient . state . & . later . for . the . Alterations . & . repairs . executed . 1871–2 . which . he . assisted . to . supervise:' These words are taken from the Hardy memorial tablet in St Juliot Church, which he himself designed in 1913. The third restoration in 1893–4 is unique, as far as I know, in that the work was carried out entirely under Hardy's direction.

Let us take the Stinsford restoration first. Hardy was associated with the church and parish of Stinsford all his life, so it is not surprising to find the name of Stinsford occurring more frequently in the Notebook than any other; see pp. 25, 44, 114, 115 and the drawing we are particularly concerned with here, inserted between pp. 115 and 116. A comparison of this sketch with the much rougher ground plan on p. 114, which Hardy presumably made in 1920 when contemplating the design of a new base and stem for the resuscitated Norman font, is most illuminating. Unexpectedly perhaps, the 1920 sketch is the more thoroughly professional, giving numerous measurements and showing such architectural details as the tower arch mould, respond north aisle (the respond to the south aisle had already been most handsomely sketched on p. 25) and on p. 115 the chancel arch moulding. In the sketch of the church before the 1840–42 alteration on the other hand, the antiquarian in Hardy predominates and he has been careful to give prominence to features that no longer exist. These two contrasting sketches, then, tell us a great deal about the history of the church since before Hardy's birth in 1840.

The most striking feature in the 1842 sketch is the churchyard path leading to the sole entrance in the north wall. Today the public enters by a west door in the tower. Another obvious difference is indicated by the dotted line showing the position of the west gallery which was not removed until some time later before the end of the century (only to be rebuilt in 1996, see above). It has long been known that the Hardys had been leading members of the church band at Stinsford for nearly forty years before it was finally wound up in 1841 or 1842 (according to *The Life,* p. 9) so that the sketch of the church before the 1842 restoration is of special interest, being a record of the building as it looked when the church band was in its heyday, as it looked indeed when from the body of the church his mother first beheld her future husband up in the west gallery 'ardent, young and trim, Bowing "New Sabbath" or "Mount

Ephraim" ' as Hardy records in his poem 'A Church Romance'. Similarly, in *Under the Greenwood Tree*:

> Dick [who is in the gallery] cast his eyes over his grandfather's shoulder, and saw the vision of the past night [Fancy Day] enter the porch door…

The Mellstock Church of the novel cannot therefore, strictly speaking, have been modelled on the Stinsford Church Hardy knew. Of this particular restoration he wrote in his *Notes on Stinsford Church*:

> Most of the seating, wainscoting, &c., that is decayed and loose seems to be the parts made of deal that were inserted at the disastrous restoration about 1840, when the excellent oak pews of Caroline or early Georgian date were swept away, some re-arranged portions of them being replaced, the entrance by a north door having been changed to west at the same time.

Lady Susan O'Brien (1743–1827), whose name appears on the sketch and who was buried next to her actor husband William O'Brien (1738–1815) in Stinsford Church, would have made a perfect Hardy heroine. However, Hardy's interest in her was probably aroused through what he had learnt of her romantic life from his father. After a vivid description of the burning of Stinsford House on September, 1892, Hardy comments:

> I am sorry for the house. It was where Lady Susan Strangways, afterwards Lady Susan O'Brien, lived so many years with her actor-husband, after the famous elopement in 1764, so excellently described in Walpole's Letters,…
>
> …she knew my grandfather well, and he carefully heeded her tearful instructions to build the vault for her husband and later herself, 'just large enough for us two'…
>
> My father when a boy-chorister in the gallery of the church used to see her, an old and lonely widow, walking in the garden in a red cloak.
> (*The Life*, p. 250)

Stinsford House (p. 44) and Church are very close, barely six feet separating the two buildings at one point.

The name Pitt, also written in on the sketch, would not have had such vivid associations for Hardy as Lady Susan, but there is no doubt about the importance of Kingston Maurward House and estate, the 'manor' of Hardy's childhood, according to p. 198 in Purdy. This is referred to directly or indirectly on four pages of the Notebook, namely, 44, 119–20 and 62. Again according to Purdy, James Fellowes bought Kingston Maurward in 1853 and it remained in his family into the 20th century.

The house on p. 45 is called simply Kingston House. but I am quite sure that Hardy meant Kingston Maurward precisely *because* the Maurward had been left out! Had it been Kingston Lacy or Russell, for example, which are both a long way from Stinsford and hold no childhood memories for Hardy, he would undoubtedly have named it.

The Kingston Maurward House of Hardy's plan on p. 45 presents something of a problem. It is totally unlike the house as it stands today. I now live near to it and have occasion to visit it several times a year. I see no reason to change the views I expressed in 1966. Hermann Lea suggests that Knapwater House in *Desperate Remedies* was 'probably suggested by Kingston Maurward House,' a building which Hardy describes as follows.

> The house was regularly and substantially built of clean grey freestone throughout, in that plainer fashion of classicism which prevailed at the latter end of the eighteenth century, when the copyists called designers had grown weary of fantastic variations in the Roman orders. *The main block approximated to a square on the ground plan*, having a projection in the centre of each side, surmounted by a pediment. From each angle of the inferior side ran a line of buildings lower than the rest, turning inwards again at their further end, and forming within them a spacious open court, within which resounded an echo of astonishing clearness…(my italics)
> …The natural features and contour of this quarter of the site had evidently dictated the position of the house primarily,…namely, a broad, graceful slope running from the terrace beneath the walls to the margin of a placid lake lying below,…An irregular wooded island stood in the midst of the lake; (p. 69).

This description certainly matches up more faithfully with the drawing than with the building itself. Kingston Maurward has never been adorned with more than one pediment on the south front as far as I have discovered, but there is no reason why Hardy's 'arrangement of Kingston House' for literary purposes should not have had four pediments. I contend that this drawing is Hardy's plan not of Kingston Maurward but of the mansion he was going to describe as Knapwater House in *Desperate Remedies*. I also think that H. Lea has correctly identified the fane of the novel as having been suggested by the Temple in Kingston Park. On pp. 119–120 of the Notebook Hardy has drawn the ground plan not only of the Temple but also of its water lily pond in relation to the lake beyond. The puzzle is why he should have made such a careful and elaborate sketch of this feature. I checked some of Hardy's measurements on the spot and they corresponded exactly. The Royal Commission on Historical Monuments, however, informed me that the pool and steps were probably of late 19th or early 20th-century date, the Temple itself being much earlier. Hardy was friendly with the Hanburys who occupied Kingston Maurward for over 20 years from 1914, and it is tempting to explain the purpose of this meticulous drawing – one of the few to occupy two whole pages – by saying that he himself designed the water lily pool. In the original drawing, the pool and the lake are shaded in blue crayon.

The St Juliot restoration (see pp. 38, 39 and 75) is the most fully documented of any with which Hardy was concerned, but this information is *not* to be found in the Architectural Notebook. Readers can refer to *The Life* and to my recent publication (2004) *The Part Played by Architecture in the Life and Work of Thomas Hardy* where, among other documentation, photographs are reproduced of the drawings I found in the Weymouth offices of Crickmay & Sons in 1958. (Almost all of these were subsequently sold, and are now in the library of the University of Texas.)

Finally we come to the last restoration, that of West Knighton Church (pp. 109–12), which is the most important of the three for it was openly attributed to Hardy. The facts are as follows, taken from *The Builder*, 26 May 1894, p. 411:

Repair of West Knighton Church

The ancient church of West Knighton, which was closed for repairs in August last, has just been re-opened. The chancel roof which was decayed, has been removed and a new roof with stone tiles erected. The inner walls have all had the old plaster cleaned off and been cemented throughout. Mullions and tracery have been added to the windows on the north side, and both windows have been made uniform.

This restoration was carried out under the direction of Mr. Thomas Hardy. A little window has been re-opened in the chancel. All the windows have been reglazed except two that contained painted glass. An irregular little window with a wooden frame in the upper part of the south wall has been built up, and a sky-light has been opened to light the gallery. When removing the plaster from the south wall of the nave an old arch with pillar and a portion of a second arch were discovered. These have been restored. Traces of old frescoes were discovered on the wall of the south transept and over the church door, and inscriptions on the south wall of the nave. The gallery has been removed, and a new gallery has been put in its place. The font, which was under the gallery, has been placed near the church door. The floor has been laid throughout with encaustic tiles...

On p. 109 of the Notebook there is a neat sketch of a window on the north side from the outside. Underneath Hardy has written:

Jamb good to springing – above, the inner member is inserted roughly – evidently when tracery was taken out.

Hardy's proposed tracery has been sketched in but not the mullions as at this stage it had not been decided whether to have a two-light or a three-light window. The latter was in fact chosen. The second piece of restoration for which Hardy was directly responsible on the evidence of the Notebook (a fact not mentioned in *The Builder* article above) was the insertion of a new window in the tower west wall. With this in view Hardy obviously made a careful study of the Early English window in the west wall of the transept for the purpose of making the new window correspond to it in style. On pp. 111 and 112 of the Notebook there are sketches relevant to the proposed new window.

As a result of this restoration, Hardy wrote a note in pencil in the margin of his copy of Hutchins (which is in the keeping of the Dorset County Museum), next to the paragraph on Knighton Church. After the sentence 'As observed by Hutchins, it contains nothing remarkable', Hardy's little * takes us to his marginal note: * This statement is not now correct. Recent examination & repairs have uncovered much interesting early architecture. (*The History and Antiquities of the County of Dorset* by John Hutchins. Third Edition, Vol. II, p. 503)

In the first edition of this Notebook (1966) I chose to consider the restoration of Stratton Church (1889–91), in which Hardy had participated as a member of the Society for the Protection of Ancient Buildings, before discussing West Knighton. In the case of Stratton, the SPAB and the Hon. Mrs Ashley, the most important benefactor, were involved, together with the architect, G.R. Crickmay, Ewan Christian of the Ecclesiastical Commission and others. In what had seemed to me a very unhappy restoration I wrote that 'the chief culprit was the lady of the manor who contributed most of the money'. Now as a result of further research I can absolve Mrs Ashley of all blame in the matter. (Readers interested in the Stratton restoration will find it fully treated in my book *Thomas Hardy: Conservation Architect*, published in 1995.) The situation at West Knighton was very different. Hardy was in charge, his brother Henry was the contractor, and the SPAB apparently had no part in the proceedings.

Hardy's restoration of West Knighton was the work of a seasoned campaigner. He knew what he was doing. He was well aware of William Morris's manifesto reprinted in full in every report of the SPAB.

What if Hardy did make the two windows on the north side uniform and – sackcloth and ashes – what if he did pierce the west wall of the tower with an 'Early English' window! The proof of the pudding is in the eating. Repairs had to be carried out at West Knighton Church and these were done in the most unobtrusive way possible.

Let us remind ourselves of the date of this restoration, namely, 1893–4. Was it a coincidence that while he was restoring West Knighton Hardy was also engaged in writing *Jude the Obscure*? In his bibliographical study of Thomas Hardy, Purdy wrote:

> ...The scenes [of the novel] were revisited in October 1892; the narrative was in outline in 1892 and the spring of 1893 and at full length,...from August 1893 onwards into the next year; the whole,...being in the hands of the publisher by the end of 1894. (p. 89)

Until the discovery of this Notebook and the article in *The Builder* quoted above – (Peter Ferriday kindly informed me of its existence in about 1961) – critics could only assume that in the restoration scenes of the novel Hardy was drawing on his experiences between the years 1856 and 1872. Yet the following from the novel:

> He examined the mouldings, stroked them as one who knew their beginning, said they were difficult or easy in the working, had taken little or much time, were trying to the arm, or convenient to the tool.
> (*Jude the Obscure*, p. 97)

might equally apply to the successful middle-aged novelist unobtrusively at work on the restoration of West Knighton Church. I am suggesting that there is a link between the two processes, that of craftsman at work in stone and in the writer with the pen. What a wonderful release from frustration it must have been for Hardy to feel the mouldings once again...

> When the gates were shut, and he could no longer get into the quadrangles, he rambled under the walls and doorways, feeling with his fingers the contours of their mouldings and carving.
> (*Jude the Obscure*, p. 92)

...and to know that for the first time (as far as is known) he was in complete charge of a restoration. At the same time by the creative act of writing *Jude the Obscure* he was exorcising the demon of restoration which tormented him for so long. In one of his reports to the SPAB on Stratton Church he wrote:

> Irregularity is the genius of Gothic architecture...

Does not this aspect of Gothic art provide Hardy with an extended image running right through *Jude the Obscure*? As he restored West Knighton – wisely avoiding a spontaneous irregularity which is not the prerogative of a restorer – he must have felt that

> ...there in the old walls were the broken lines of the original idea; jagged curves, disdain of precision, irregularity, disarray.
> (*Jude the Obscure*, p. 98)

Very few buildings are described in *Jude the Obscure* but there are Gothic details in profusion: saints and prophets, crocketed pinnacles, porticoes, gurgoyles, (Hardy's spelling) window-tracery, mullions, east windows etc., – just the kind of details Hardy sketched in the Notebook, just the kind which a master-mason would stamp with his personality as he was working in the stone, and so produce a unique effect of spontaneity or unexpectedness. Such details form a subtle accompaniment to Sue Bridehead's elusive personality, which Hardy said in *The Life* (p. 272) was a difficult one to portray. In 1893 he wrote:

> I consider a social system based on individual spontaneity to promise better for happiness than a curbed and uniform one under which all temperaments are bound to shape themselves to a single pattern of living
> (*The Life*, p. 258)

At one point in *Jude the Obscure* Sue exclaims mournfully: 'We must conform!' (p. 413) Such an attitude is correct in church restoration. Hardy fully realised that at West Knighton he was only 'copying, patching and imitating' (*Jude the Obscure*, pp. 98–9). By all means make the two windows uniform, for as Ruskin said in *The Seven Lamps of Architecture*, 'The Lamp of Memory': '...restoration...is a Lie from beginning to end'. But the same principles do not apply to the living in whom uniformity tends to mean the death of original thought, the quenching of the spirit.

The proper restraint that Hardy exercised in the restoration of West Knighton, the negative qualities he so skilfully displayed, contributed by contrast, as it were, to a greater awareness of his own ideal as expressed in the spontaneity of Gothic art. In *The Life* we read:

> He knew that in architecture cunning irregularity is of enormous worth, and it is obvious that he carried on into his verse,...the Gothic art-principle in which he had been trained – the principle of spontaneity, found in mouldings, tracery, and such like – resulting in the 'unforeseen'... character of his metres and stanzas, that of stress rather than of syllable, poetic texture rather than poetic veneer;... (p. 301)

The letter killeth (quoted on the title-page of *Jude the Obscure*), but the Gothic art-principle, the principle of spontaneity, results in the unforeseen, in the creation of a character like Sue Bridehead.

The Importance of the Notebook

With the exception of a few pages, the Notebook's contents are almost equally divided between Hardy's Gothic studies and interests, and work done for strictly domestic and functional purposes. Which of these two groups is likely to interest us more? I suggest the second group, and principally those pages concerned with secular buildings which he must have done while working for G.R. Crickmay of Weymouth between about April 1869 and the end of April 1871. All these pages show Hardy as a learner, eager – or at least anxious – to acquire new architectural techniques and even some knowledge of engineering.

Significantly, this side of Hardy's work for Crickmay is not mentioned in *The Life*. This was a crucial time in Hardy's career: he wanted to marry, his first novel *Desperate Remedies* (1871) had not been a financial success and, through a misunderstanding, the publication of *Under the Greenwood Tree* (1872) was unnecessarily delayed.

> He consulted Miss Gifford [his fiancée] by letter, declaring that he had banished novel-writing for ever, and was going on with architecture henceforward.
> (*The Life*, p. 86)

Her reply, in which she showed unshakeable faith in Hardy as a writer, only made him the more eager, paradoxically, to pursue architecture as a profession 'being obviously the quick way to an income for marrying on' (p. 87). Hence the importance of all those new techniques he was learning at Crickmay's. To imagine Hardy as he then was, we must think of him in his early thirties, anxious to make a success of architecture. Drains were now more important to him than fonts. We must picture him, for example, in the noise and clatter of a railway yard carefully looking both ways before stepping over the lines rather than striding about silent churchyards and stumbling over the occasional tombstone. All this experience would have stood the future architect in good stead. The man 'of measuring eye' was no longer required to judge the height of a church tower or the width of a porch but to gauge the size of a carriage door or the length of a girder. This too was the age of social reforms. New hospitals, schools and prisons were being built. Hardy was no longer concerned only with the seating arrangements of a church but with the more urgent problem of how much space should be allocated to each individual man or woman in a large institution such as a hospital.

While the Notebook as a whole is important because it provides information about Thomas Hardy that can be obtained nowhere else, the pages dealing with Hardy's non-ecclesiastical work at Crickmay's are outstandingly so. This information is not only fresh but totally unexpected and shows us an energetic young man who, for all he could tell at the time, was about to make architecture his lifelong career. Indeed his work with Crickmay paid early dividends for it must have helped him to obtain what turned out to be his last commission as a professional architect but which in another sense might have been his first, namely his work as Roger Smith's assistant in the designing of Board Schools in 1872.

If I were asked to select the three or four most important pages in the whole Notebook as opposed to any group of pages, I should unhesitatingly select those dealing with West Knighton. When Hardy agreed to direct the West Knighton restoration he must have used the Notebook for the first time since leaving Crickmay some twenty years previously. He was also in the middle of composing his last major long novel. As he turned over the pages of the Notebook to find a blank space to record his measurements and make his sketches he must assuredly have been reminded – among other things – of those hectic years in London. He may indeed already have deliberately consulted the Notebook to refresh his memory of the past. *Jude the Obscure* is, in my view, Hardy's greatest novel. It is extraordinary to think that Hardy's humble work at West Knighton – virtually unknown until recent years – should have been a living part of the novel and so be in a measure to blame for the explosion of notoriety that burst in upon Hardy following its publication. As Hardy worked his way through and beyond the problems of restoration in that little church – West Knighton is still relatively remote and unvisited – so in the novel did he tackle honestly and ruthlessly the problems of modern life, not least of which was his own, and a more general, loss of faith. The common factor was the stonemason's craft, that of working in stone, and this for Hardy was a more powerful remembrancer than any Notebook.

Sir Albert Richardson, who had met Hardy in 1923 at Max Gate when he was architect to the Duchy of Cornwall, told me that he was the author of Hardy's obituary in *The Builder*, 28 January 1928. It was entitled 'The Master Craftsman'. The Architectural Notebook is a major contribution to our understanding of this term when applied to Thomas Hardy both as writer and architect.

Appendix: Further Details

1. Details of pp. 173–76

The greater part of p. 173 has been pasted in on yellow tracing paper; all drawings on pp. 174 and 175 are on yellow tracing paper; on p. 176 the panel marked 'Celtic' is on yellow tracing paper while most of the other drawings have been pasted in on white tracing paper. The following is a list of the figures and motifs on these pages of the Notebook which I have identified as having been taken from *The Grammar of Ornament*, by Owen Jones (1856), one hundred folio plates, drawn on stone by F. Bedford.

Page 173

- Figure, top centre, taken from Plate XXXV, no. 16, Arabian.
- Figure, top extreme left, possibly taken from Plate XXXV, no. 15, Arabian.
- The four calligraphic figures beginning with a vertical line are Turkish, Plate XXXVII.

Page 174

- All the patterns are Arabian.
- From top to bottom and from left to right where appropriate the patterns were taken from Plate XXXI, nos 29, 28, 27, 2, part of 6 (the horn shape), 10, 36 and 4.
- The two remaining patterns are incomplete tracings of no. 13 (left) and no. 23 (right) of Plate XXXII.

Page 175
- Motif, top centre second row down, taken from Plate XLIX, no. 2, Indian.
- Flower motif, extreme right third row down, taken from Plate XLIX, no. 19, Indian.
- Motif, bottom left, almost certainly taken from Plate LV, no. 5, Indian.
- The 2nd and 3rd motifs from the bottom left were taken from the same pattern, Plate XVIII, no. 21, Greek.
- The leaf and flower motif occupying the right hand corner, taken from Plate XVIII, no. 15, Greek.
- The fan-like motif with 18 petals, 2nd row from the bottom 3rd from the left, taken from Plate LIV, no. 6, Indian.
- The filigree motif, extreme left 4th from the top, taken from Plate LI, no. 10, Indian.

Page 176
- The three-stemmed papyrus-like motif was taken from the title page.
- Just below and to the centre is an Arabian motif, taken from Ch.VIII, p. 3.
- The Celtic design was taken from the Aberlemno Cross on Plate LXIII.
- Above left is the head of a New Guinea canoe traced from figure in Ch. I, p. 3.
- To the right of this, part of an Egyptian motif taken from Plate X, no. 19.

2. Technical details

For those interested in technical details, here are some points to look out for.

On p. 3 the process now known as 'shuttering' or 'form work' is described as 'temporary wood bearing pieces'. On p. 4 there is a left-hand thread (bottom right corner), a rare example of carelessness. Notice the trouble taken over a metal weather bar (full size) on p. 19 and also, on p. 21, a special detail to enable ventilation at the middle of a sash window without causing a draught at the bottom. (The taper at the top allows the air to enter while at the bottom the window and frame are drawn in contact thus showing how draught is excluded.) On p. 37 three technical problems are being tackled; note particularly the batten spacing formula in the centre and the water bar under the door at the bottom. The plate glass bedded in wash leather on p. 42 suggests superior workmanship, as does the cavity wall on p. 47 with, by modern standards, a double thickness of outer wall. Two methods of sound insulation can be studied at the bottom of p. 52 and, on p. 61, notice the piles driven into the ground to support the extra weight of the tower. The highly professional details on p. 84 refer to key points on the roof structure drawn on p. 83. The fact that each step of a staircase (p. 161) is to be made of solid oak is unusual.

3. Hardy and Victor Hugo

It is perhaps worth noting, especially in view of Hardy's strong admiration and affection for Victor Hugo, that Trinity Schools (Weymouth) are actually mentioned in his last great work *L'Homme qui Rit* on p. 225. The editor of this novel states that Victor Hugo was in Weymouth on 9 October 1866 and bought a map of Portland in a local bookshop. A final essay called 'La Baie de Portland' originally figures as the first chapter of the novel and was considered by the critics worth preserving in this way. Many other localities in the area are also mentioned by Hugo including Ringstead, Saint-Thomas Street, Melcomb-Regis, Radipole, Dorchester, Wyke Regis, Chess-Hill (sic), etc. Hardy would be delighted, I am sure, to share part of Wessex with so great a precursor. Asked for his tribute to the genius of Victor Hugo on the centenary of his birth Hardy wrote:

> 'His memory must endure. His works are the cathedrals of literary architecture, his imagination adding greatness to the colossal and charm to the small.'
> (*The Life*, p. 311)

The Architectural Notebook of Thomas Hardy

Note on the Pagination and the Facsimile

Pagination of the Reproduction of the Notebook
Hardy's pagination is retained throughout. The pagination is as follows:

Pages 1–73, then 70, 71, 72, 73 again; the page which comes after 73 and before 76 (which is blank and once had something pasted over it and later removed) is unnumbered; pp. 77–115; a ground plan of Stinsford Church has been inserted between pp. 115 and 116; pp. 116 and 117; p. 118 is blank; pp. 119 and 120; pp. 121–156 are blank; pp. 157–183; p. 184 is blank; pp. 185–190.

Hardy's Notebook is reproduced here in the exact size of the original.

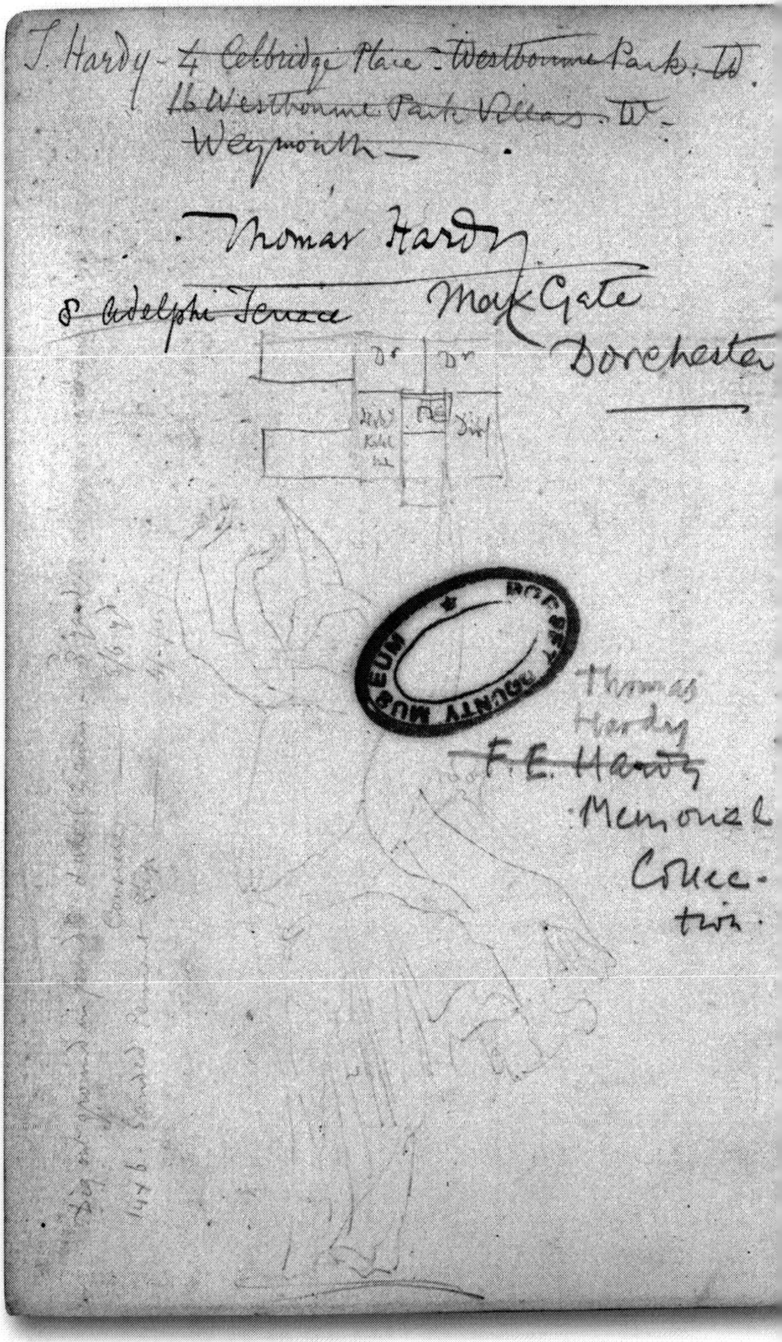
T. Hardy - 4 Celbridge Place - Westbourne Park. W
16 Westbourne Park Villas. W -
Weymouth -
Thomas Hardy
8 Adelphi Terrace
Max Gate
Dorchester
DORSET COUNTY MUSEUM
Thomas
Hardy
F. E. Hardy
Memorial
Collec-
tion.

1

Pine Timber.

The Red Fir or Pine is the "pinus sylvestris" common to the north of Europe – by our people called Scotch fir: in commerce it is called Baltic fir, Riga Fir, Memel Timber, &c. It grows also in British America & the north of the United States; and is called Red Pine in commerce: it appears to be identical with the Red Fir of the north of Europe, but seems to grow quicker, being a freer wood, with fewer knots. The European is always called in shipbuilding Fir; the British American, Pine.

The white Pine is the "Pinus Strobus" & is a softer & much freer wood, shows scarcely any fibre, & is indigenous to the North American continent only, especially to Canada & New Brunswick. This is the largest of the pines or firs of commerce, & par excellence the house carpenter's wood. The deals from it are the largest import of wood stuffs. The finest growth is from the entrance of the Gulf of St Lawrence to Quebec, & frequently called Yellow pine. Its colour inclines to a pale yellow....

The white wood of Europe is the Norway Spruce ("Abies") from which the ordinary deals of commerce called White Spruce, are manufactured – the inferior qualities being very knotty. The same or very nearly the same wood is found in North America especially in New Brunswick; but the reduction of the duties on foreign wood is greatly interfering with their import. As to strength or value in ship or housebuilding, the red & the white differ greatly – the Red fir & pine being the hardest, the strongest & least subject to decay or rot. The White Pine is far inferior in strength, & more subject to rot; but, in fact, the most useful. The Spruce seldom comes in size for timber & when used in shipbuilding is given to very early decay.

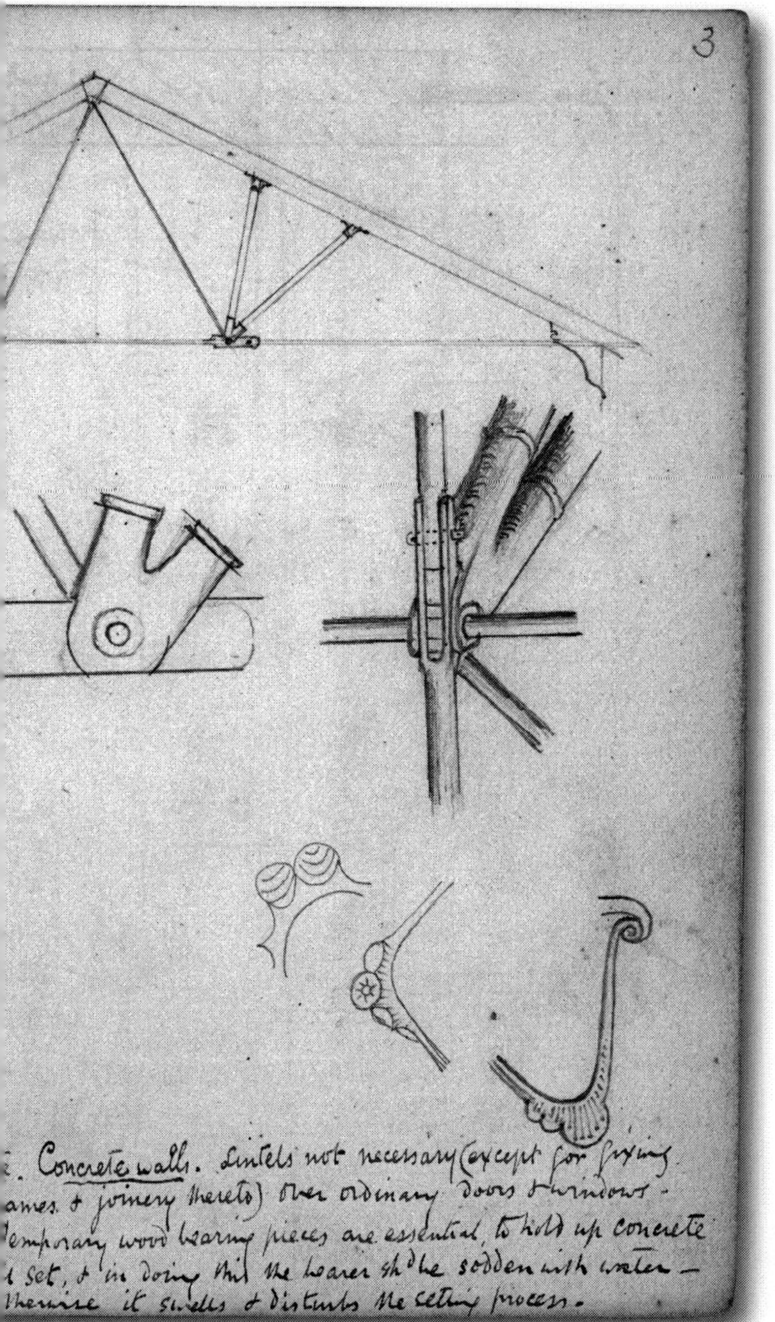
3
. Concrete walls. Lintels not necessary (except for fixing
ames. & joinery thereto) over ordinary doors & windows -
emporary wood bearing pieces are essential, to hold up concrete
l set, & in doing this the bearer sh^d be sodden with water —
therwise it swells & disturbs the setting process.

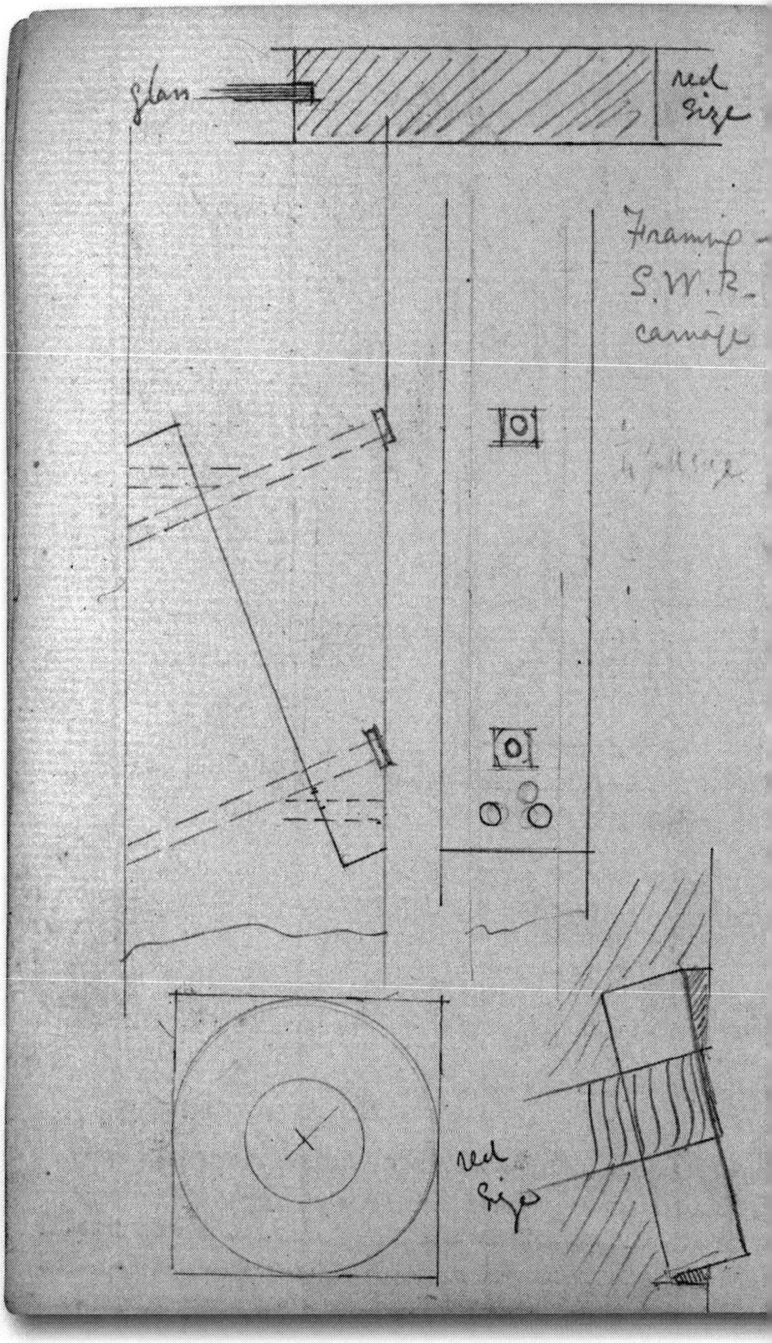
glass
red
size
Framing
S.W.K.
carriage
red
size

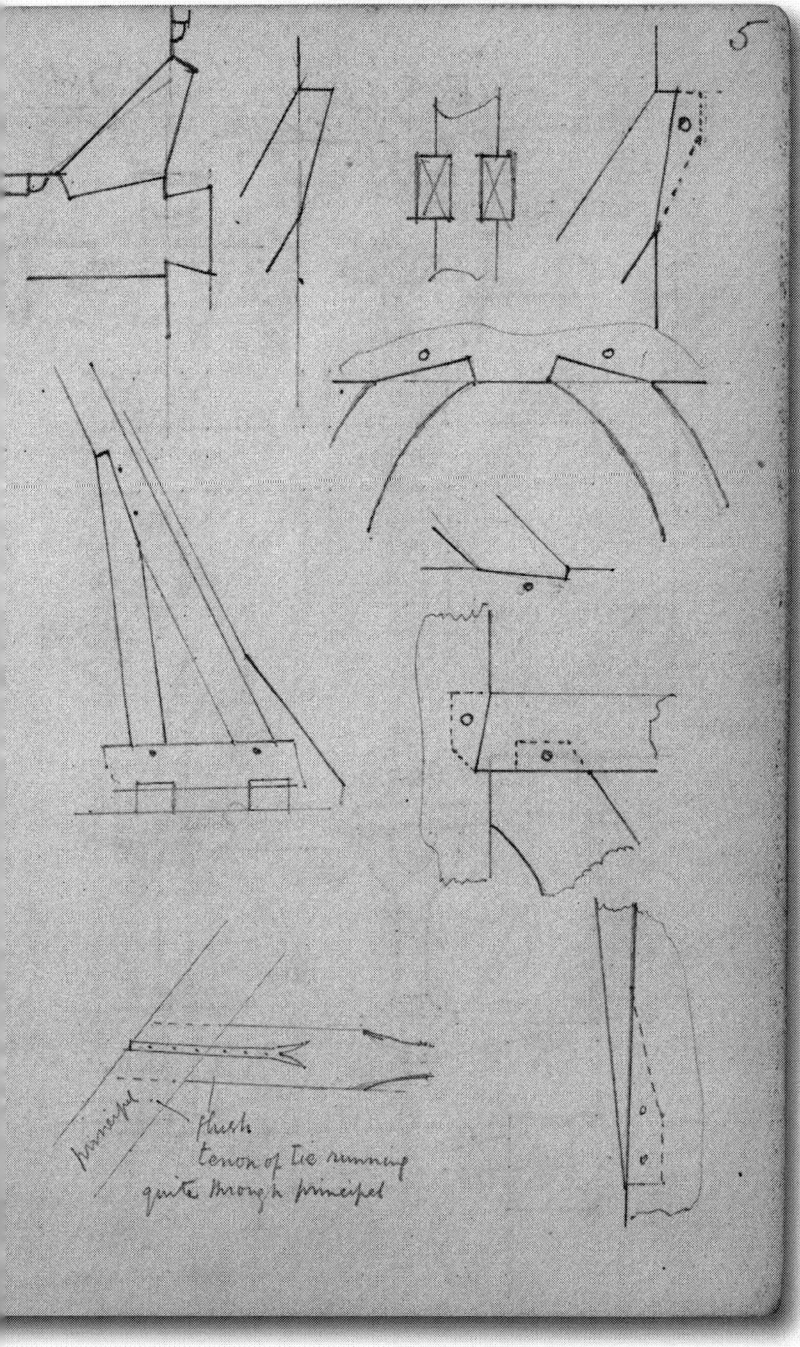
5
principal
flush
tenon of tie running
quite through principal

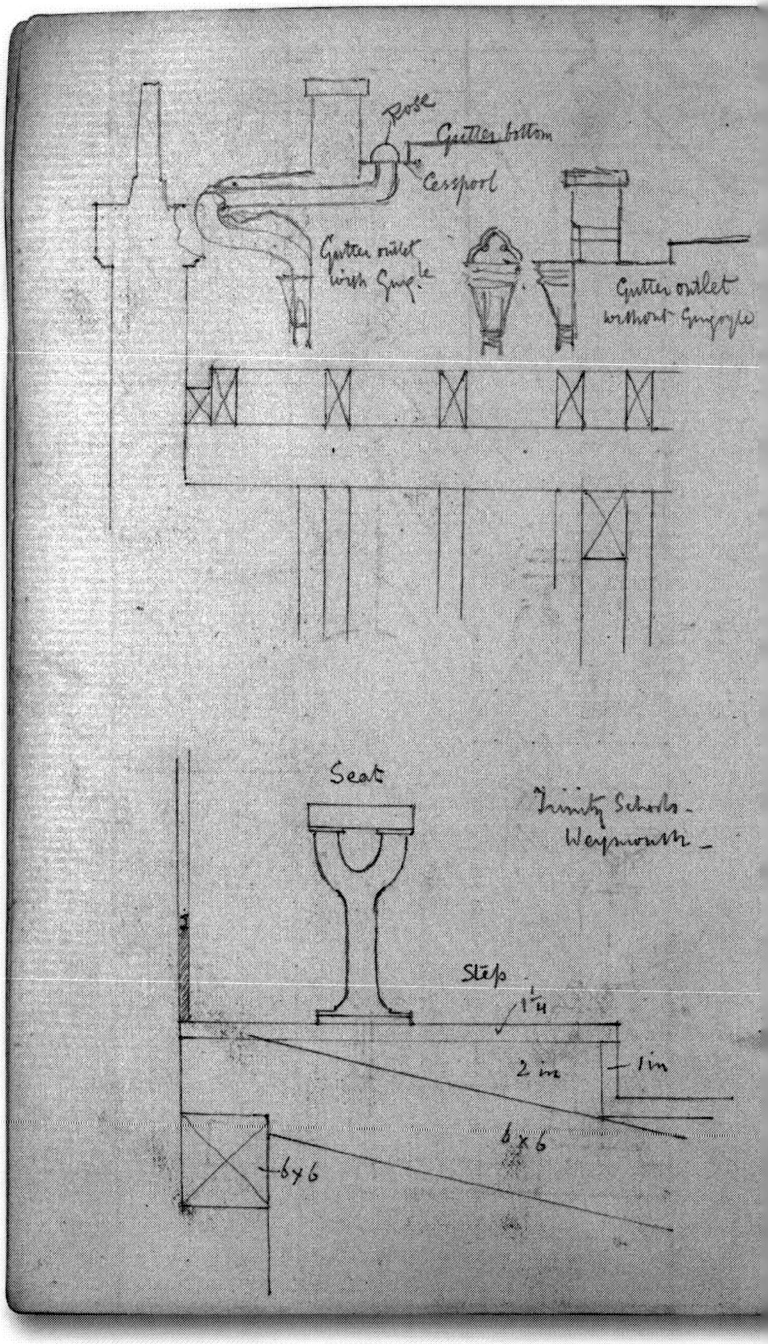
Rose
Gutter bottom
Cesspool
Gutter outlet with Gurg.le
Gutter outlet without Gurgoyle
Seat
Trinity Schools -
Weymouth -
Step
1¼
2 in
1 in
6 x 6
6x6

7
Alkham
Kent.
Verona
Verona
Angel
Supporting

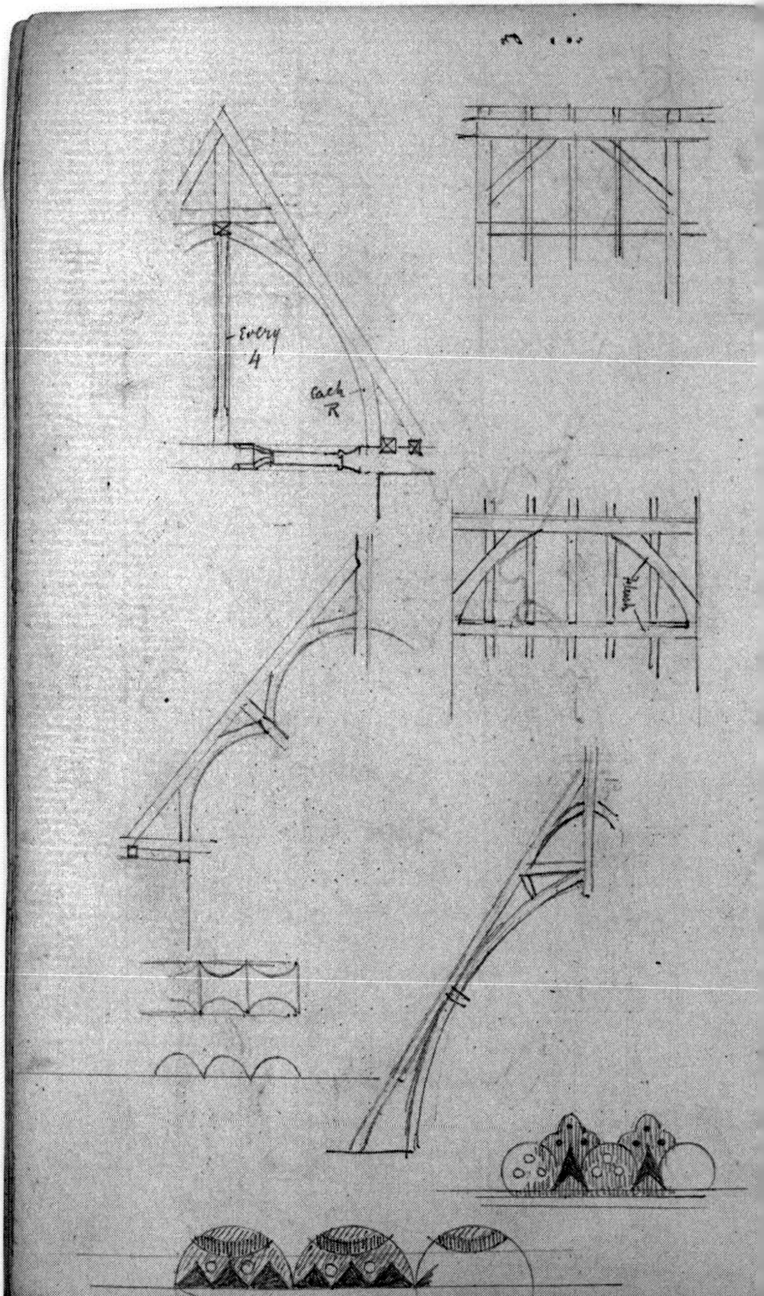
every
4
each
R

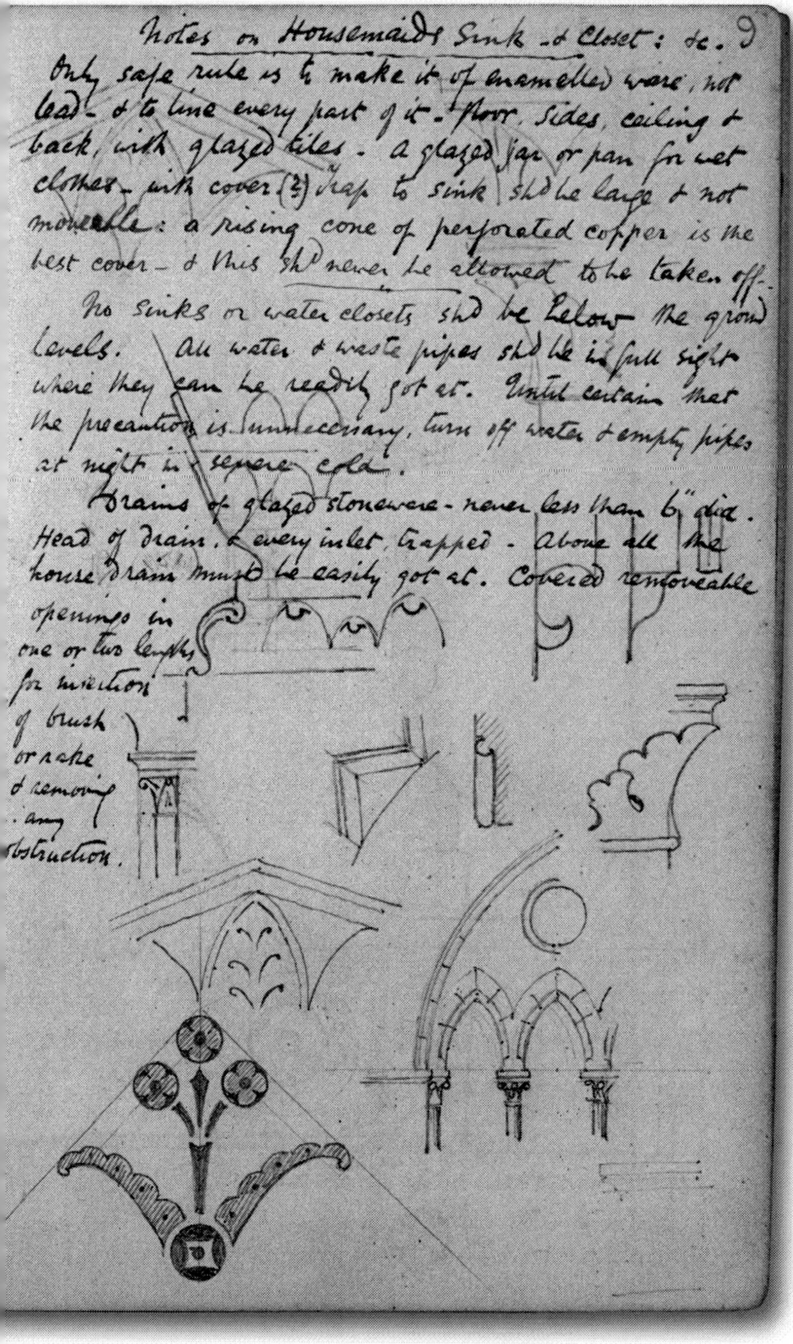

Notes on Housemaids Sink & Closet: &c. 9

Only safe rule is to make it of enamelled ware, not lead – & to line every part of it – floor, sides, ceiling & back, with glazed tiles. A glazed jar or pan for wet clothes – with cover (?) Trap to sink shd be large & not moveable: a rising cone of perforated copper is the best cover – & this shd never be allowed to be taken off.

No sinks or water closets shd be below the ground levels. All water & waste pipes shd be in full sight where they can be readily got at. Until certain that the precaution is unnecessary, turn off water & empty pipes at night in severe cold.

Drains of glazed stoneware – never less than 6" dia. Head of drain, & every inlet, trapped – Above all the house drain must be easily got at. Covered removeable openings in one or two lengths for insertion of brush or rake & removing any obstruction.

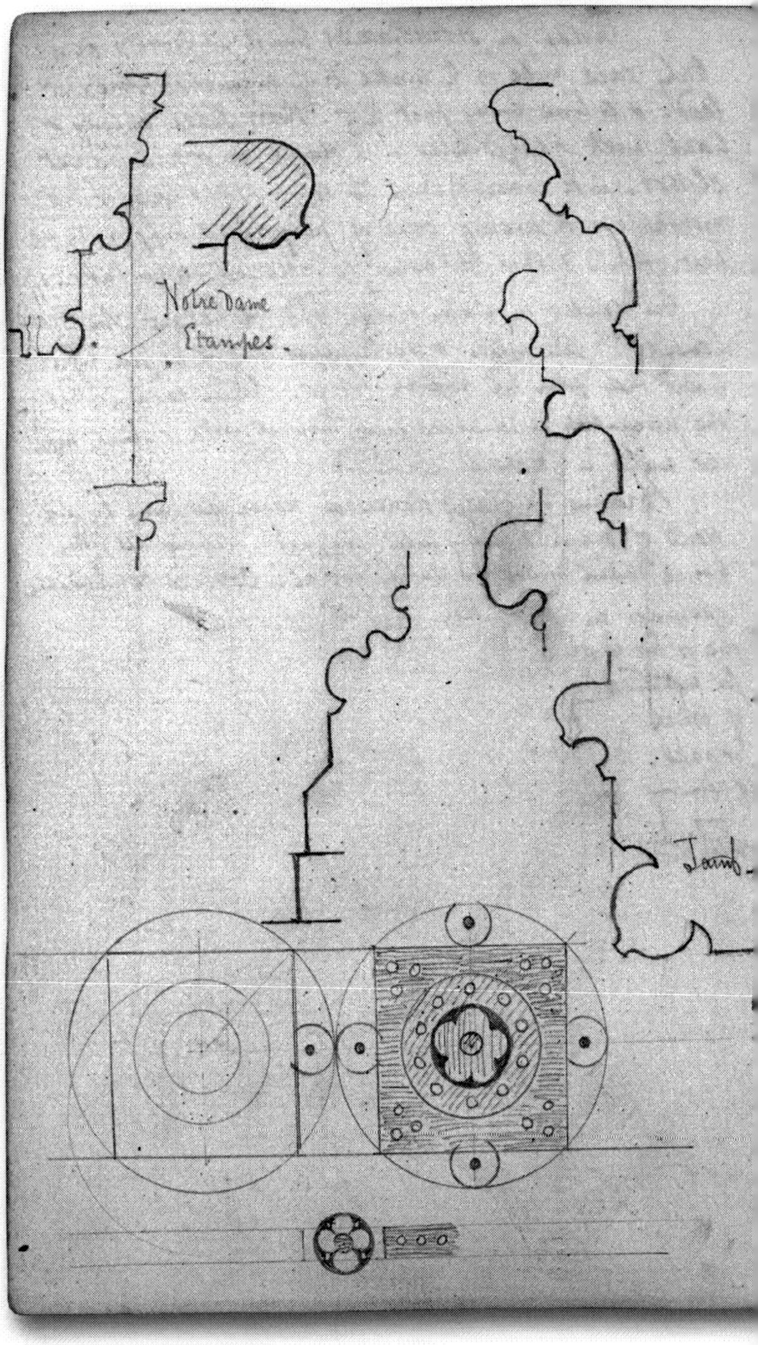
Notre Dame
Etampes.

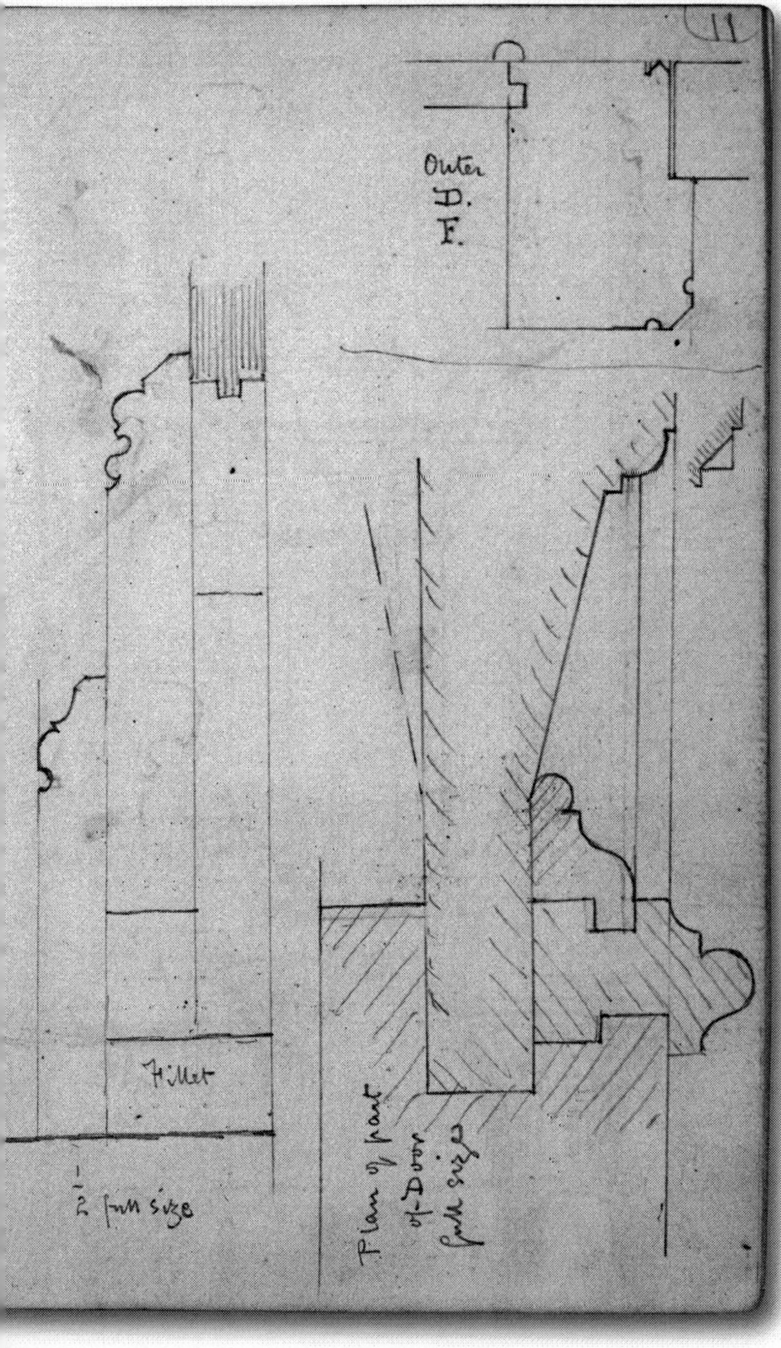
11
Outer D. F.
Fillet
½ full size
Plan of part of Door full size

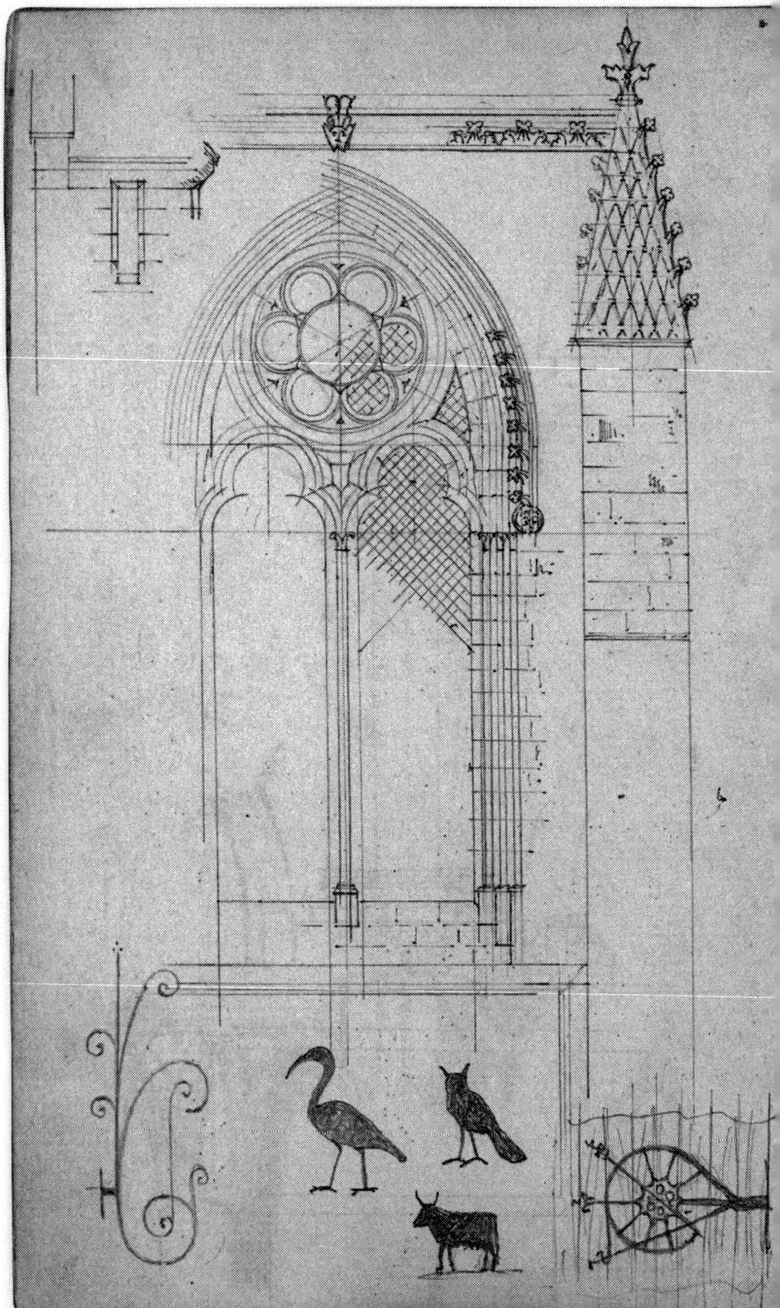

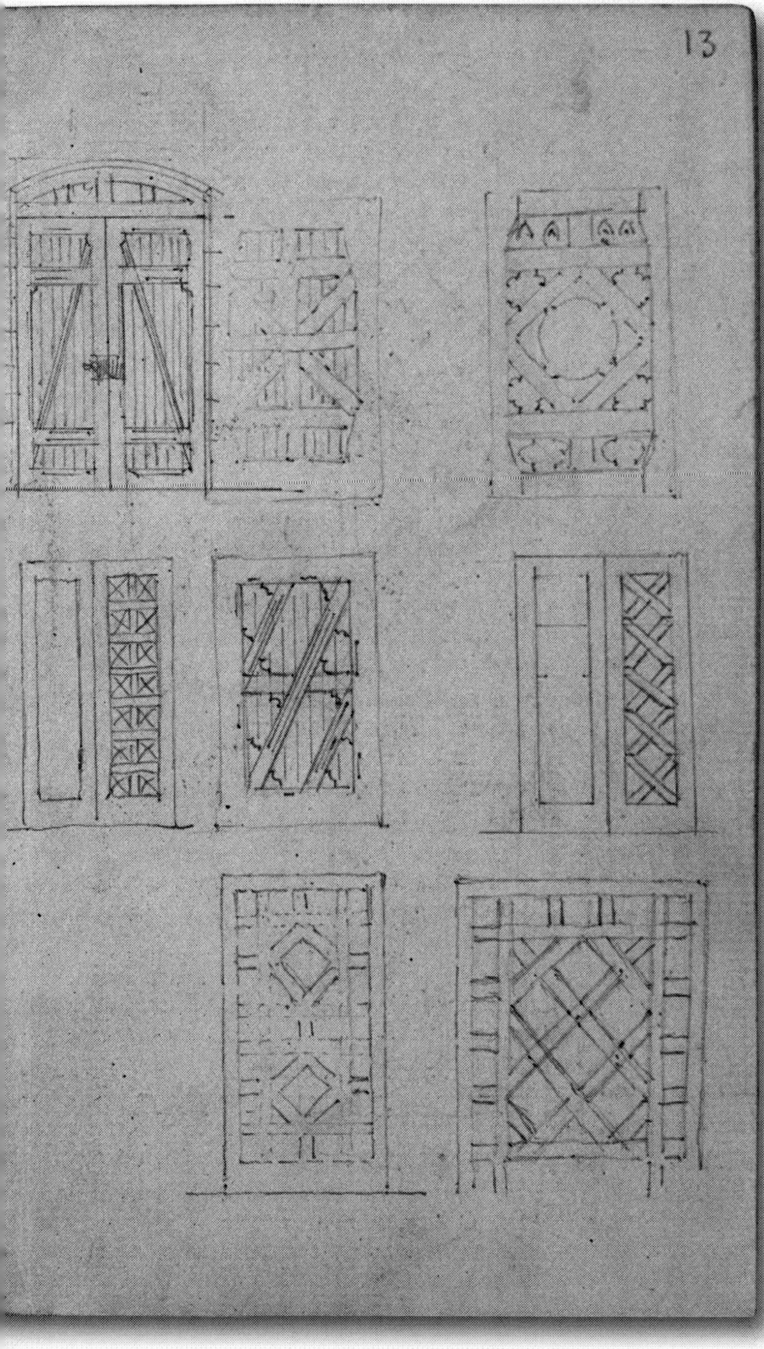
13

pp. 014 – 015

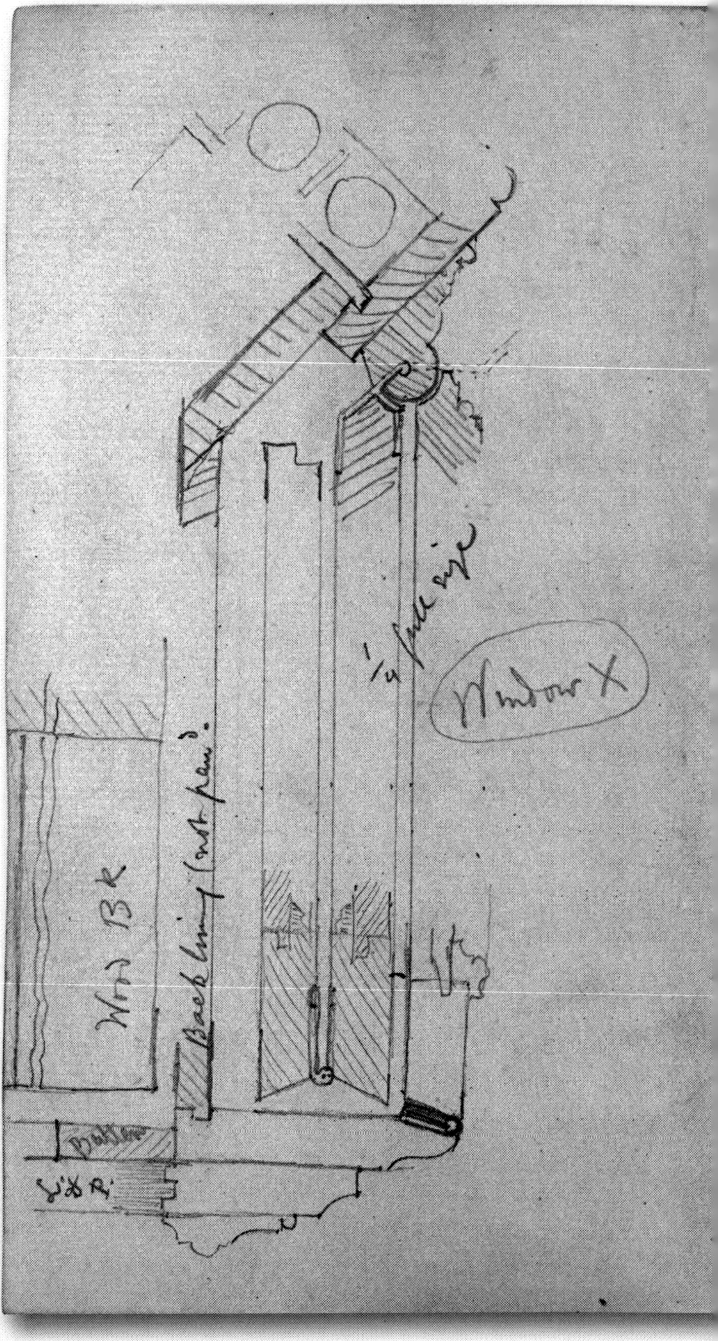

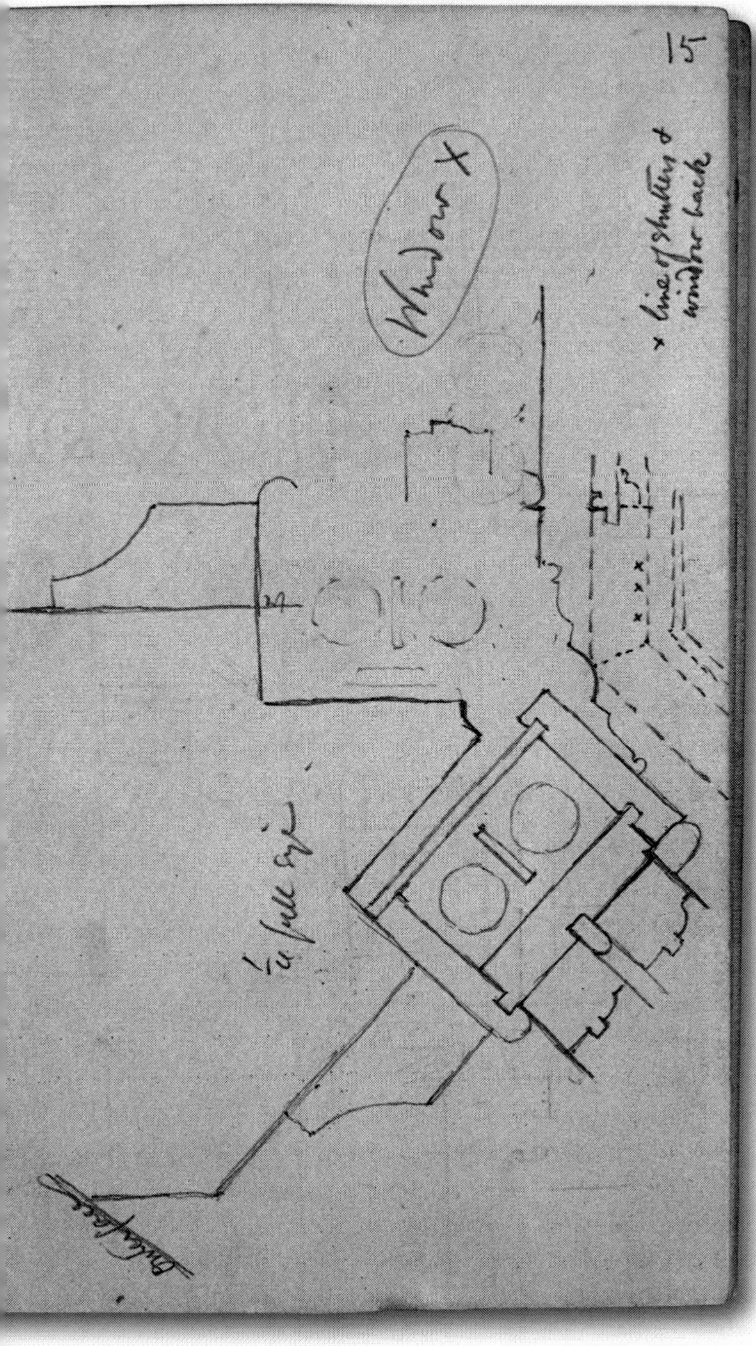
15
Window X
× line of shutters & window back

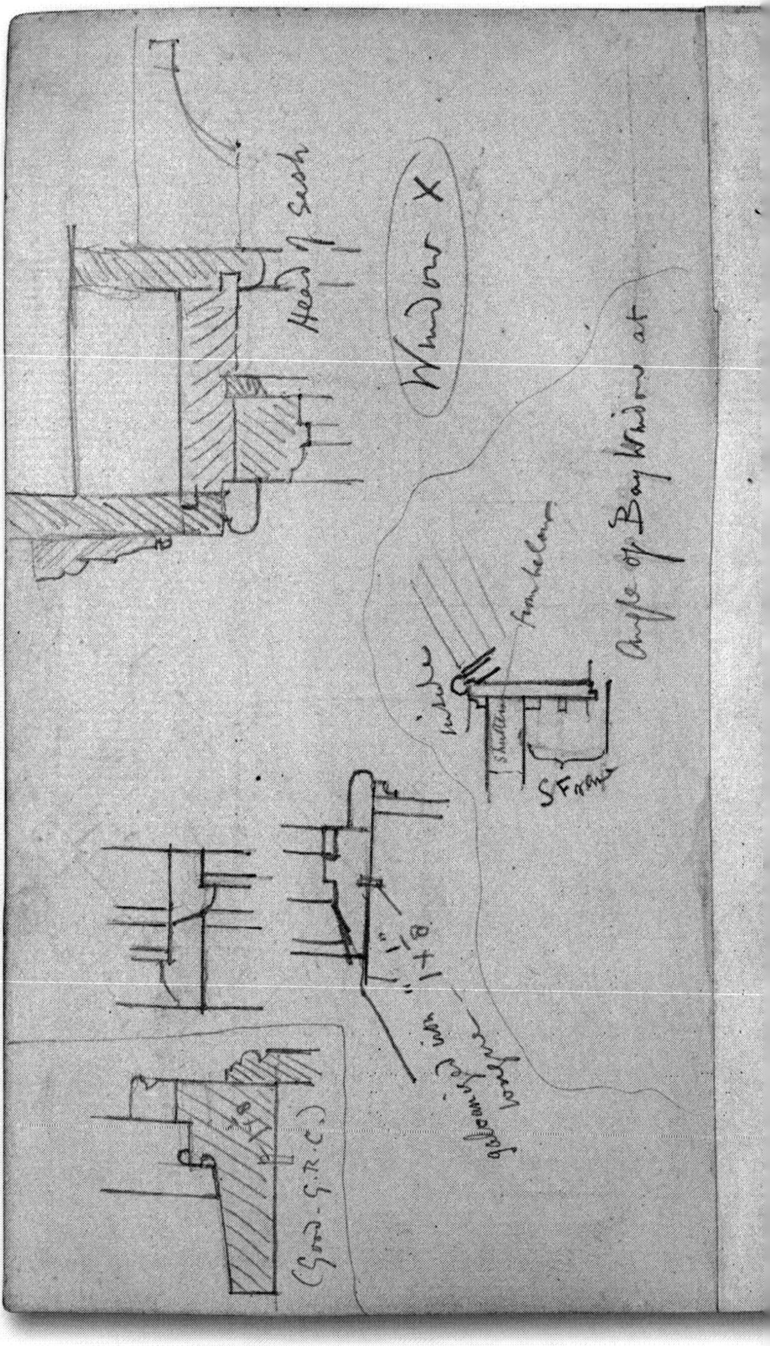
Head of sash
Window X
Angle of Bay Window at
from below
shutter
S Frame

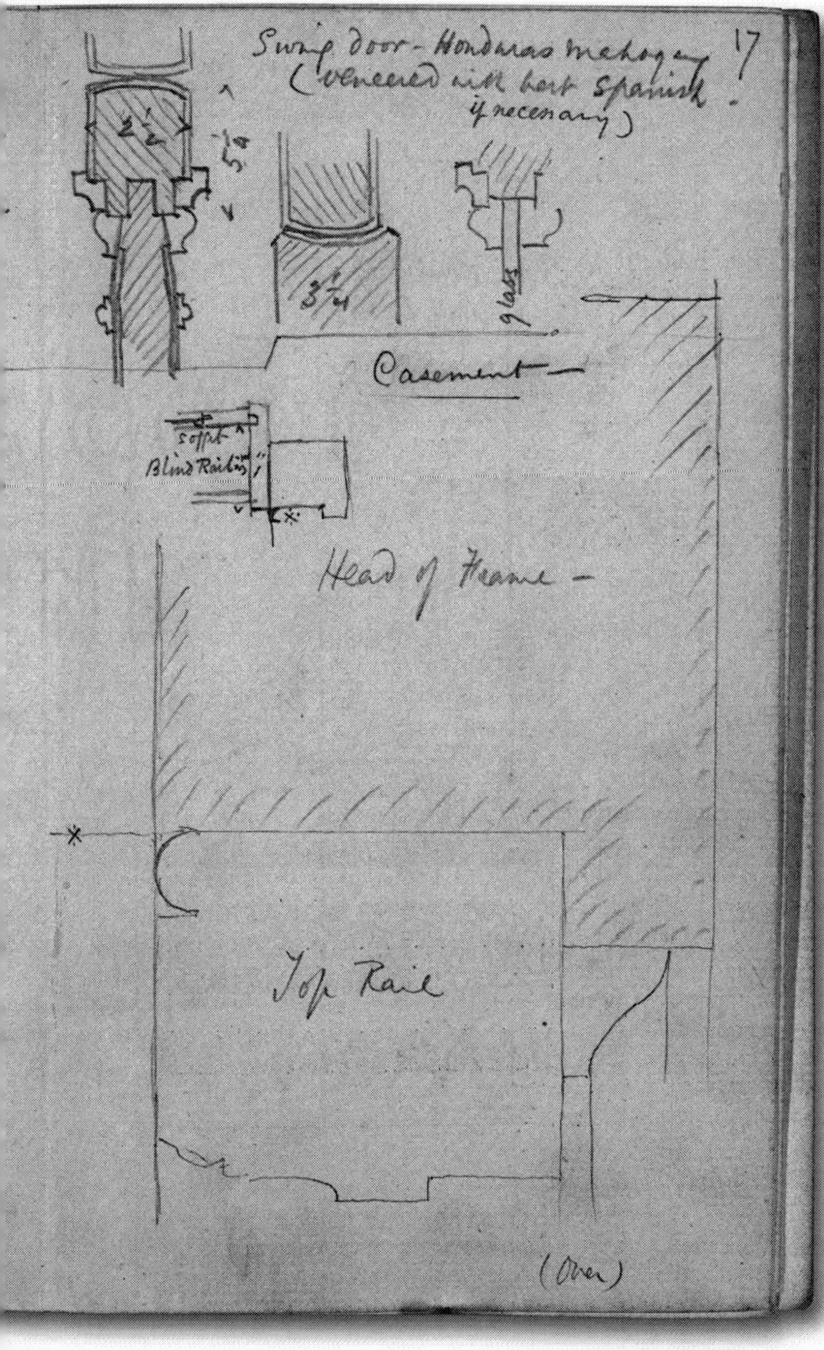
17
Swing door - Honduras mahogany
(veneered with best Spanish
if necessary)
2½
5⅛
3½
glass
Casement -
soffit
Blind Railing
Head of Frame -
Top Rail
(Over)

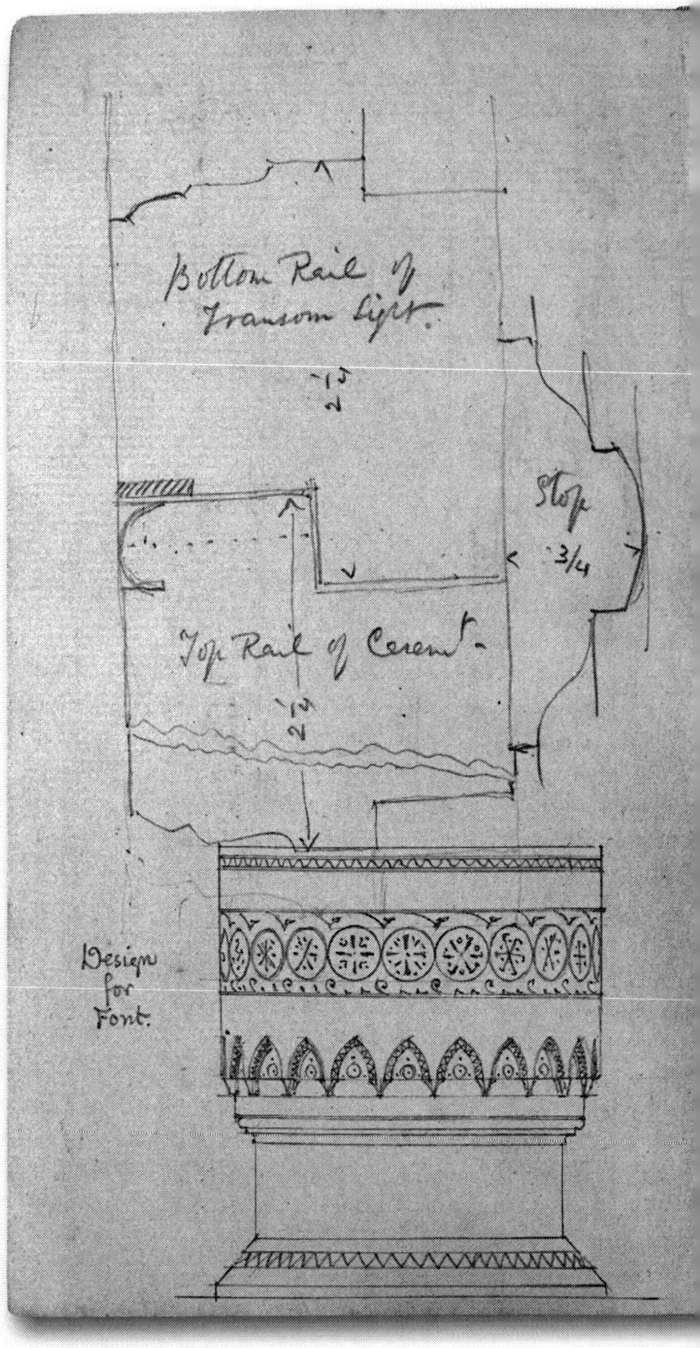
Bottom Rail of Transom Light.
Stop
3/4
Top Rail of Casemt
Design for Font.

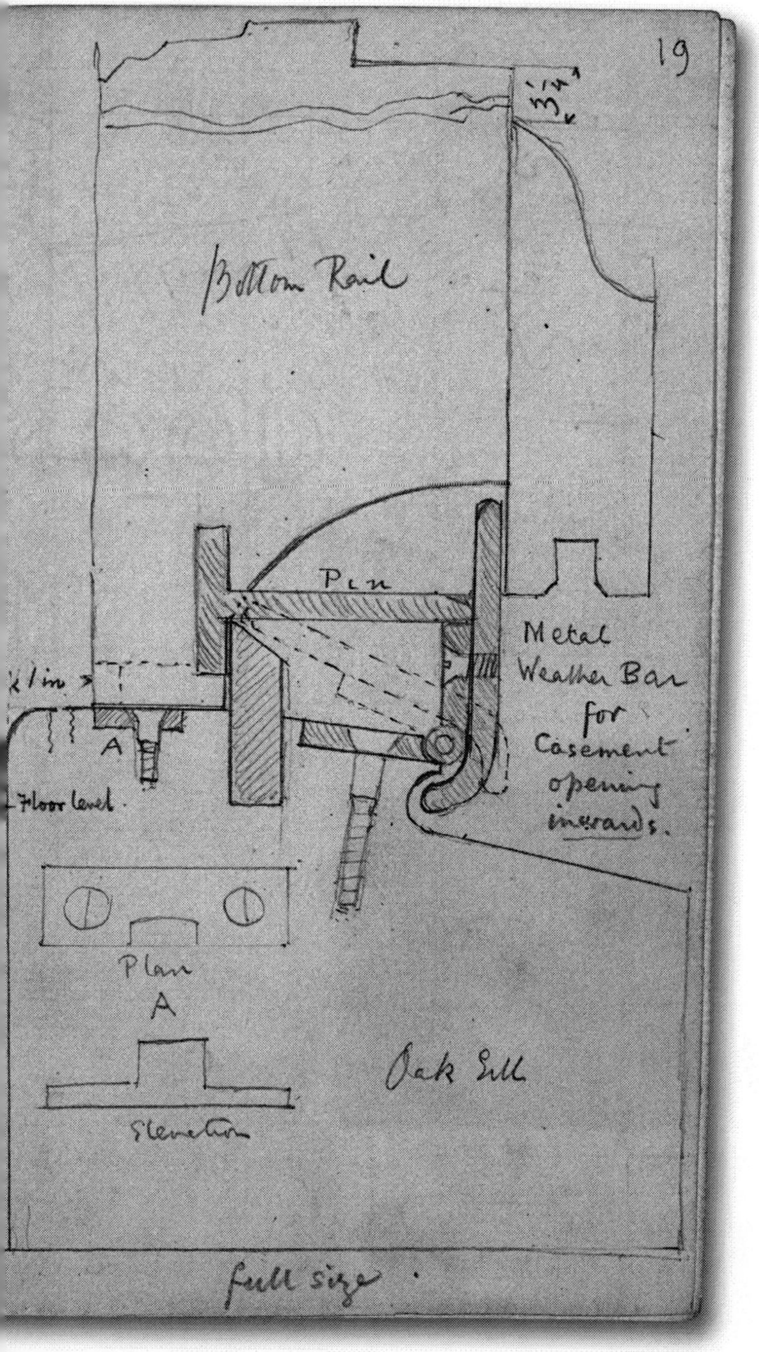
19
Bottom Rail
Pin
Metal
Weather Bar
for
Casement
opening
inwards.
Floor level
A
Plan
A
Elevation
Oak Sill
full size

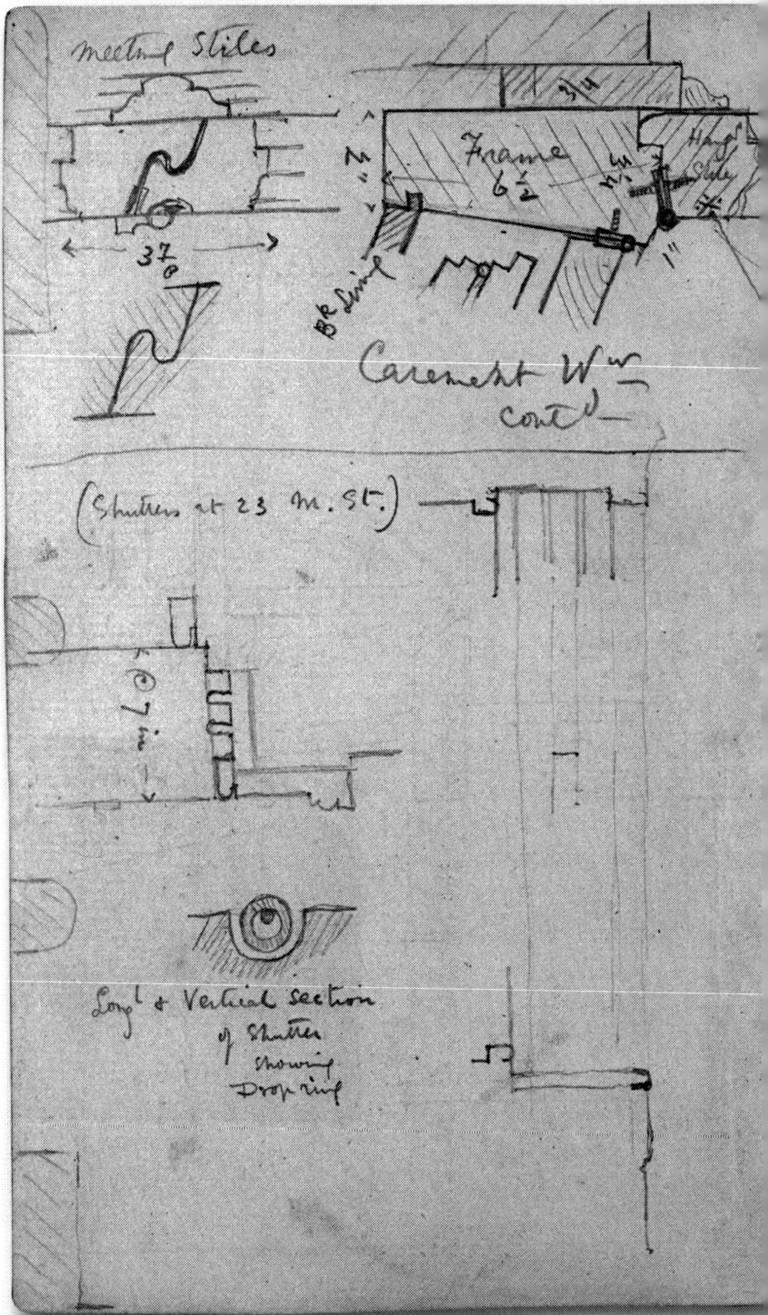
meeting Stiles
Frame
Casement Wdw
contd
(Shutters at 23 M. St.)
Long' & Vertical section
of Shutter
showing
Drop ring

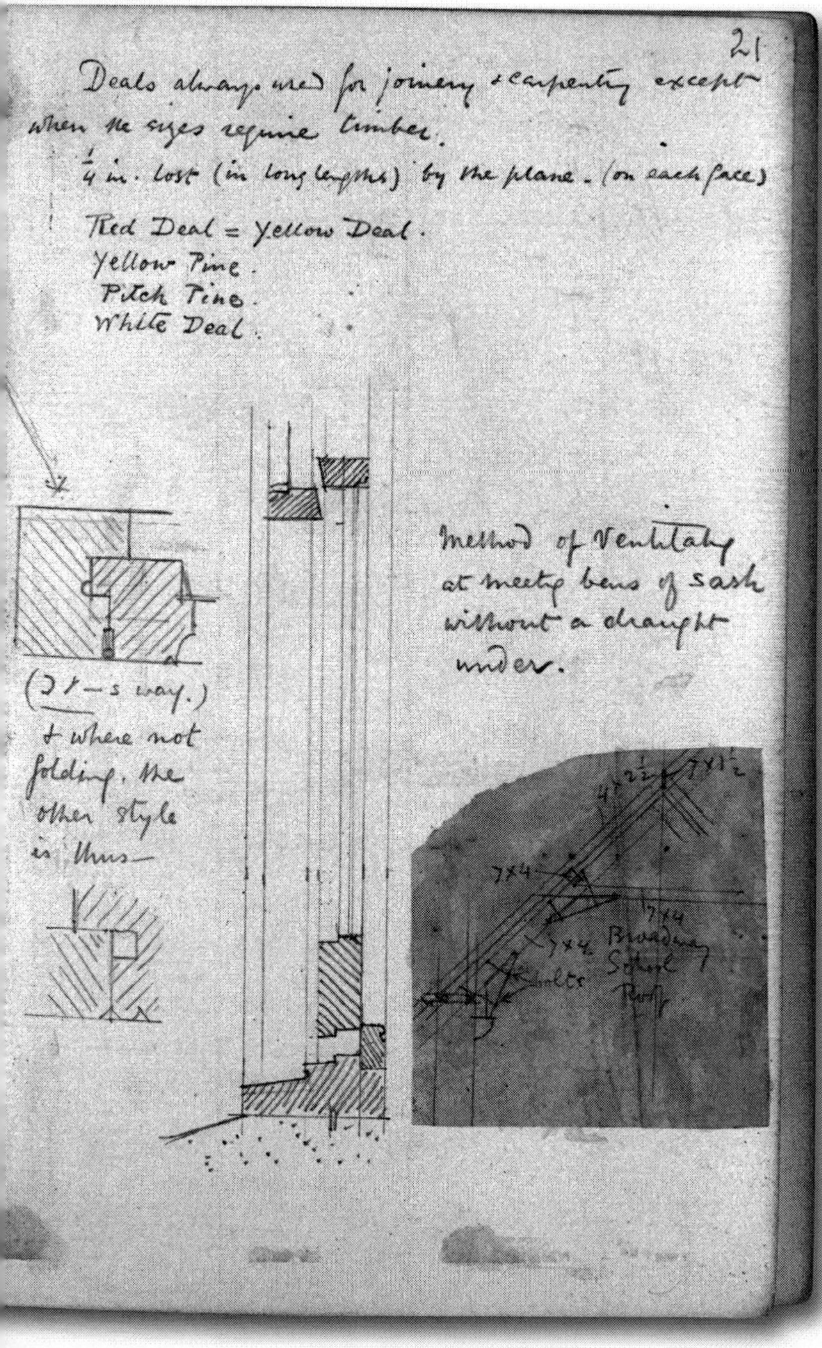
21

Deals always used for joinery & carpentry except when the sizes require timber.

$\frac{1}{4}$ in. lost (in long lengths) by the plane. (on each face)

Red Deal = Yellow Deal.
Yellow Pine.
Pitch Pine.
White Deal.

(3/– s way.)
& where not folding, the other style is thus—

Method of ventilating at meeting bars of sash without a draught under.

Ch. near the Downs. From the hill.
1866

23
Design for Font
3'-6
Officiating step
Roof of Common Street House ¼ scale.

25
Stinsford Church – Dorset –
Respond to South arcade –
1-0½
6"
3½
6½
5½
5½
Sketched from the Original.
T. H.

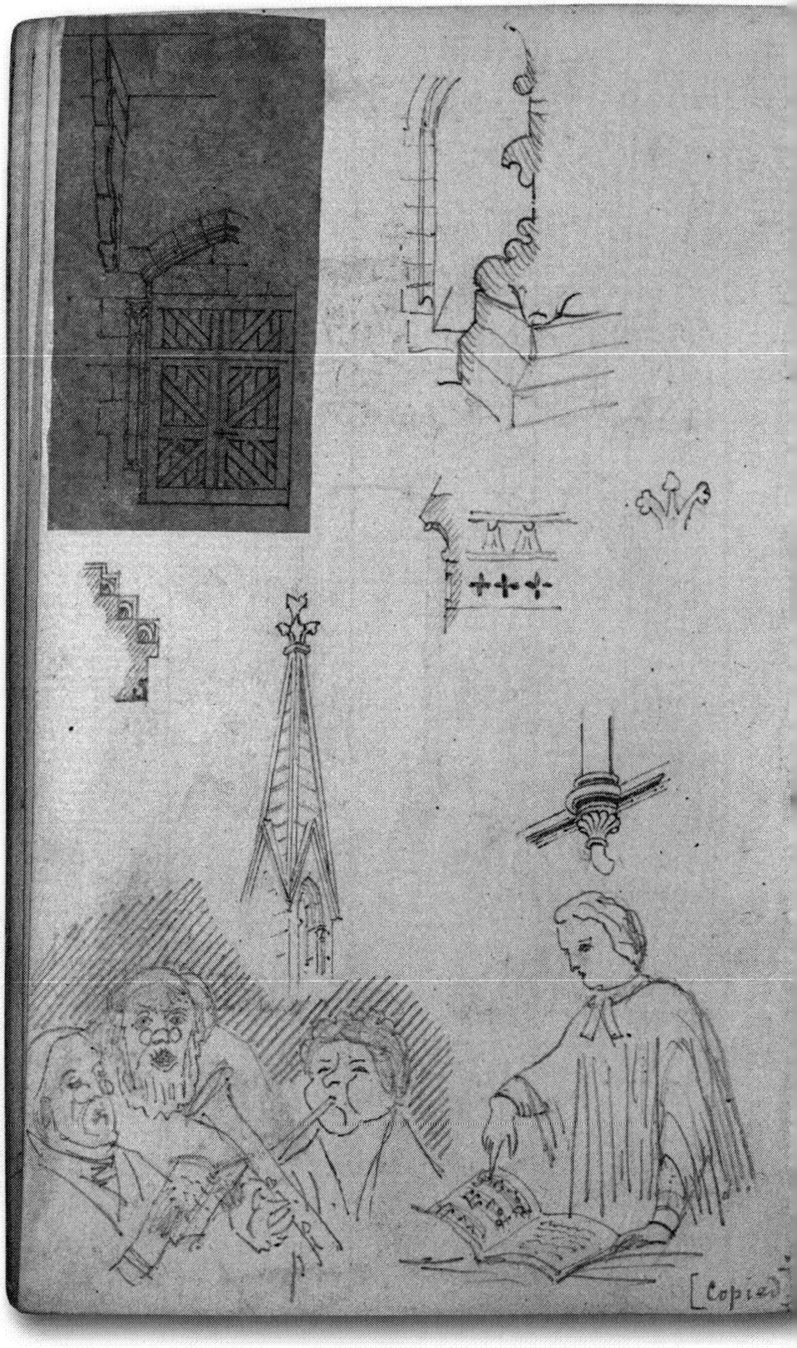
[Copied]

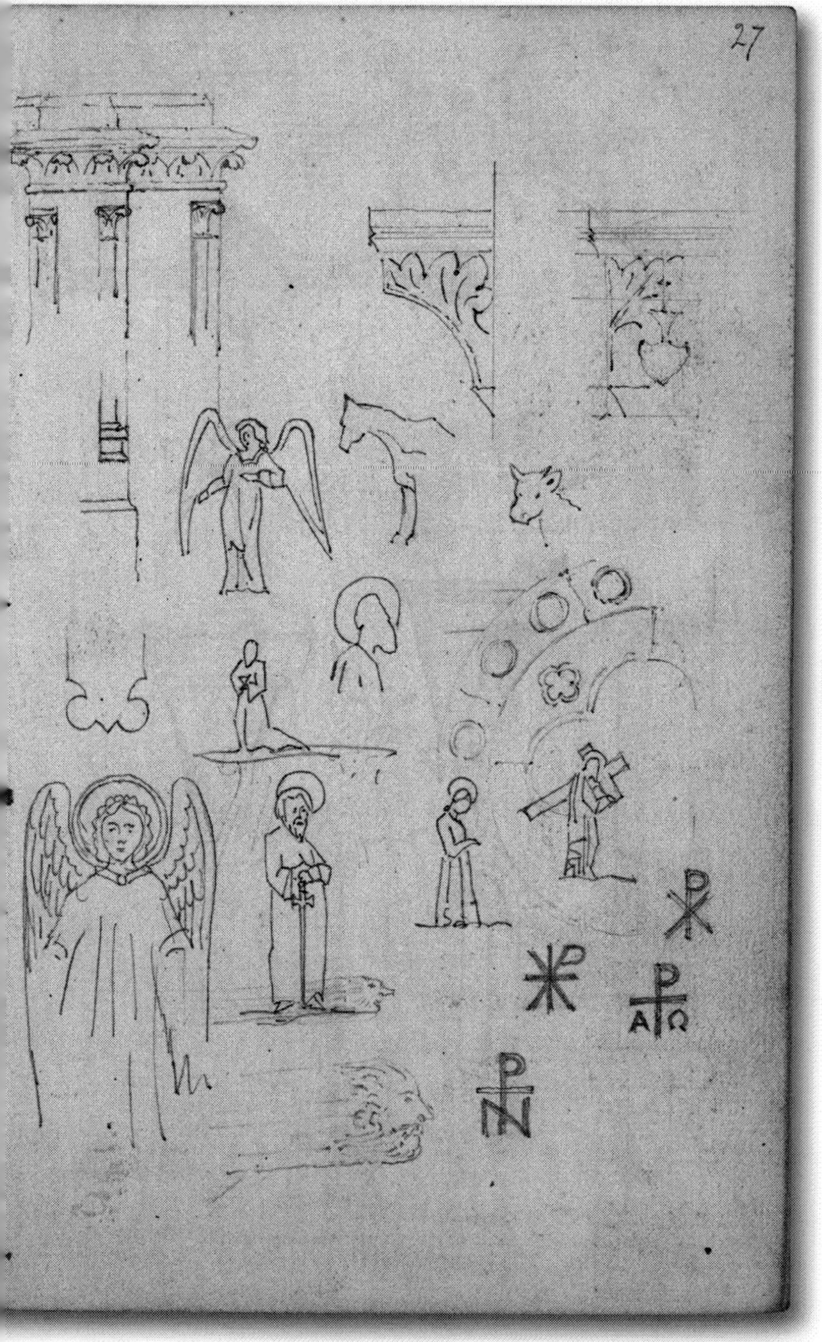
27
AΩ

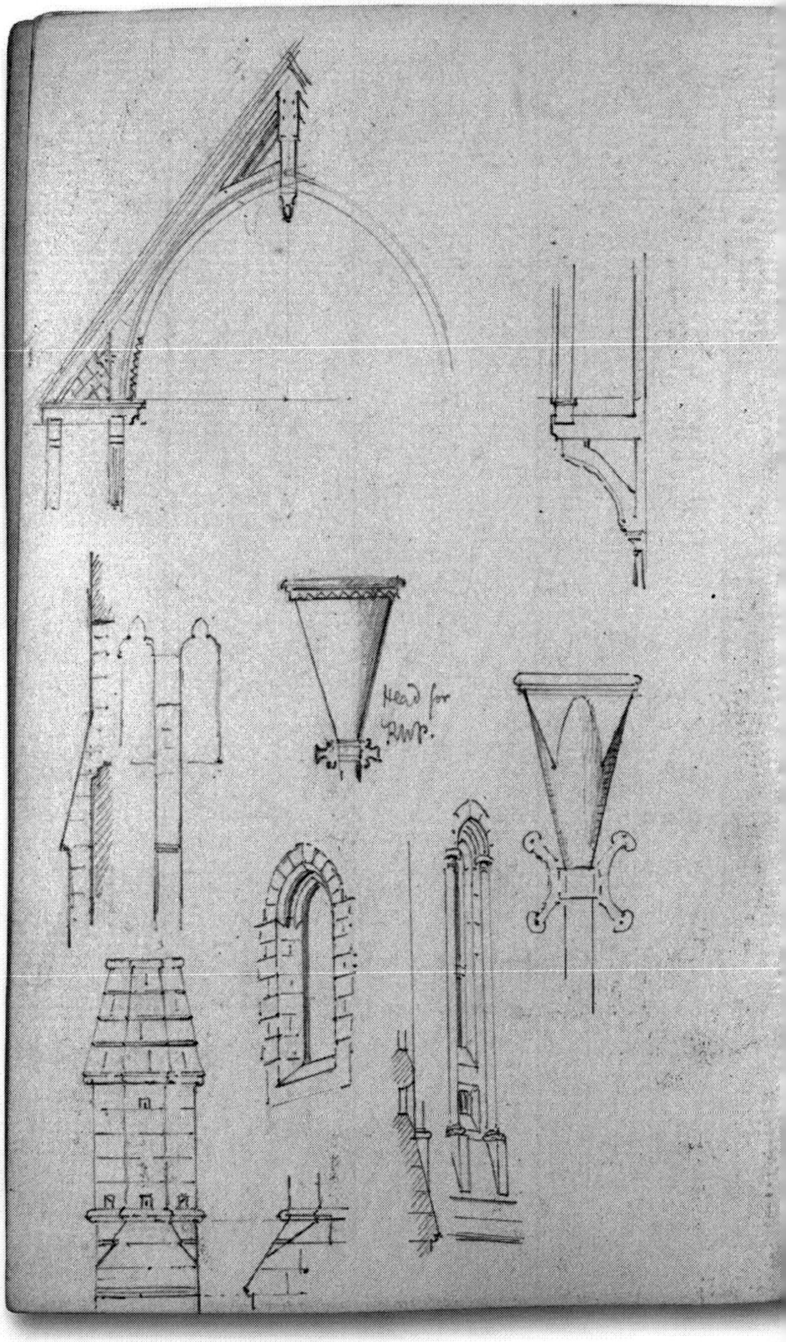
Head for RWP.

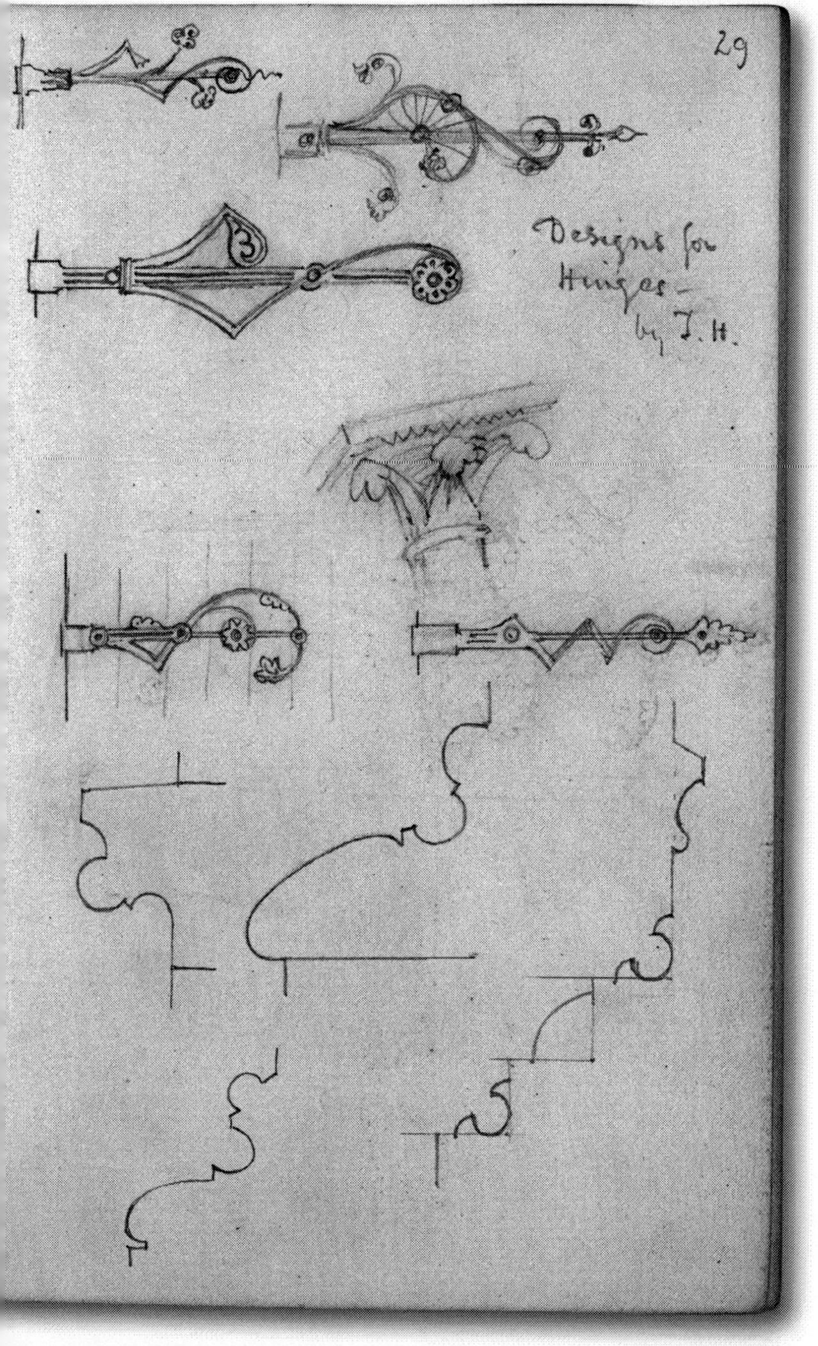
29
Designs for Hinges — by T. H.

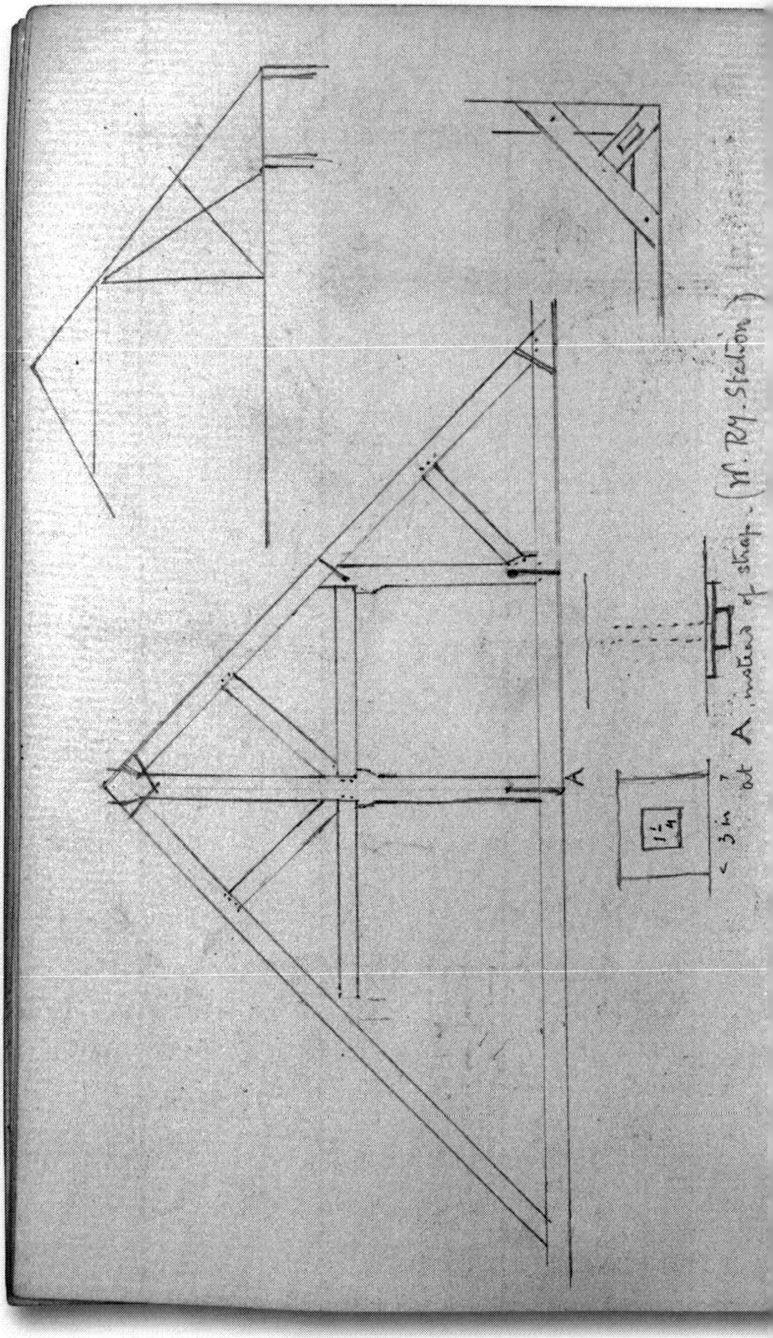
A
3 in
at A instead of strap. (W. Ry. Station)

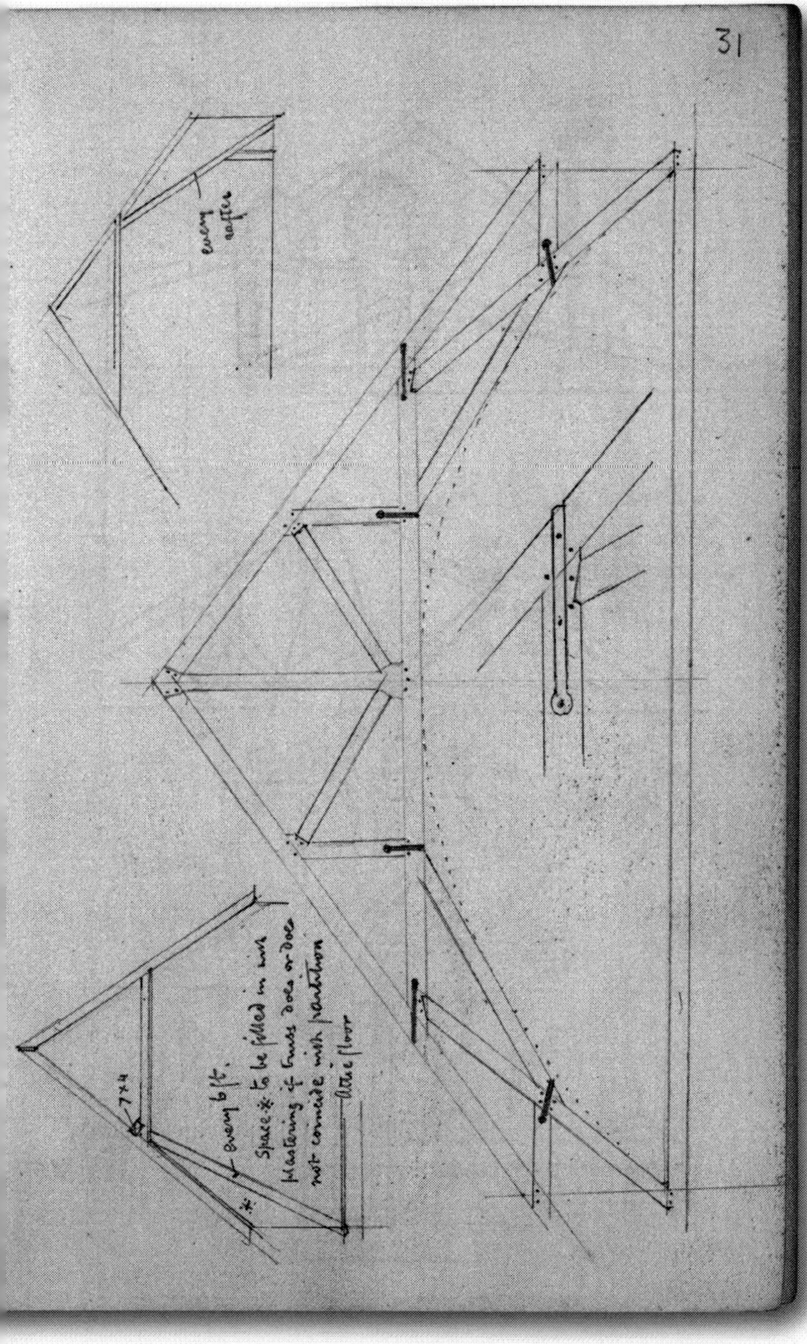
31
every rafter
7x4
every 6 ft.
Space * to be filled in with plastering if truss does or does not coincide with partition
Attic floor

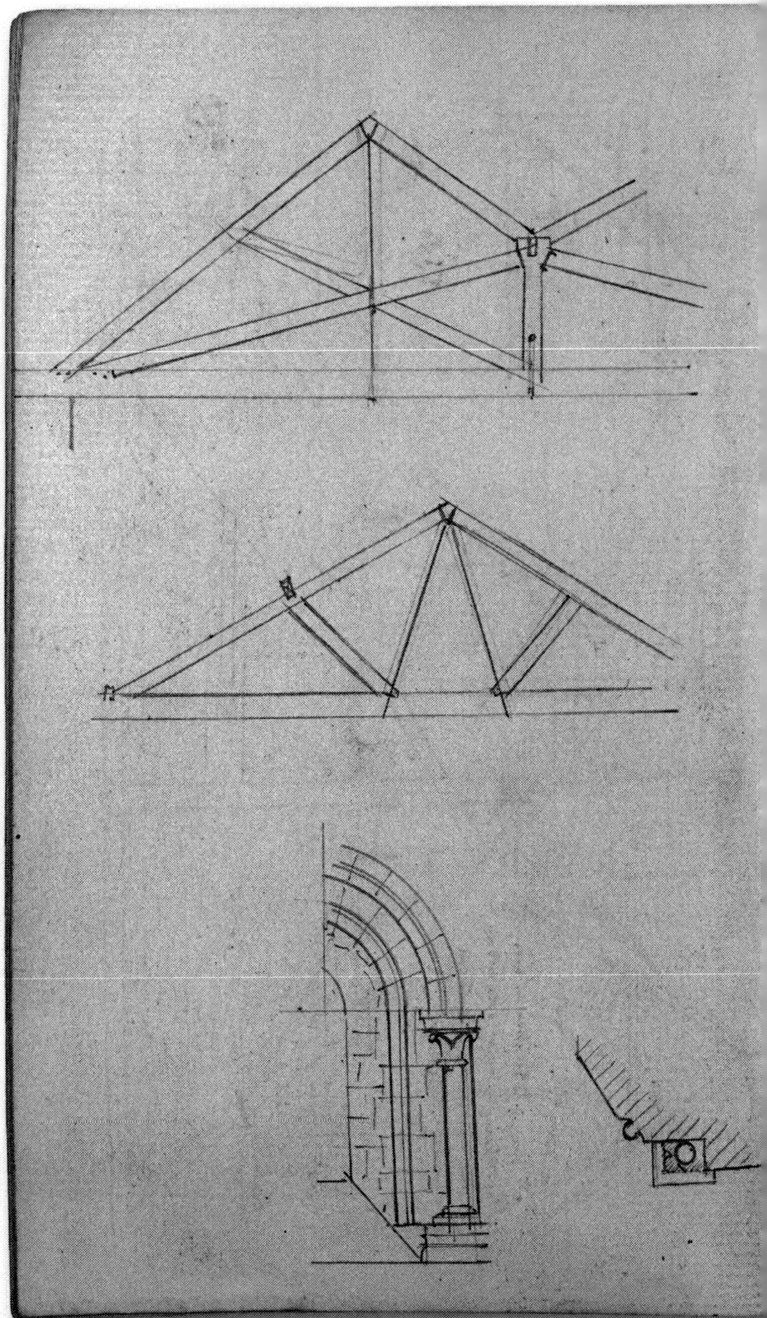

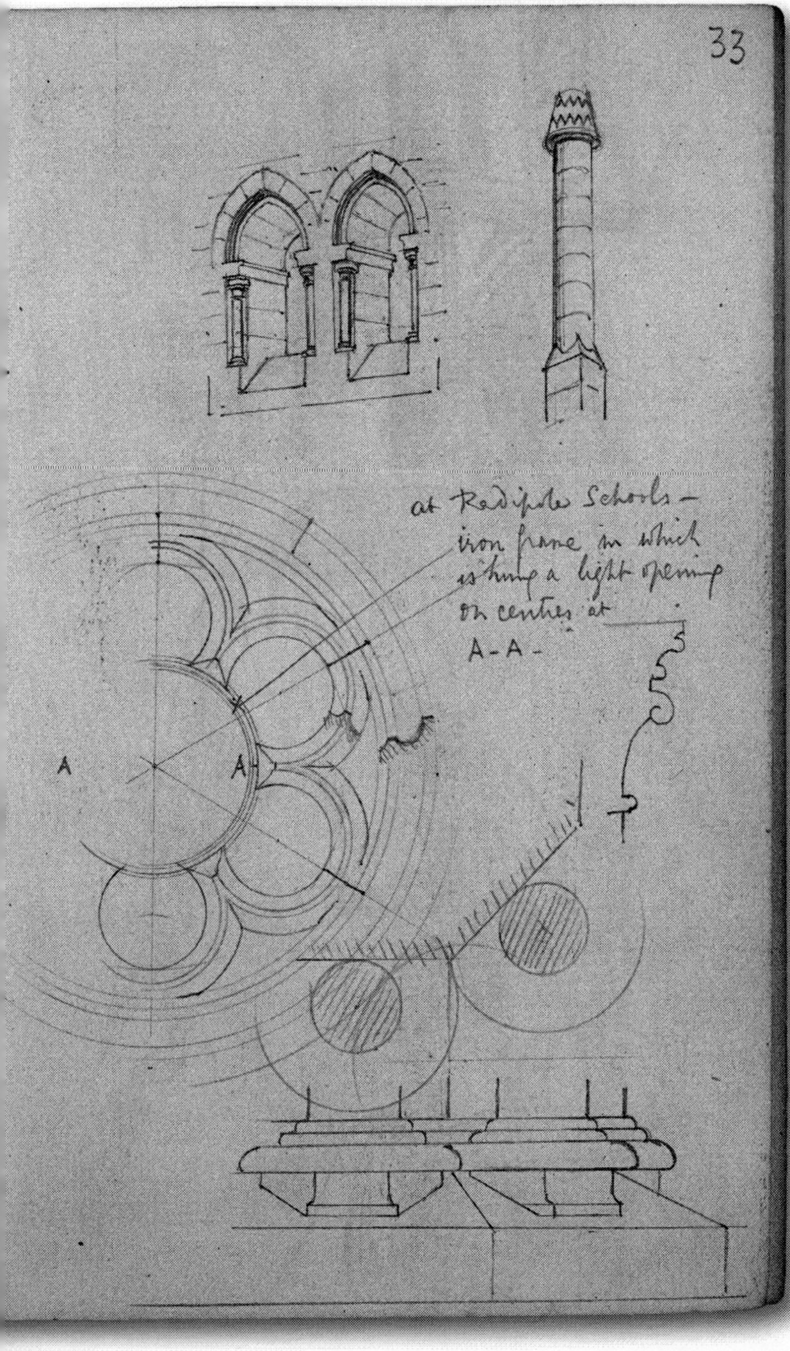
33
at Radipole Schools –
iron frame in which
is hung a light opening
on centres at
A-A-
A
A

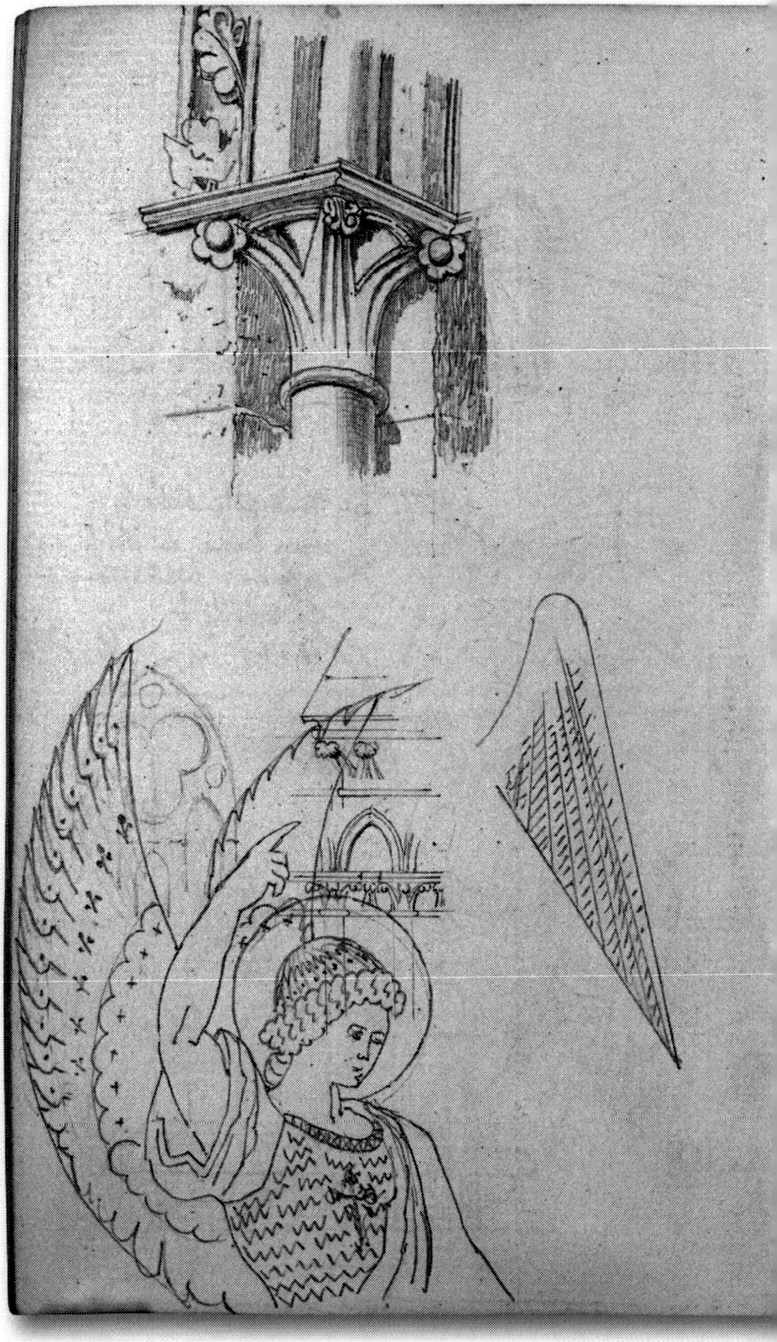

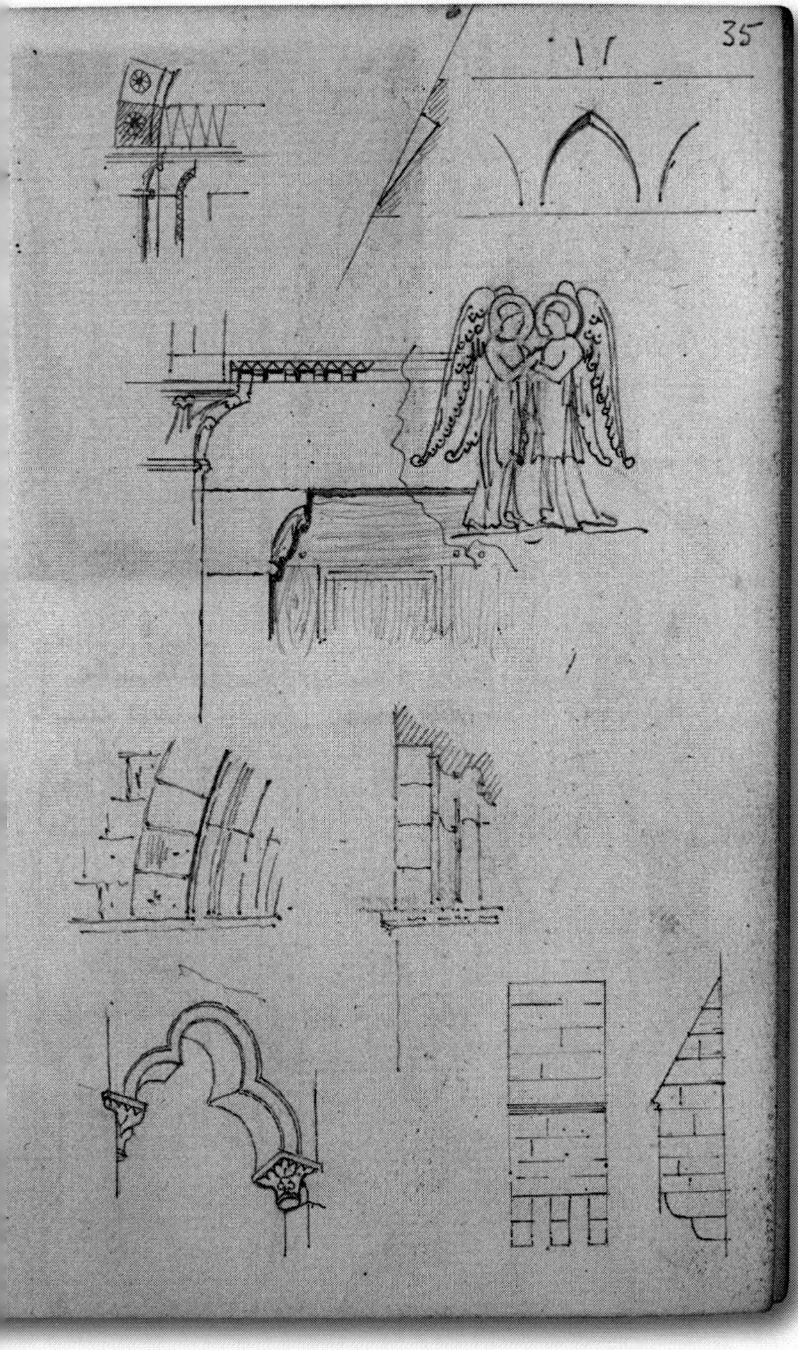
35

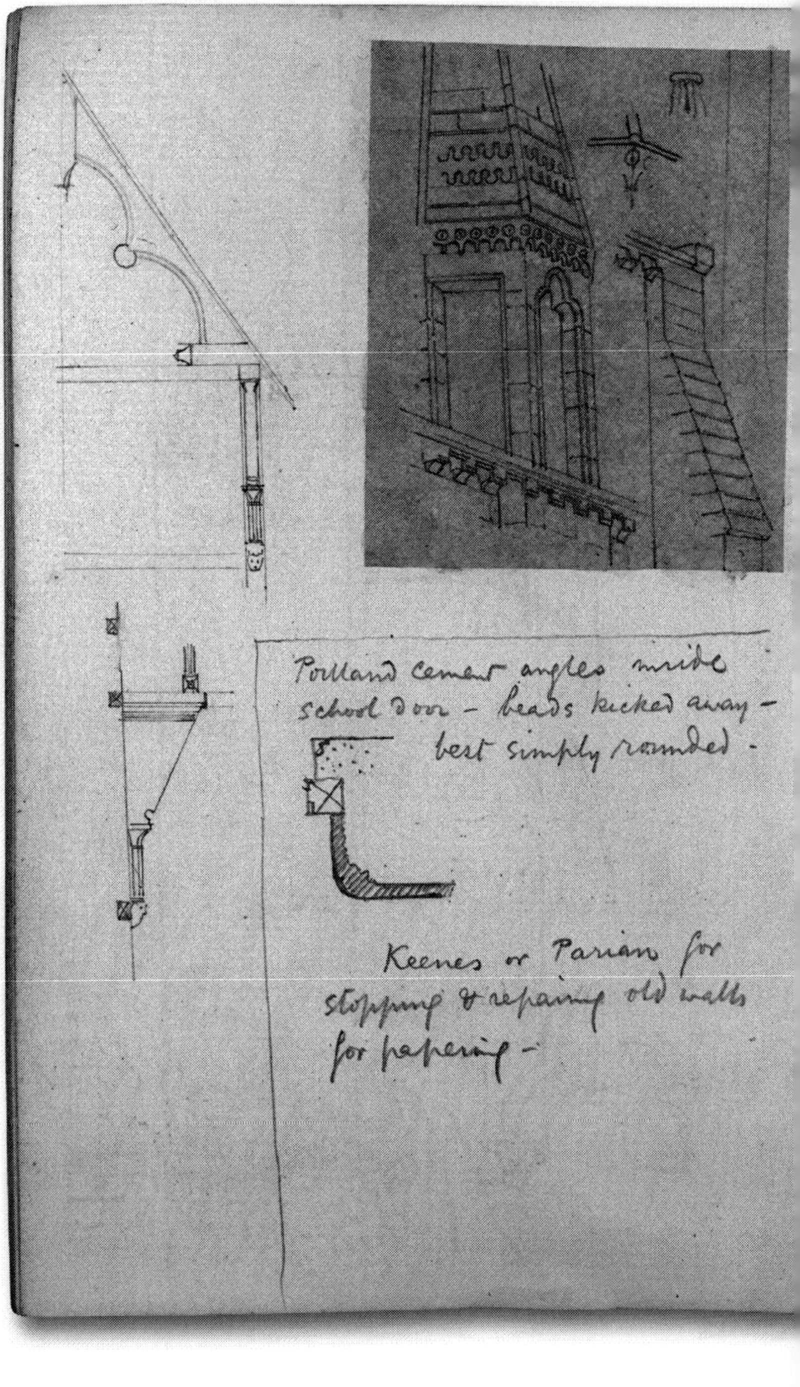
Portland cement angles inside
school door – beads kicked away –
best simply rounded –

Keenes or Parian for
stopping & repairing old walls
for papering –

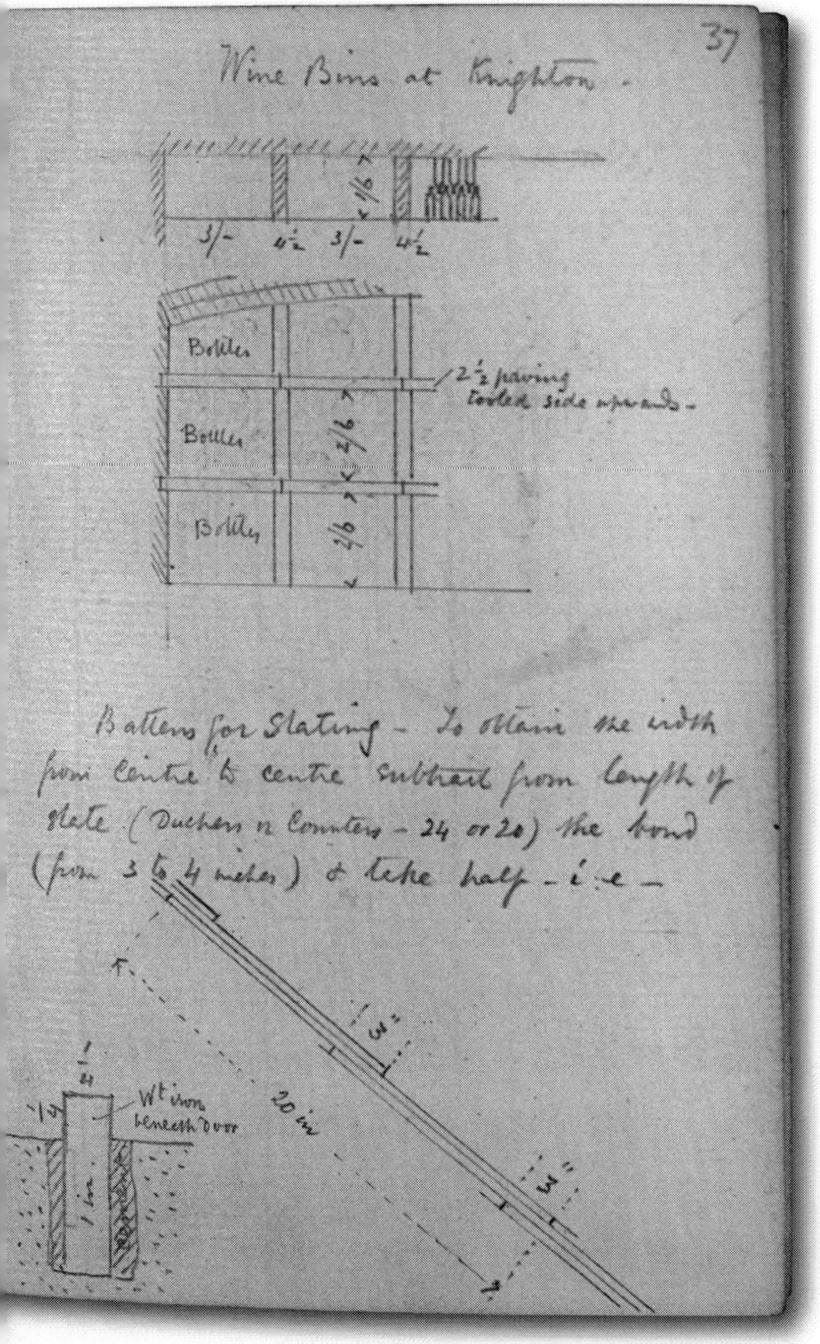
37

Wine Bins at Knighton -

3/- 4½ 3/- 4½ 1/6

Bottles

Bottles

Bottles

2½ paving tooled side upwards -

2/6

1/6

Battens for Slating - To obtain the width from centre to centre subtract from length of slate (Duchess or Countess - 24 or 20) the bond (from 3 to 4 inches) & take half - i.e -

3"

20 in

3"

¼

½

Wt iron beneath Door

1 in.

Seat Ends - St Juliot Church - Cornwall -
1870

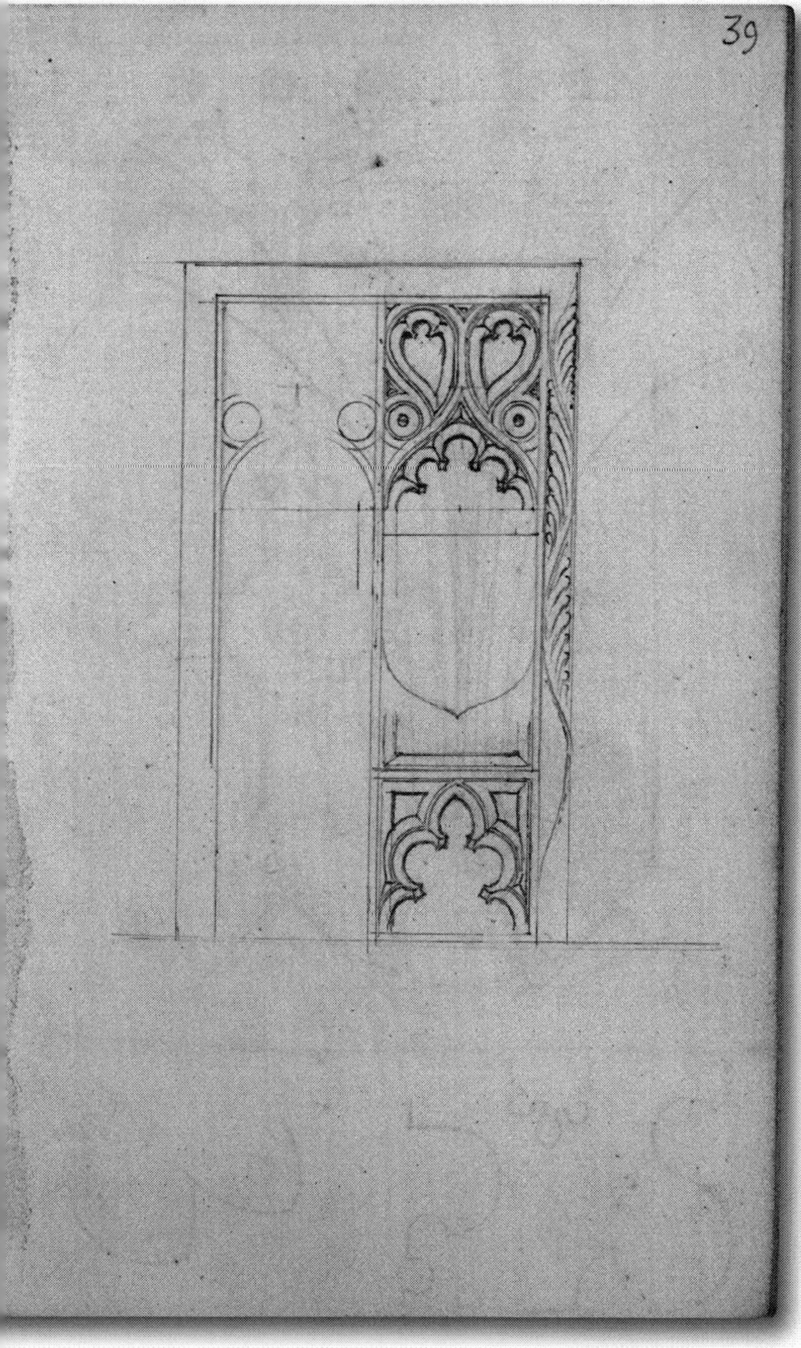

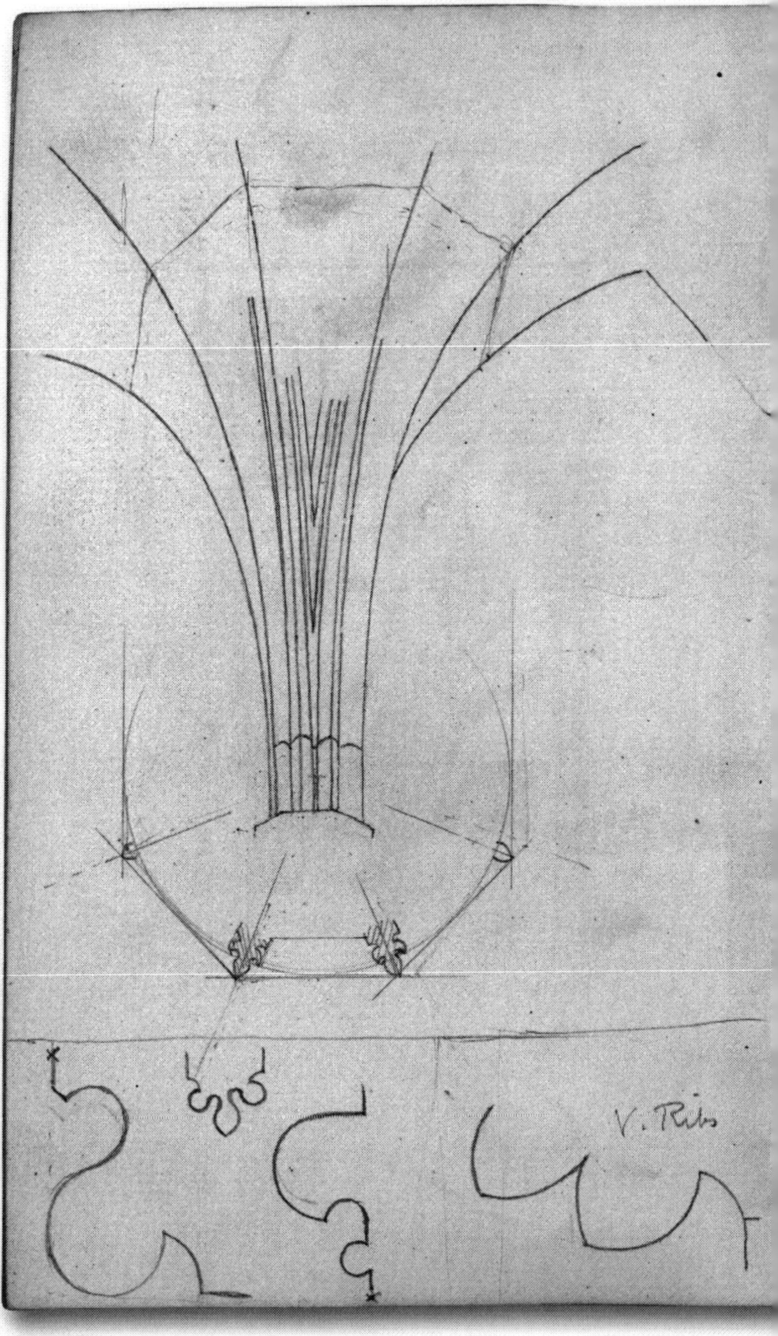
V. Ribs

41

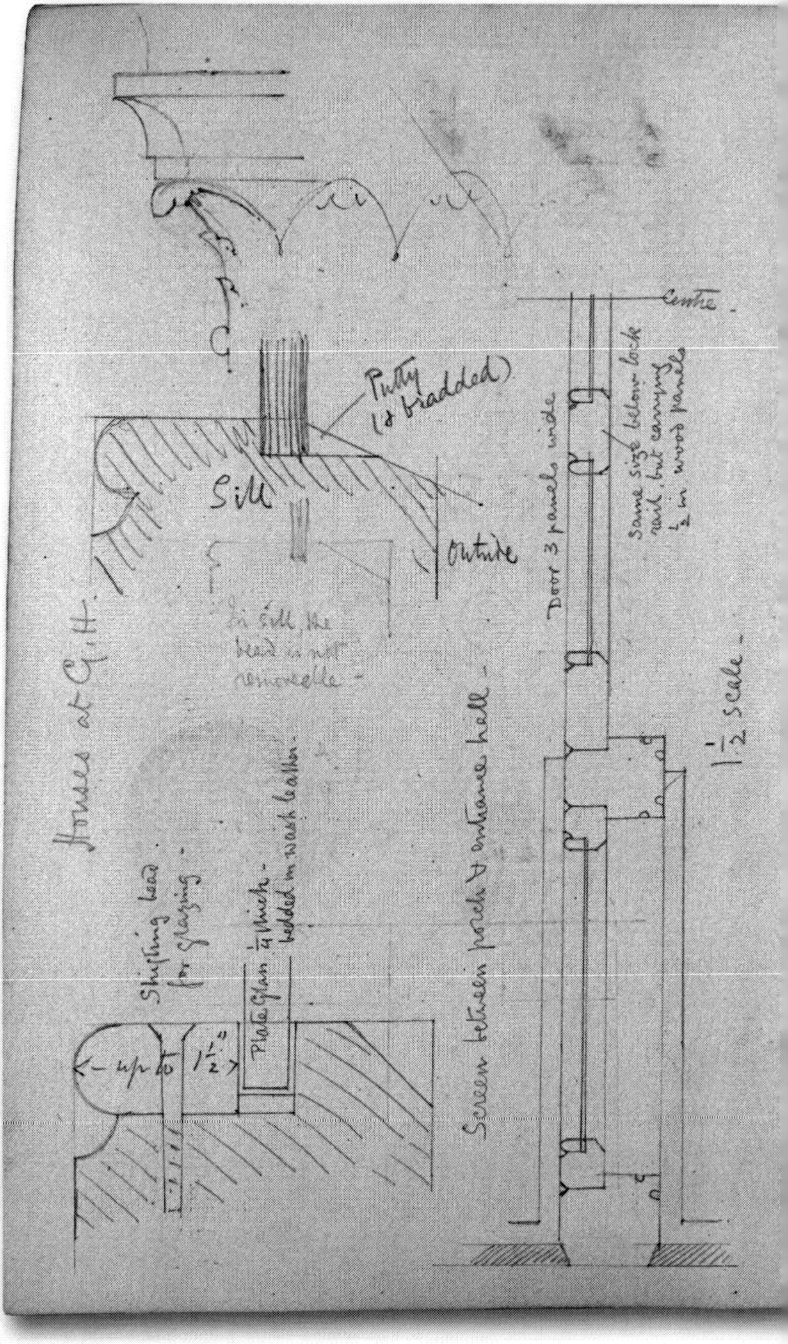
Houses at G.H.
Putty (& bradded)
Sill
Outside
In sill, the bead is not removeable -
Shifting bead for glazing -
Plate Glass 1/4 thick - bedded in wash leather.
4 to 10
1 1/2"
Screen between porch & entrance hall -
Centre -
Door 3 panels wide
Same size below lock rail, but carrying 1/2 in. wood panels
1 1/2 scale -

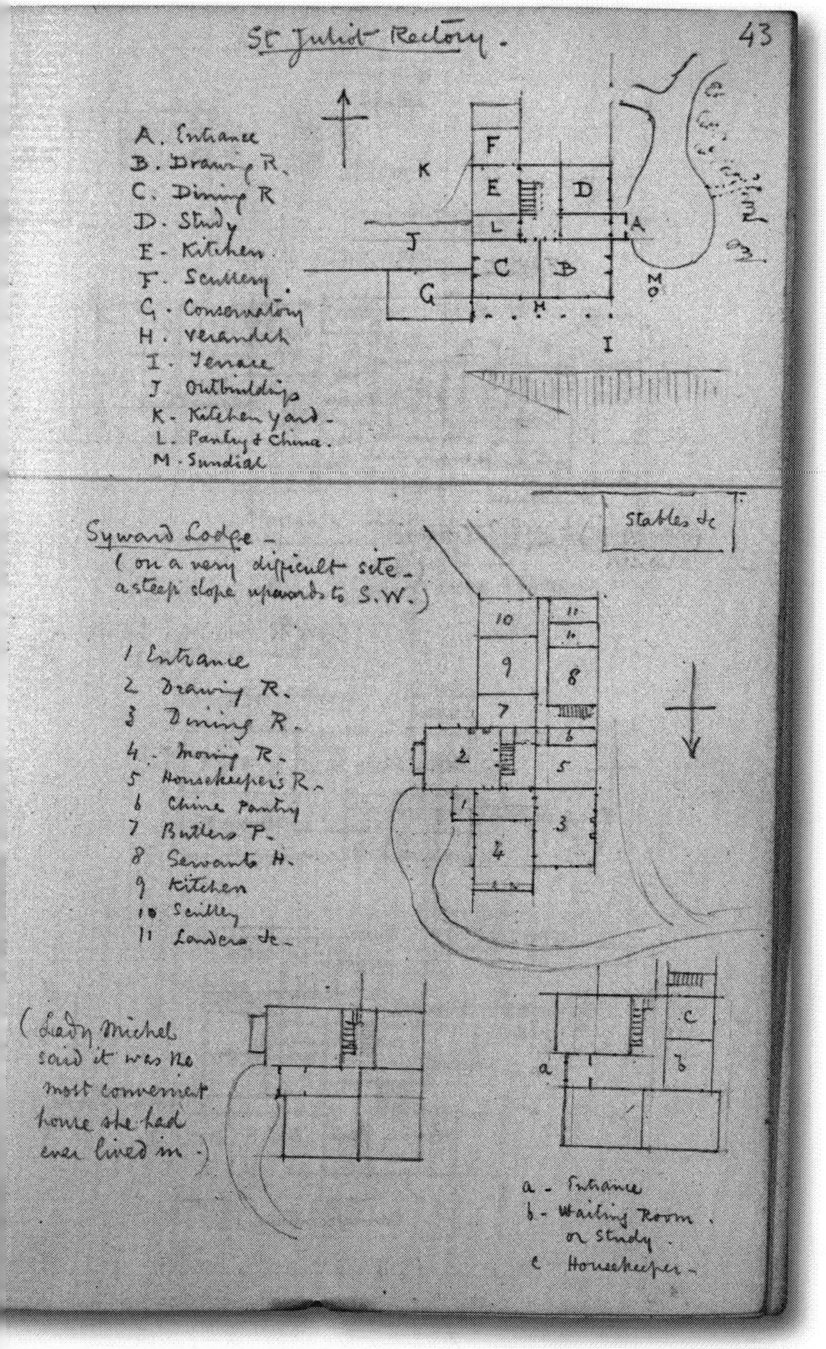
St Juliot Rectory.
43
A. Entrance
B. Drawing R.
C. Dining R
D. Study
E - Kitchen.
F. Scullery.
G. Conservatory
H. Verandah
I. Terrace
J Outbuildings
K - Kitchen yard.
L. Pantry & China.
M. Sundial
Syward Lodge -
(on a very difficult site - a steep slope upwards to S.W.)
1 Entrance
2 Drawing R.
3 Dining R.
4 Morning R.
5 Housekeeper's R.
6 China Pantry
7 Butlers P.
8 Servants H.
9 Kitchen
10 Scullery
11 Larders &c.
Stables &c
(Lady Michel said it was the most convenient house she had ever lived in.)
a - Entrance
b - Waiting Room or Study.
c Housekeeper -

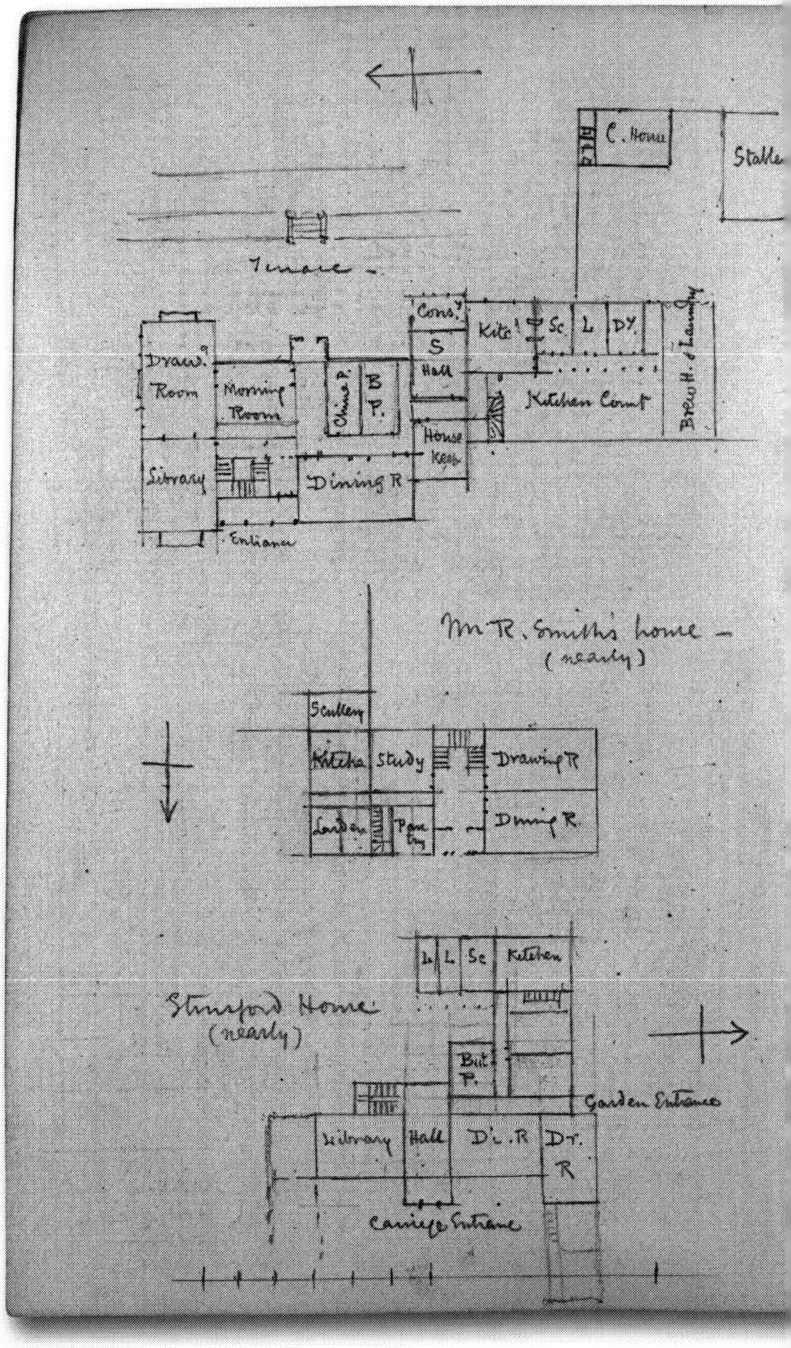
C. House
Stables
Terrace
Cons.y
Kitc.
Sc.
L
DY.
Brew H. & Laundry
Draw.g Room
Morning Room
China P.
B P.
S
Hall
Kitchen Court
House Keep.
Library
Dining R
Entrance
Mr R. Smith's house – (nearly)
Scullery
Kitchen
Study
Drawing R
Larder
Pantry
Dining R.
L
L
Sc
Kitchen
Stinsford House (nearly)
But. P.
Garden Entrance
Library
Hall
D'.R
Dr. R
Carriage Entrance

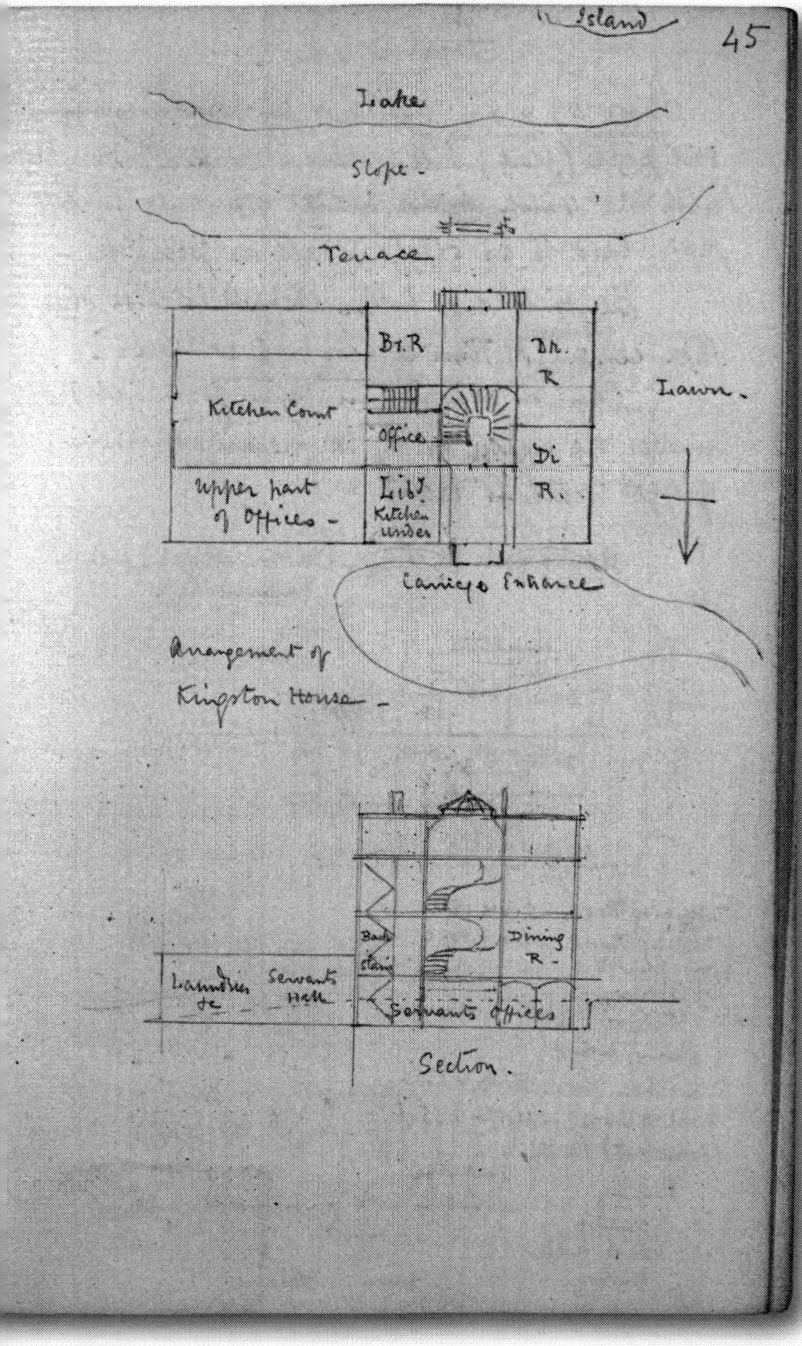
45
Island
Lake
Slope
Terrace
Br. R
Dr. R
Lawn
Kitchen Court
Office
Di R.
Upper part of Offices
Lib. Kitchen under
Carriage Entrance
Arrangement of Kingston House
Back stairs
Dining R.
Laundries &c
Servants Hall
Servants Offices
Section.

Drains &c.

Chase 4½ x 4½ sufficient for ~~lead~~ descending soil pipe (galvanized cast-iron or lead). An elbow connects this with the 4 inch ~~drain~~ glazed stoneware socket pipe, laid to as steep a fall as possible –

The joints are better stopped in with clay than cement (?) Run to cesspool or sewer –

Common 4in drain pipes from RWP's – unless the water is to be preserved, when glazed socket is better –

Hawkhurst Rectory – (Rector delighted with its convenience) –

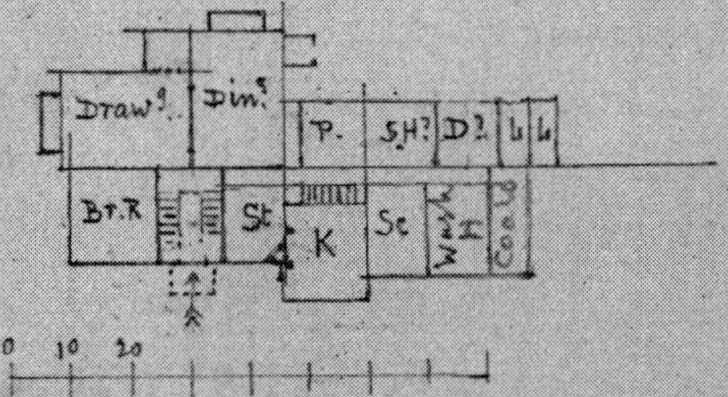

Drawing Room 20.2 x 15.2
Dining Room 21.0 x 16.0
Breakfast R or Library } 15.6 x 12.2
Study or Waiting Room } 11.6 x 10-6
Kitchen — 15.6 x 13.6
Hall & Stairs — 11.2 x 15.6

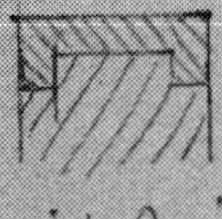

Brick Quoins in cellar –

Servants Hall | Larder
Pantry | Coals
Scullery
Wash house
Dairy

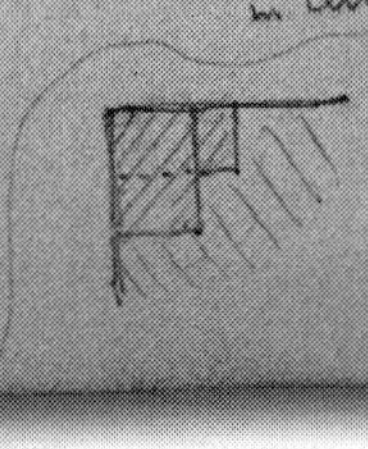

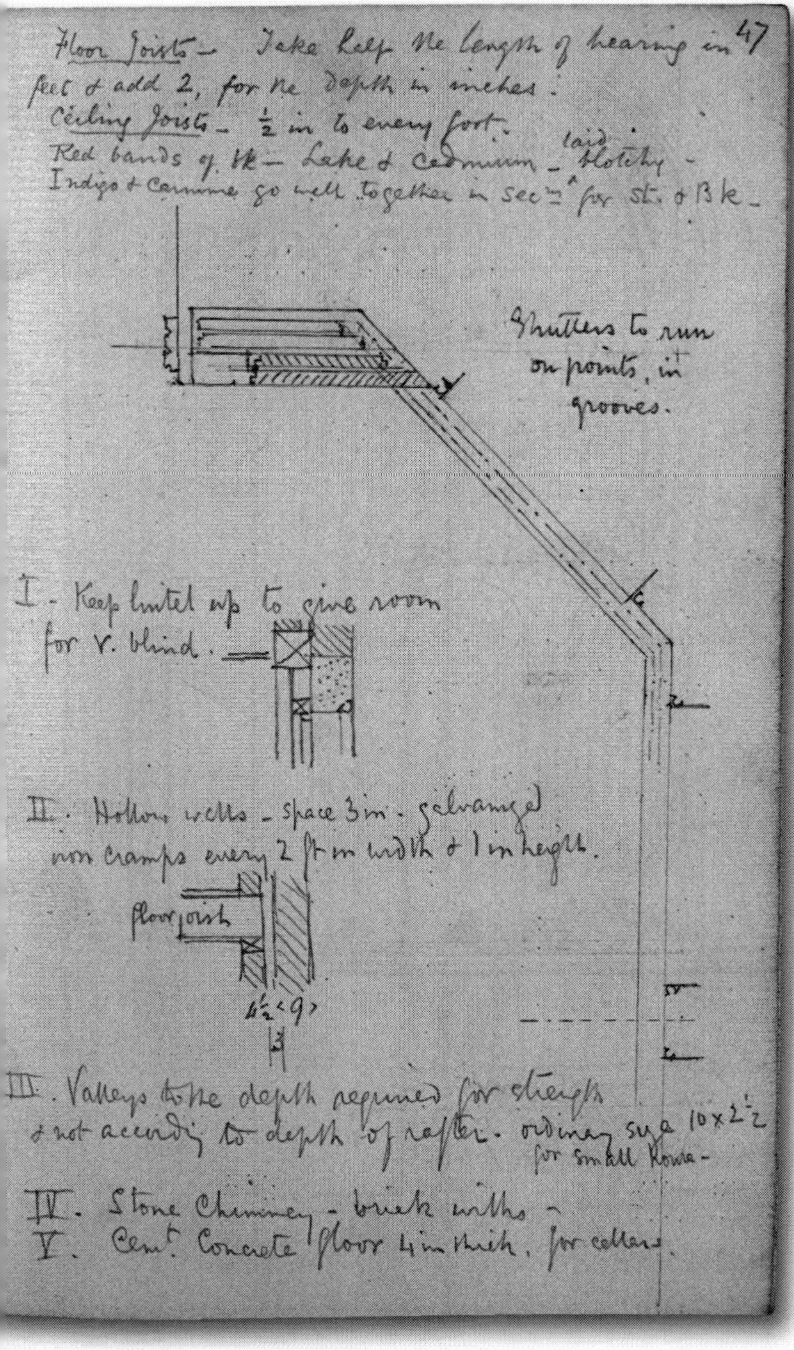

Floor Joists – Take half the length of bearing in 47
feet & add 2, for the depth in inches.
Ceiling Joists – ½ in to every foot.
Red bands of bk – Lake & Cadmium – laid blotchy –
Indigo & Carmine go well together in secn for st. & Bk –

Shutters to run on points, in grooves.

I. – Keep lintel up to give room for v. blind.

II. Hollow walls – space 3 in – galvanized iron cramps every 2 ft in width & 1 in height.

floor joist

4½ < 9 >

3

III. Valleys to be the depth required for strength & not according to depth of rafter. ordinary size 10 × 2½ for small house –

IV. Stone Chimney – brick withs –

V. Cemt. Concrete floor 4 in thick. for cellars.

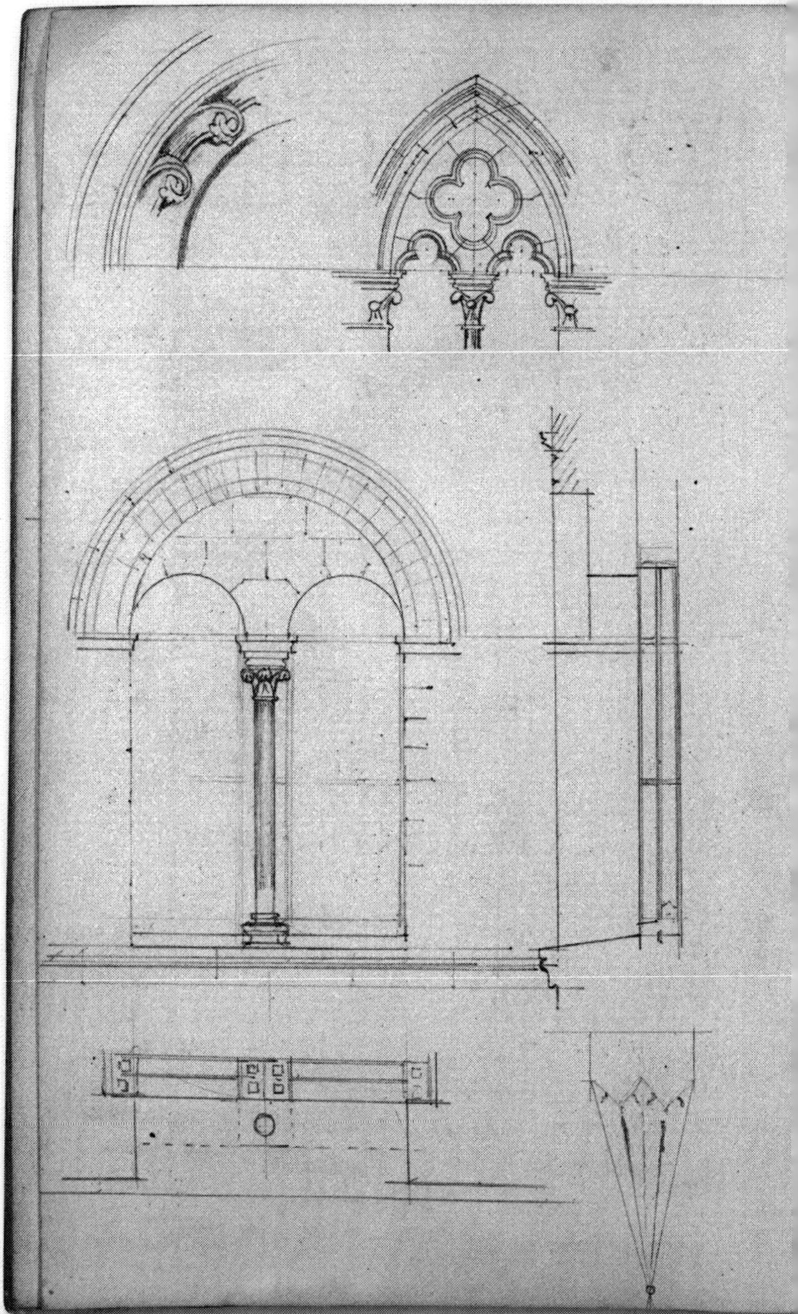

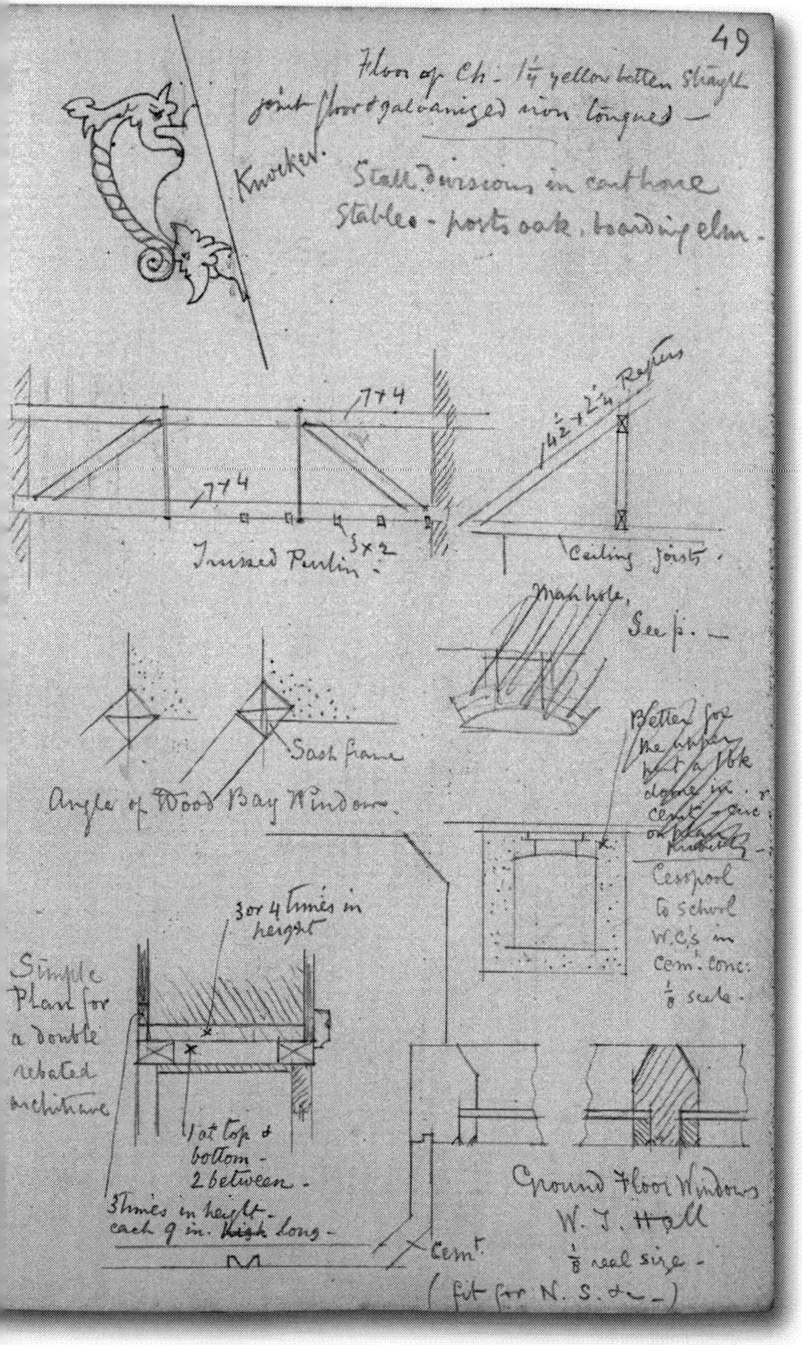
49
Floor of Ch. – 1¼ yellow batten straight joint floor & galvanized iron tongued –
Knocker.
Stables – posts oak, boarding elm.
7 × 4
7 × 4
3 × 2
Trussed Purlin.
Rafters
Ceiling joists.
Man hole,
See p. –
Sash frame
Angle of Wood Bay Window.
Cesspool to school W.C.'s in cem.t conc:
⅛ scale.
3 or 4 times in height
Simple Plan for a double rebated architrave
1 at top & bottom – 2 between.
3 times in height. each 9 in. High long.
Cem.t
Ground Floor Windows W. T. Hall
⅛ real size.
(fit for N. S. & –)

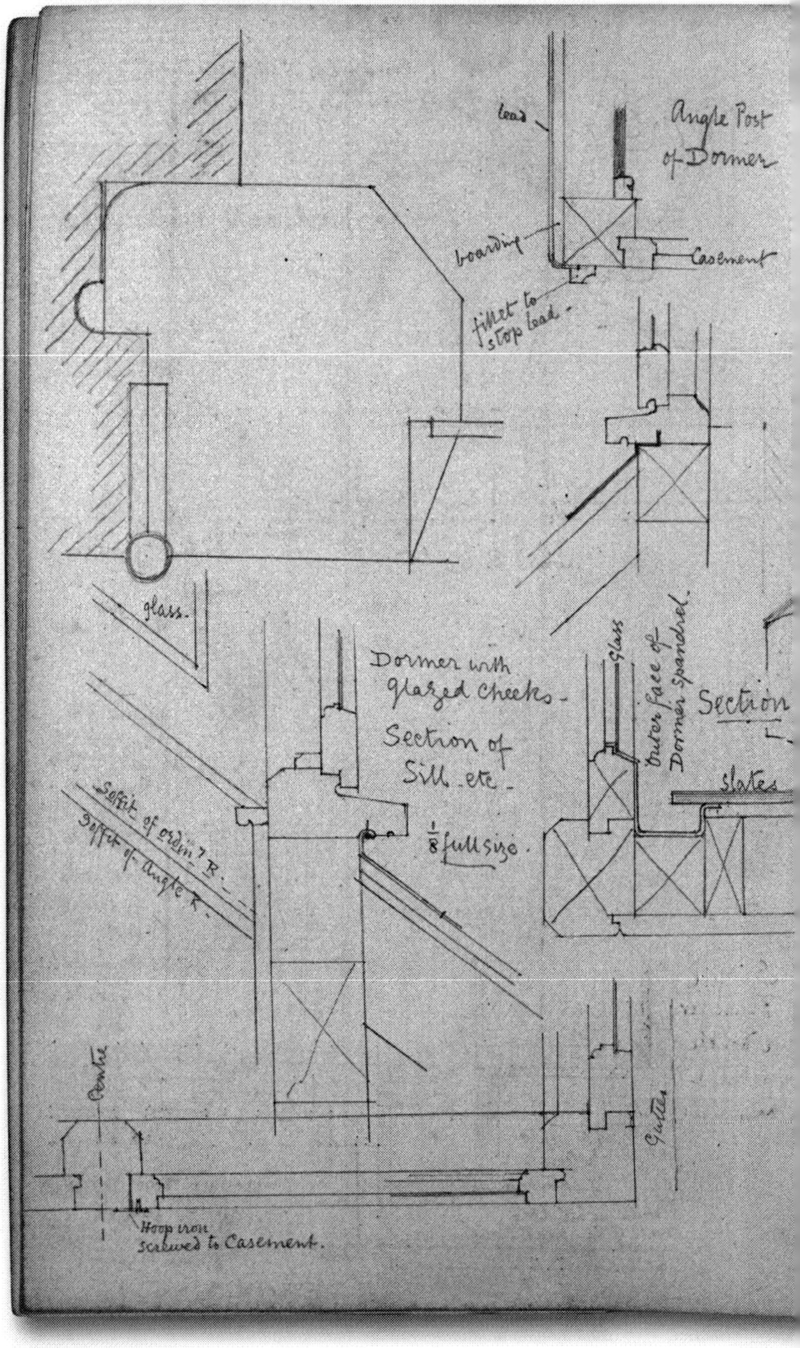
lead
Angle Post of Dormer
boarding
Casement
fillet to stop lead.
glass.
Dormer with glazed cheeks.
Section of Sill. etc.
1/8 full size.
Soffit of ordin.y R.
Soffit of Angle R.
Glass
Outer face of Dormer spandrel.
Section
slates
Centre
Gutter
Hoop iron screwed to Casement.

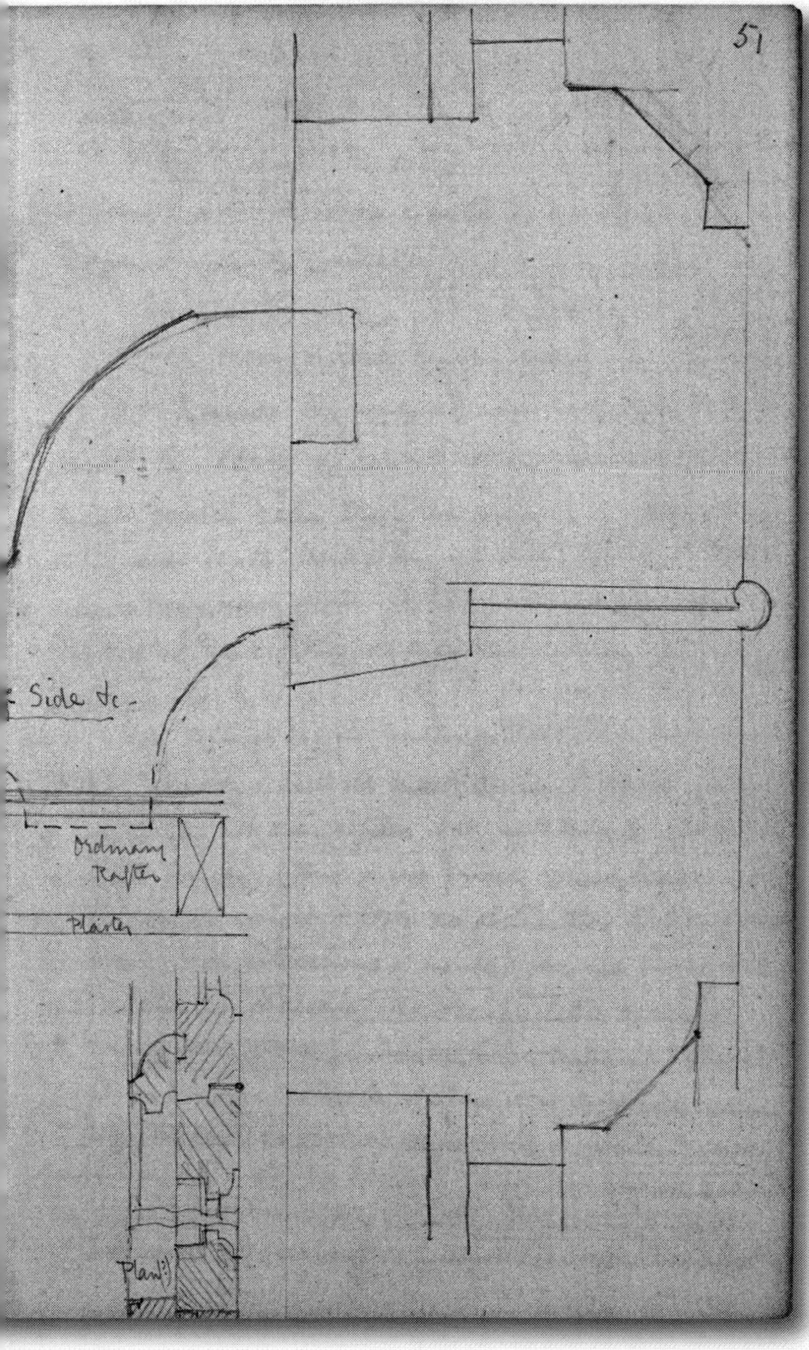
51
Side &c-
Ordinary Rafter
Plaster
Plan(?)

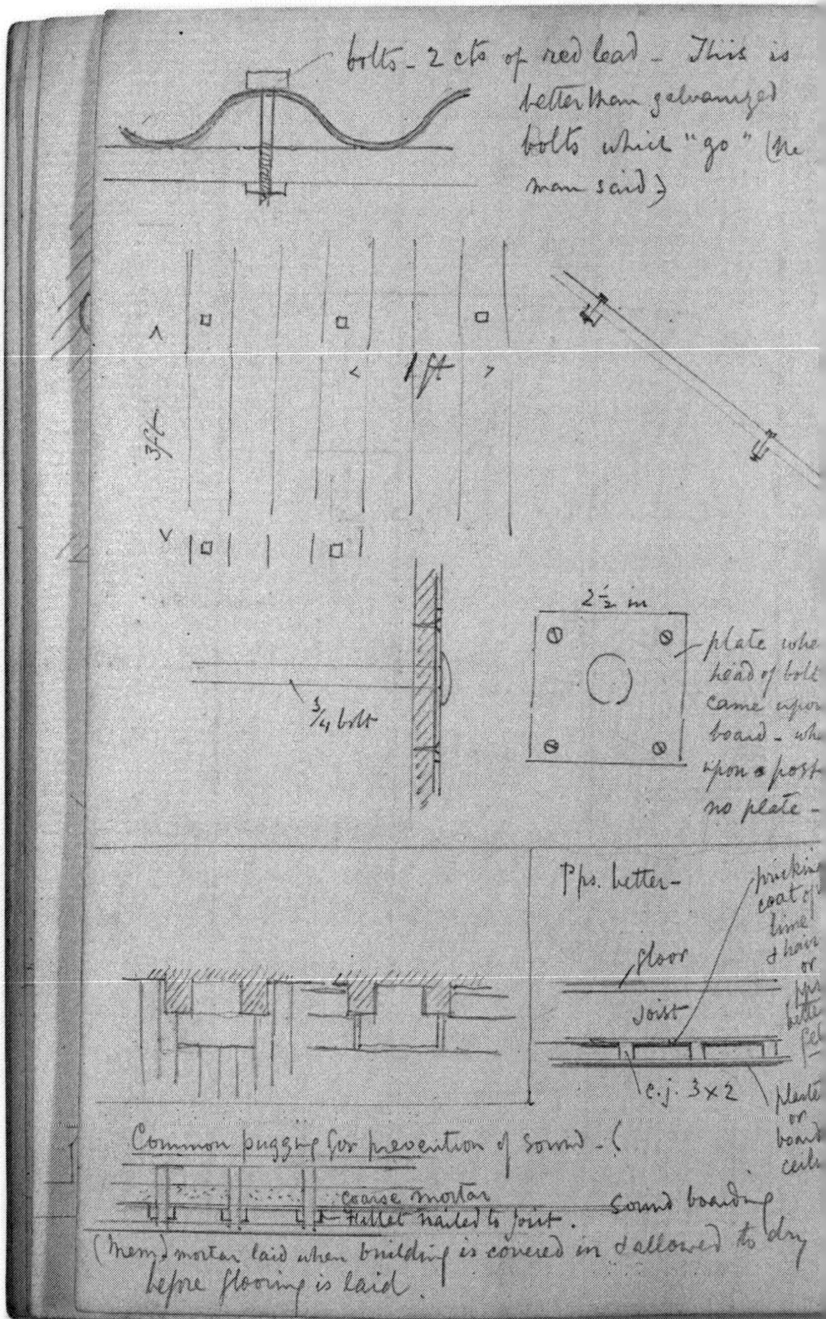
bolts - 2 cts of red lead - This is
better than galvanized
bolts which "go" (the
man said)
3 ft
1 ft
3/4 bolt
2½ in
plate
head of bolt
came
board -
no plate -
Pps. better -
pricking
coat of
lime
& hair
or
floor
Joist
c.j. 3×2
plaster
or
Common pugging for prevention of sound - (
coarse mortar
Sound boarding
Fillet nailed to joist.
(mem.) mortar laid when building is covered in & allowed to dry
before flooring is laid.

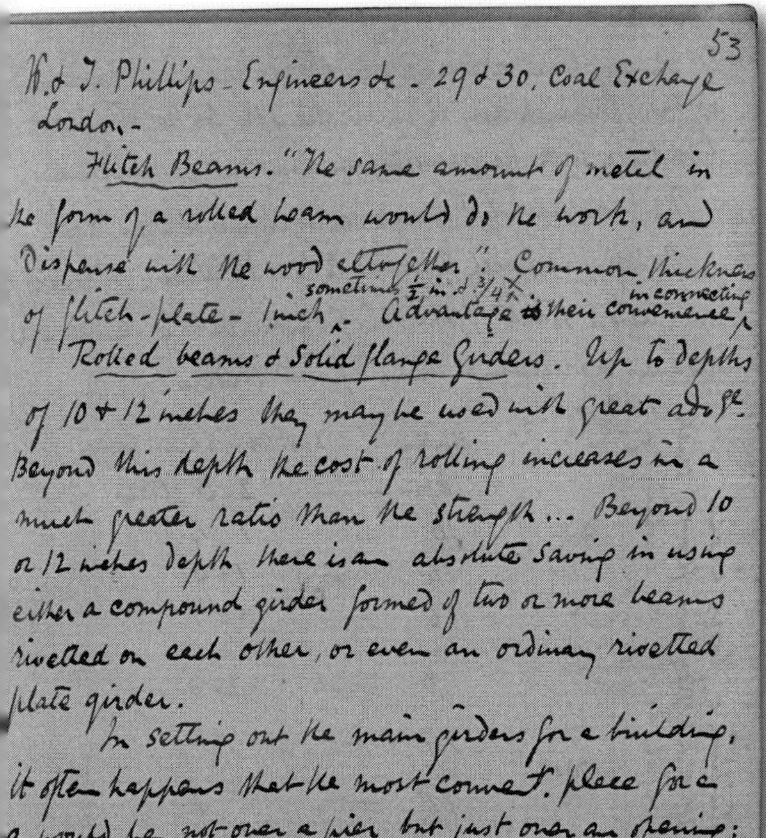

53

W. & J. Phillips – Engineers &c – 29 & 30, Coal Exchange
London. –

Flitch Beams. "The same amount of metal in the form of a rolled beam would do the work, and dispense with the wood altogether". Common thickness of flitch-plate – 1 inch (sometimes ½ in & 3/4 ×). Advantage is their convenience in connecting.

Rolled beams & Solid flange Girders. Up to depths of 10 & 12 inches they may be used with great advt. Beyond this depth the cost of rolling increases in a much greater ratio than the strength ... Beyond 10 or 12 inches depth there is an absolute saving in using either a compound girder formed of two or more beams rivetted on each other, or even an ordinary rivetted plate girder.

In setting out the main girders for a building, it often happens that the most convent. place for a g. would be not over a pier but just over an opening: a lintel formed of one or two small rolled beams wd sustain all the weight & form no obstruction to light or headway. In alterations of houses they are invaluable: used as shoring & needles they occupy little space ... In wide openings over windows in town buildings, where light is always desirable, & where it is especially necessary to keep the arch as shallow as possible a lintel of channel iron may be used, the vertical flange running up behind the brick arch constituting the facing & forming a socket to receive the ends of joists ... Another convent. applicn

× Depth 9 to 12 in.

is where stone or even wood staircases are concerned as they furnish any required strength for the strings & landings with the maximum amount of headway.

The more useful & usual sections – 6 to 8 in. deep.

Being practically limited to 10 or 12 in deep; Messrs P[illegible] invention starts from this point – taking the small beams & building them up into girders.

Light joists – suitable in construction of floors where spans are small; when placed 2ft apart they give floors of small depth. Also useful as lintels.

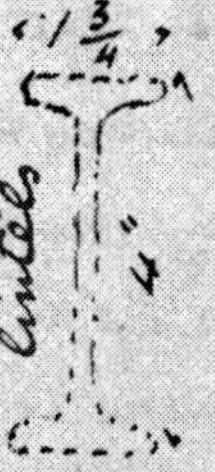

Span	Distrib^d Safe load
6ft	2.0 tons
10	1·4
14	1·0
16	0·9

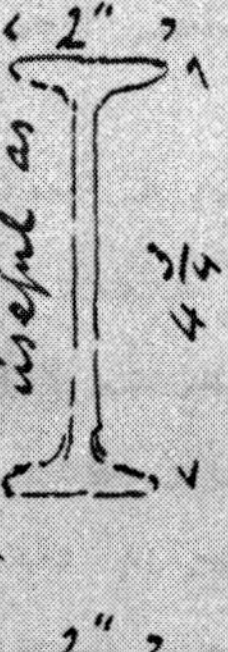

Span	Distrib^d Safe load
8	2·0
14	1·2
18	0·9

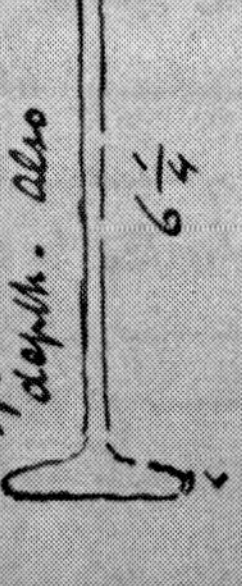

Span	Distrib^d Safe load
8	3·6
14	2·4
18	1·7

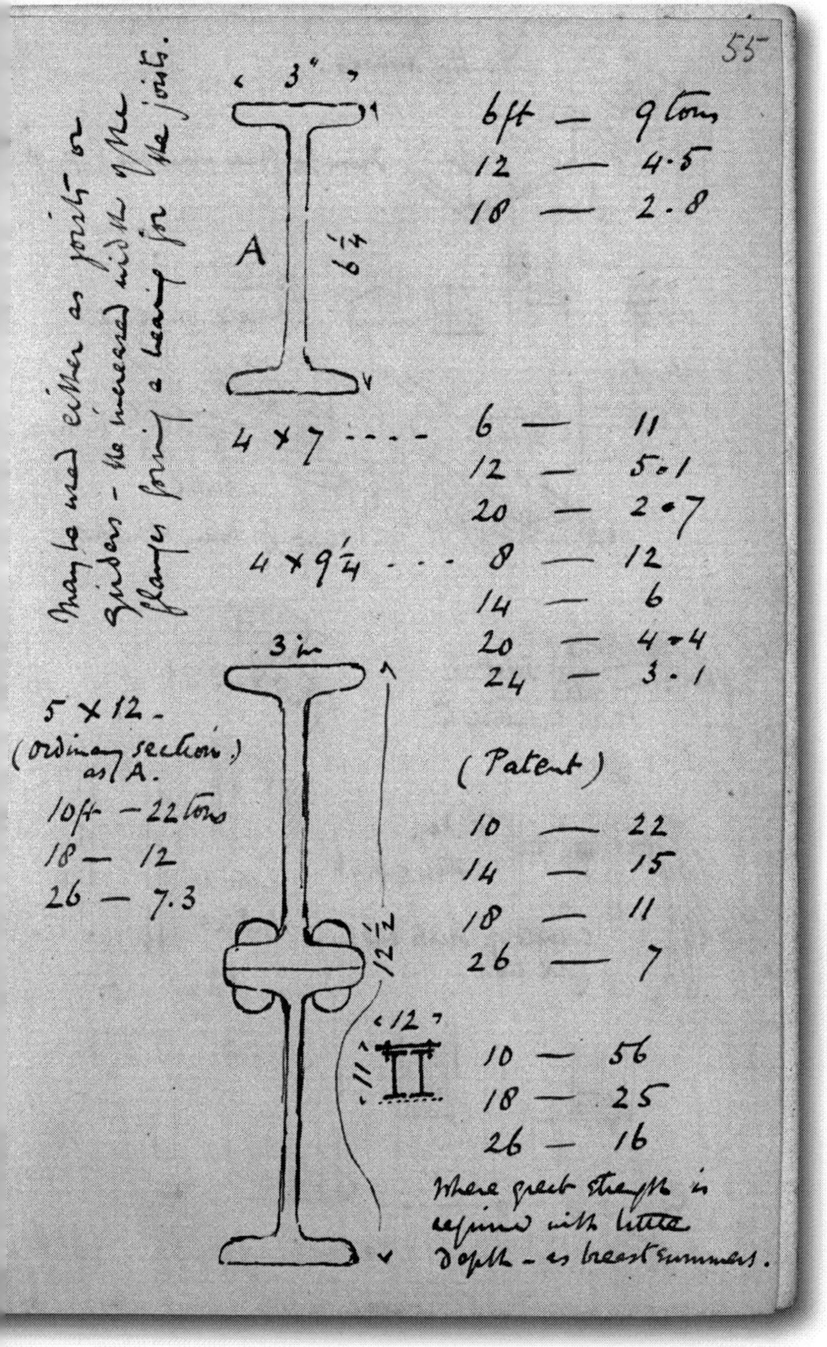
55

May be used either as joists or girders – the increased width of the flanges forming a bearing for the joists.

3"

A

6¼

6ft — 9 tons
12 — 4.5
18 — 2.8

4 × 7 .... 6 — 11
12 — 5.1
20 — 2.7

4 × 9¼ ... 8 — 12
14 — 6
20 — 4.4
24 — 3.1

3 in

5 × 12 –
(ordinary section) as A.
10ft — 22 tons
18 — 12
26 — 7.3

(Patent)
10 — 22
14 — 15
18 — 11
26 — 7

12½

12

11

10 — 56
18 — 25
26 — 16

Where great strength is required with little depth – as breast summers.

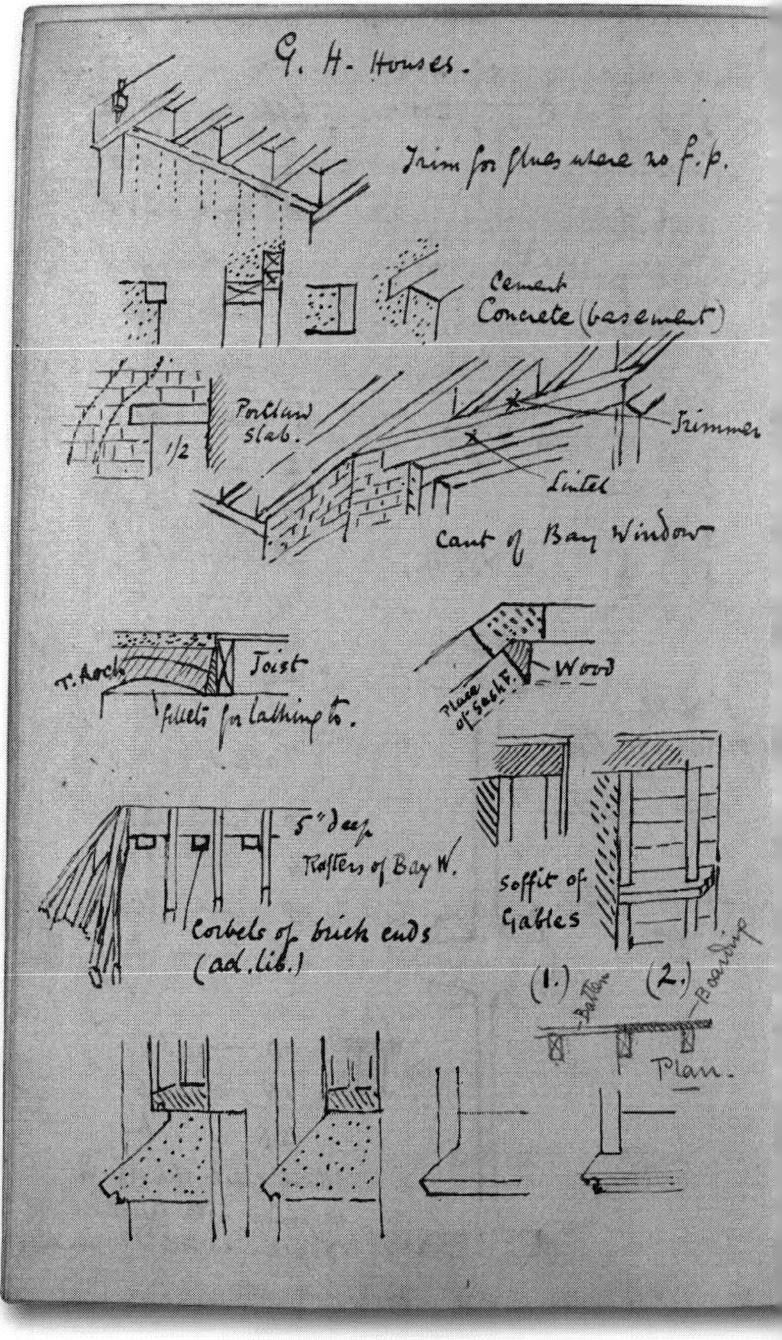
G. H. Houses.
Trim for flues where no F.P.
Cement
Concrete (basement)
Portland slab.
1/2
Trimmer
Lintel
Cant of Bay Window
T. Arch
Joist
fillets for lathing to.
Wood
Place of Sash F.
5" deep
Rafters of Bay W.
Corbels of brick ends
(ad. lib.)
Soffit of
Gables
(1.)
(2.)
Batten
Boarding
Plan.

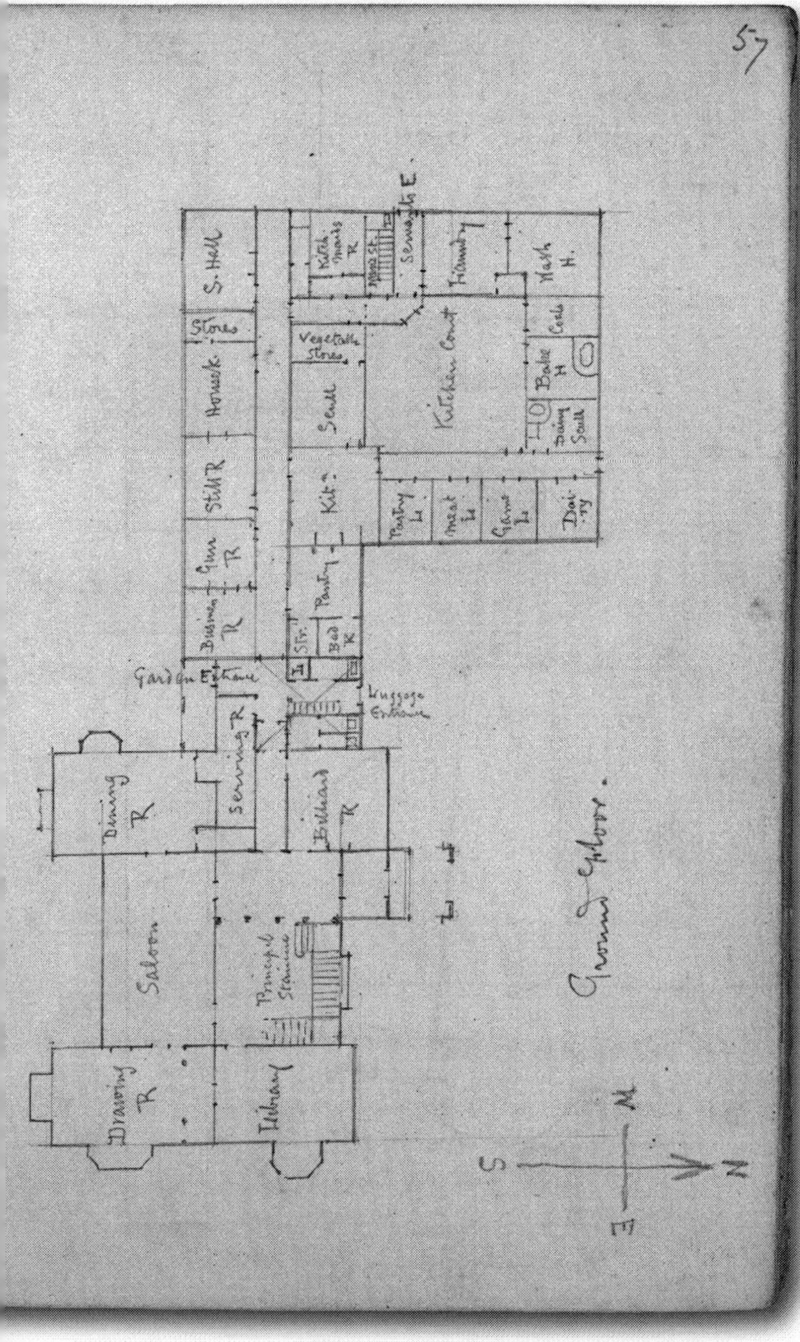
57
S. Hall
Stores
Housek
Still R
Gun R
Kit:
Pantry
Vegetable Stores
Kitchen Court
Laundry
Wash H.
Coals
Bake H
Dairy Scull
Pastry L
Meat L
Game L
Garden Entrance
Luggage Entrance
Serving R
Billiard R
Dining R
Saloon
Principal Staircase
Drawing R
Library
Ground Floor.
S
N
E

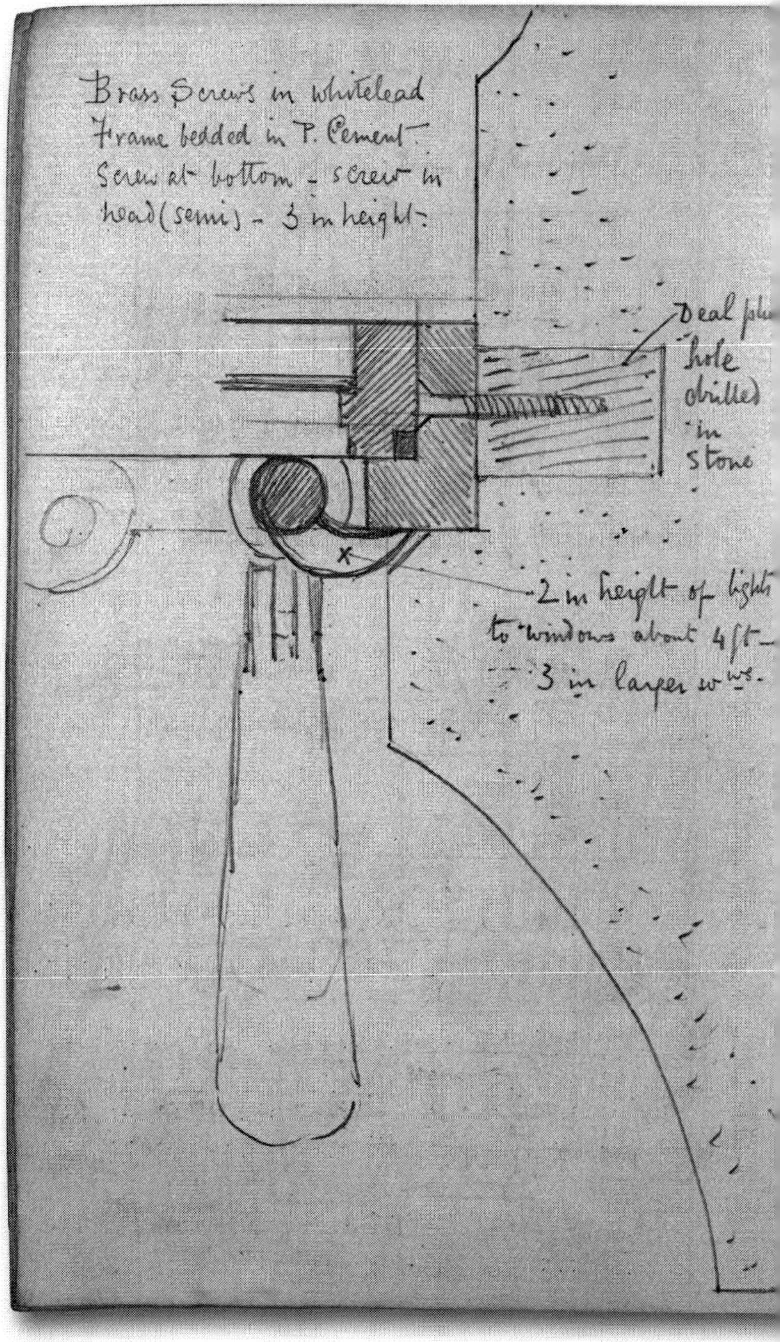
Brass Screws in whitelead
Frame bedded in P. Cement.
Screw at bottom - screw in
head (semi) - 3 in height.
Deal pl
hole
drilled
in
stone
2 in height of ligh
to windows about 4ft
3 in larger w

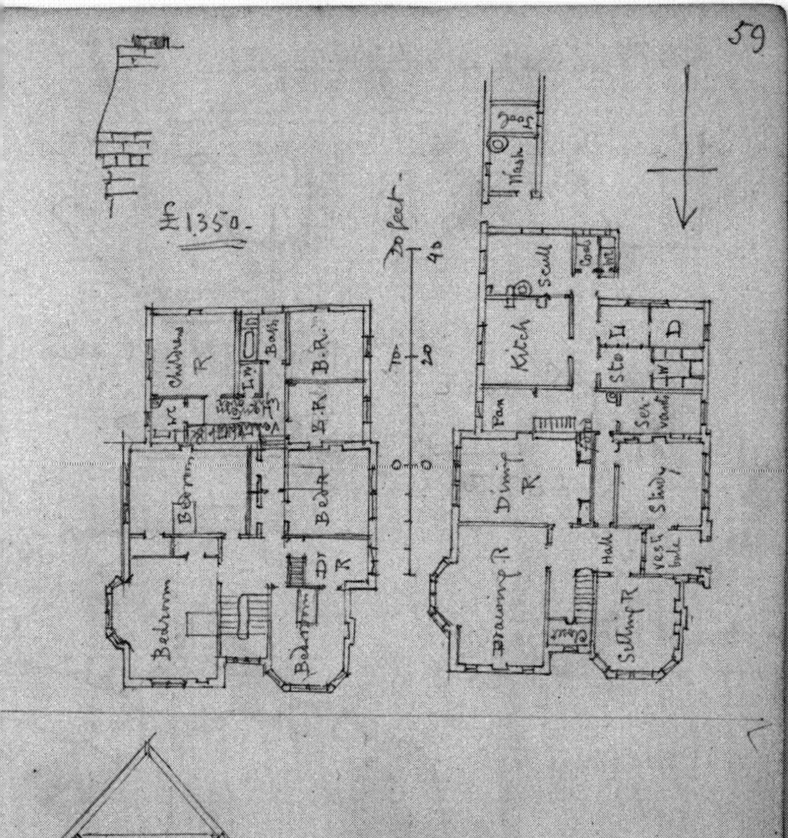

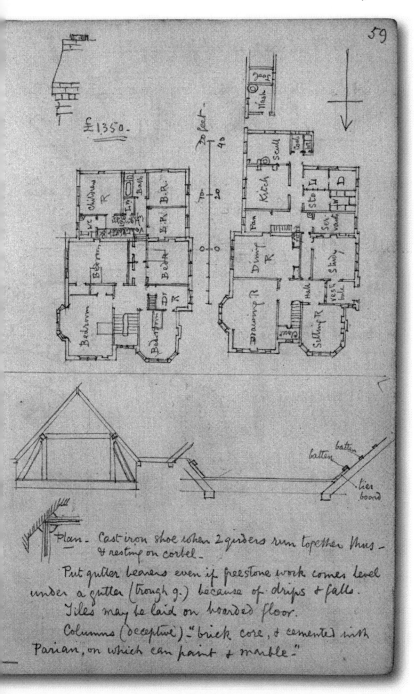

Plan – Cast iron shoe when 2 girders run together thus – & resting on corbel –

Put gutter bearers even if freestone work comes level under a gutter (trough g.) because of drips & falls.

Tiles may be laid on boarded floor.

Columns (deceptive) – "brick core, & cemented with Parian, on which can paint & marble."

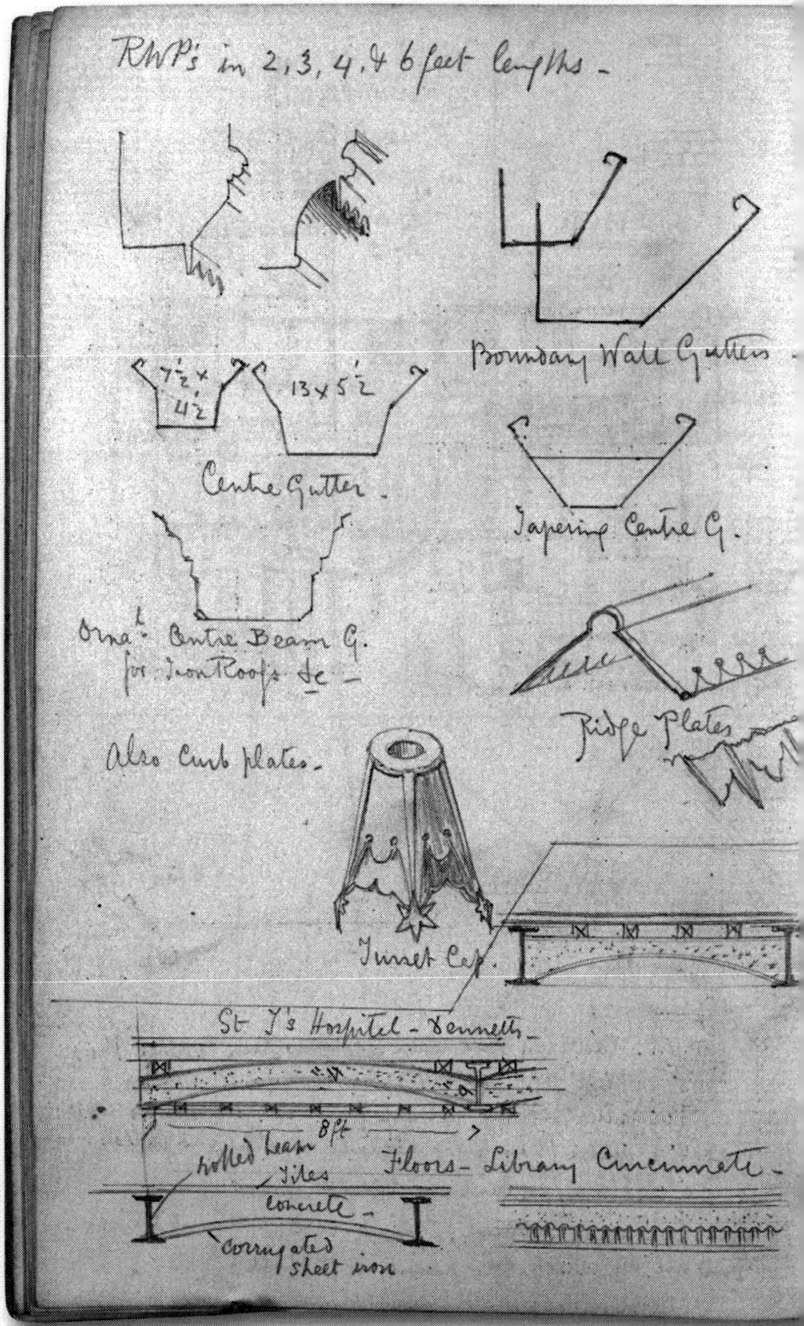
RWP's in 2, 3, 4, & 6 feet lengths –
Boundary Wall Gutters –
7½ × 4½
13 × 5½
Centre Gutter –
Tapering Centre G.
Ornal Centre Beam G.
for Iron Roofs &c –
Ridge Plates
Also Curb plates –
Turret Cap.
St T's Hospital – Tennett's –
8 ft
Rolled beam
Tiles
Concrete –
Corrugated sheet iron
Floors – Library Cincinnati –

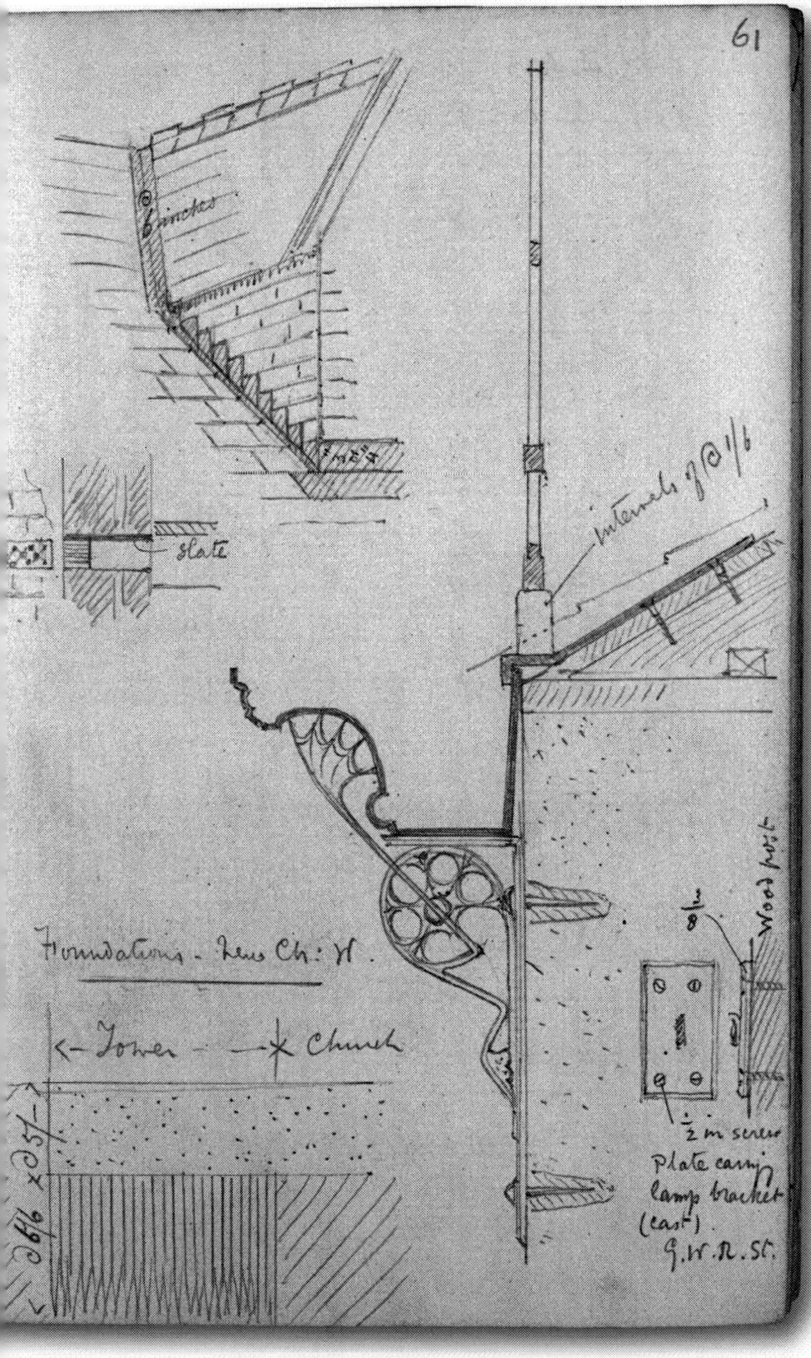
61
bricks
slate
intervals of @ 1/6
Foundations - New Ch: W
<- Tower - -x Church
Wood post
1/8
1/2 in screw
Plate carrying lamp bracket (cast)
G.W.R. St.

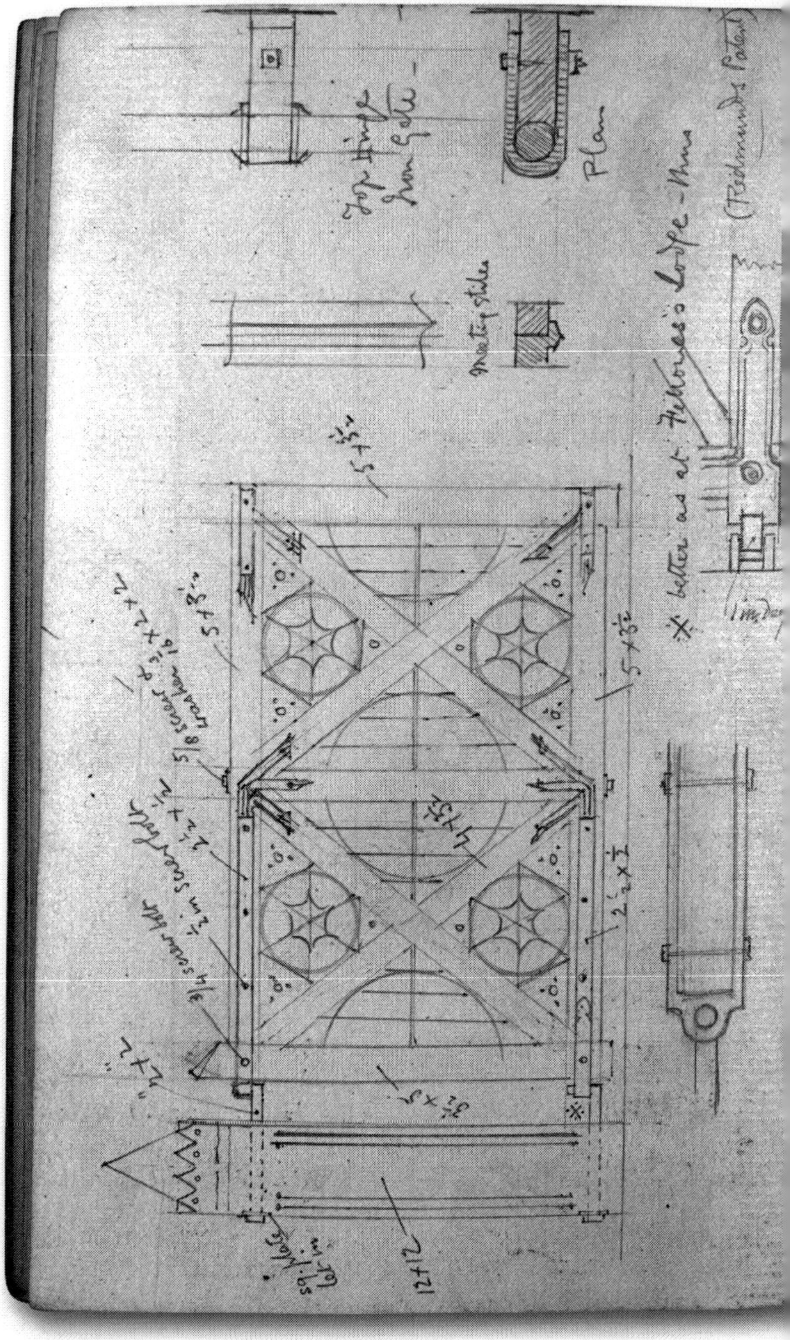
Plan
Meeting stiles
12 x 12

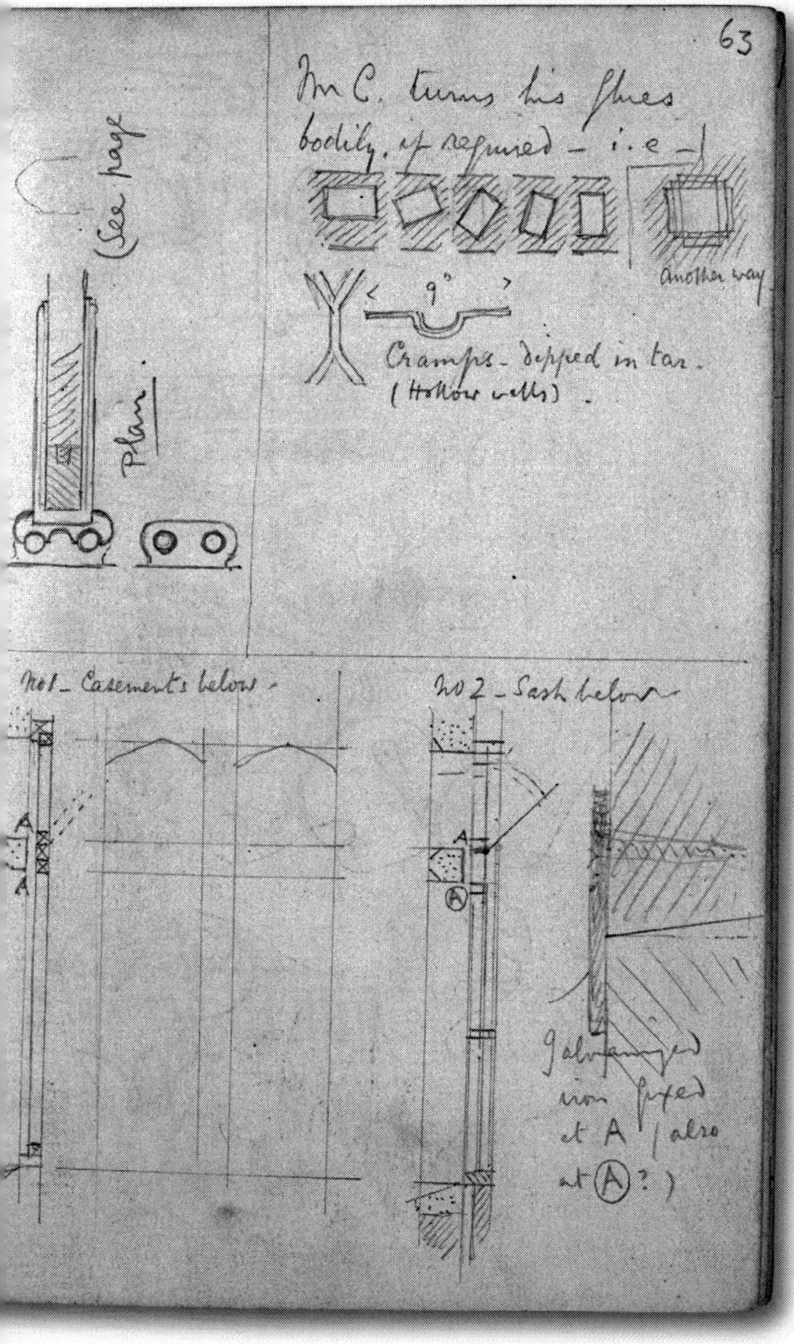
63
Mr C. turns his flues bodily, if required – i.e –
another way
9"
Cramps – dipped in tar.
(Hollow walls)
(See page
plan
No1 – Casements below –
A
A
No 2 – Sash below –
A
A
Galvanized iron fixed at A (also at A ?)

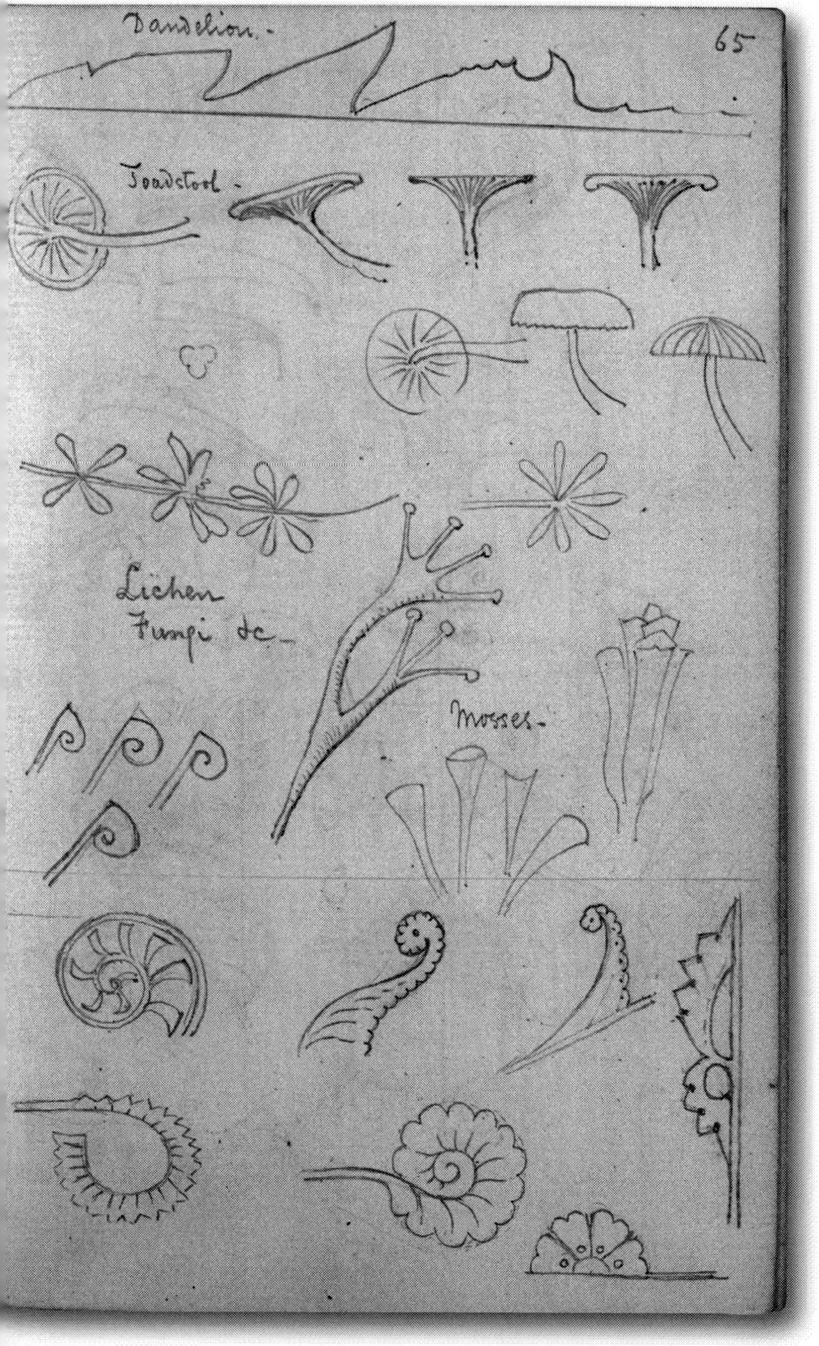
Dandelion.-
65
Toadstool.-
Lichen
Fungi &c.-
Mosses.-

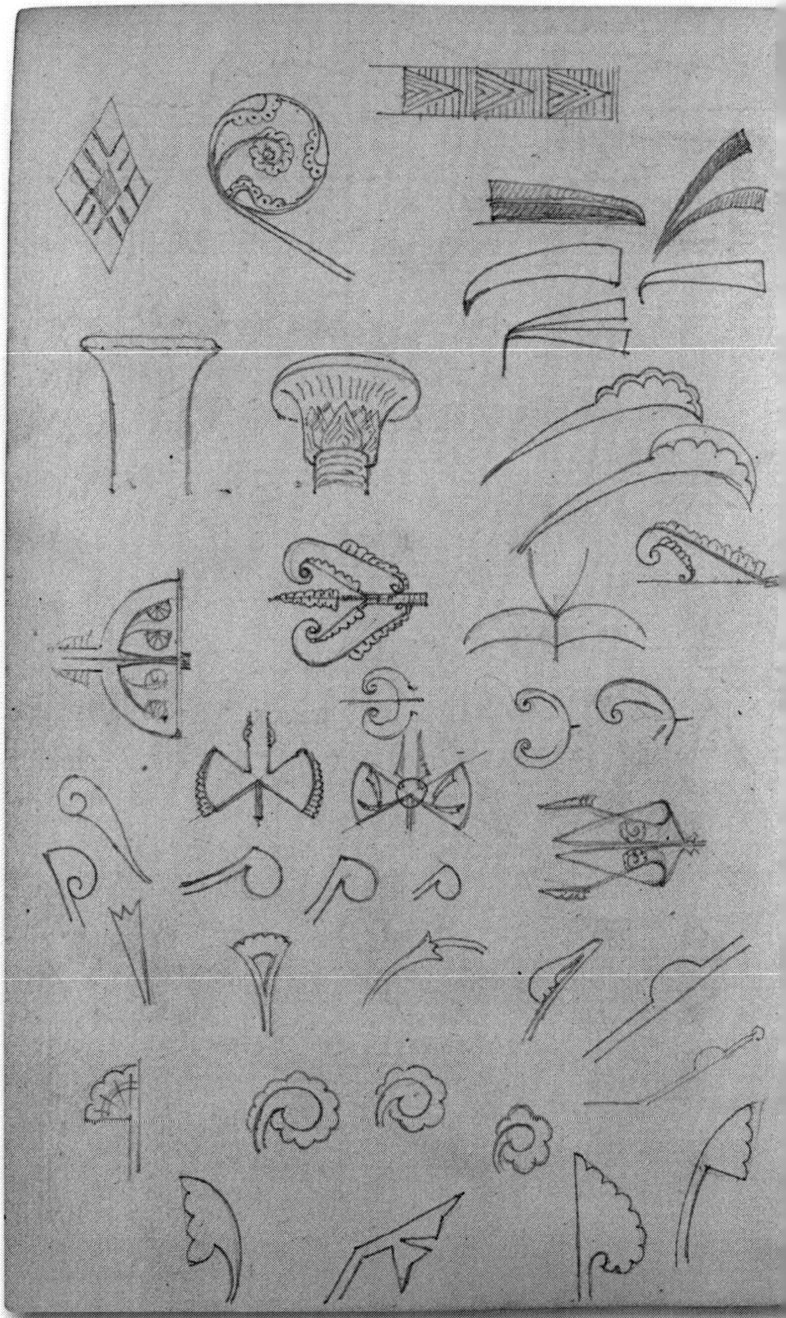

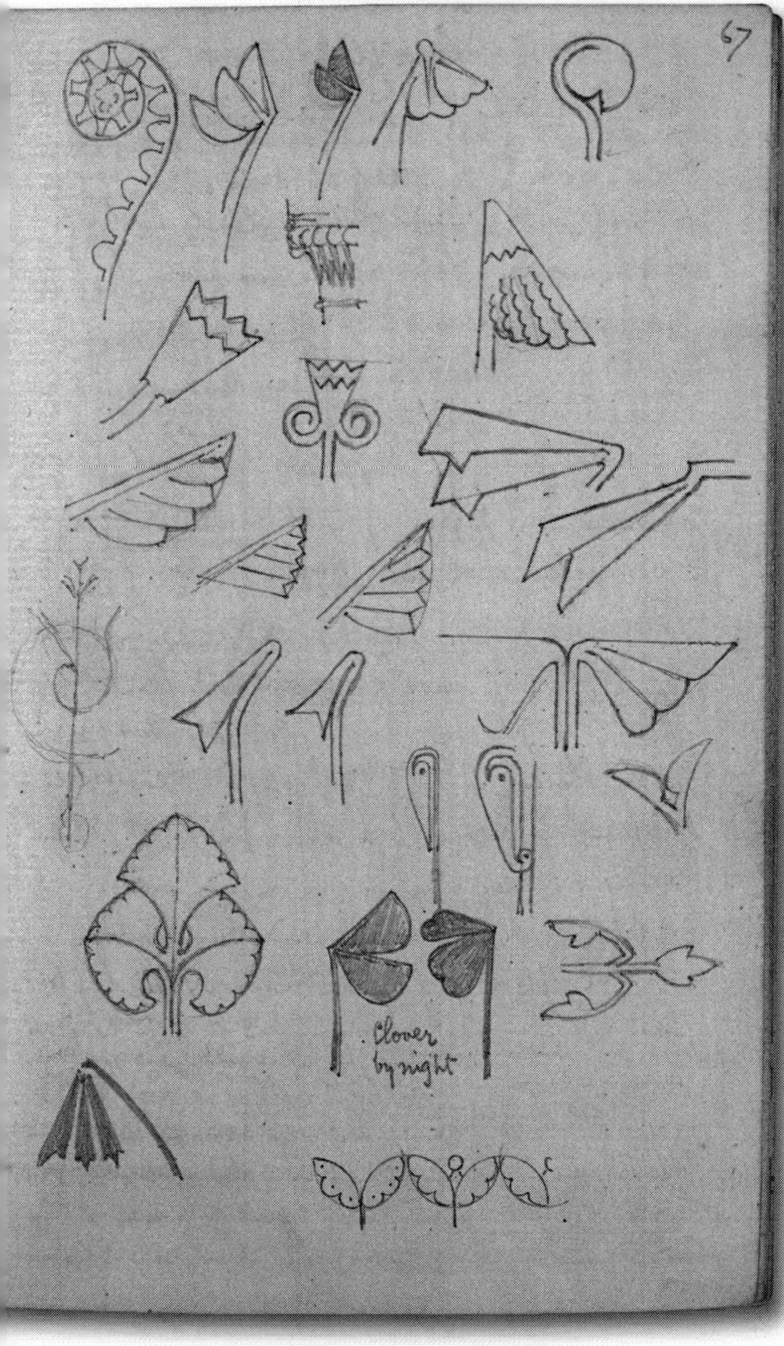
67
Clover
by night

Lead flat.

4 × 2½ bearers. inch deal boarding for lead - inch deal checking - milled lead 6 lbs to foot - 2 in. rolls - lead to turn up 9 in under slates & in no place to be more than 2/6 wide -

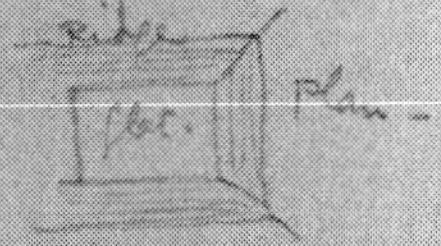

(Another place) a proper cesspool to each gutter - 3 in. pipes of 7 lb lead soldered in & connected with two stacks of 3 in RWP.

W.C. cast iron soil pipe to be carried up through the roof with an open end for ventilation & having a proper lead flashing & apron on the slates - to be in a chase in wall cut for purpose - covered with a piece of pipe casing & proper rebated grounds &c - & to fill in solid with sawdust around the same.

A W.C. floor - framed trimmer 10 × 3 - floor joists 5 × 2 - ceiling joists 3½ by 2 - lay on same an inch white battened floor & a ½ in rough floor on top of ceiling joists - the space between the two being filled in solid with sawdust

69

To excavate the ground for cesspool 5 ft dia. & 6 ft deep to spring of arch. To be lined with 1 bk walls in cement & to have a bed of concrete 18 in deep under the whole surface. To be domed over with a 1 bk. Dome in cemt. To have a manhole in the centre 2 ft dia. brought up square to the surface of the ground. to be covered with a piece of 3 in Purbeck paving. The interior to be floated with P. cemt. & trowelled to a fine face with a steel trowel. & to have a 9 in. overflow pipe from the same to the river—

Zinc

Get good falls & drips. Lay every sheet free, for contraction & expansion. sheets 8 ft by 3 ft. Lay none but {Devaux's [anybody's]} pure Vieille Montagne zinc. Thickness No 13 as the minimum, & Nos 14, 15 & 16 as the best gauges.

James W Tyler in "Builder".

[Zinc lasts abt. 35 years]

Drainage.

Not enough that house drains be made of glazed earthenware carefully put together & cemented, but they shd. be laid in a brick trough & covered with stone, or where such expenses can be afforded, [& if drain has to be carried across space] they shd be made of iron flanged pipes screwed together, with the joints caulked. In the case of ordinary glazed pipes the least inequality in soil will crush cemt. joints & allow escape of sewage gas.

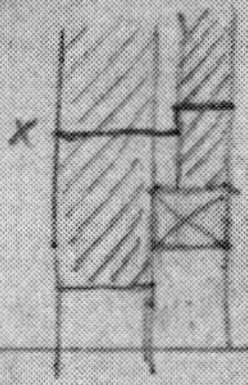

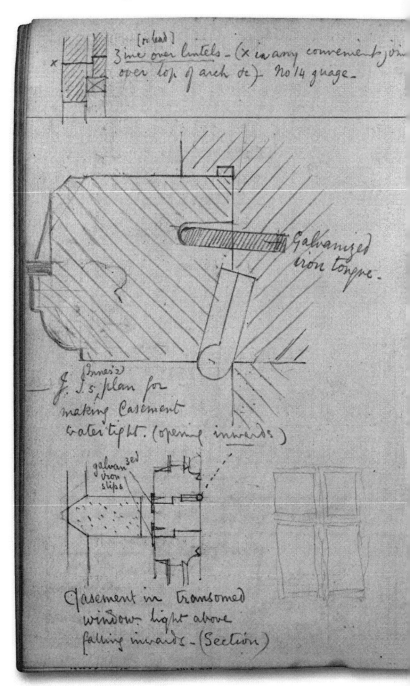

[or lead]
Zinc over lintels – (x in any convenient join[t]
over top of arch &c) – No 14 guage –

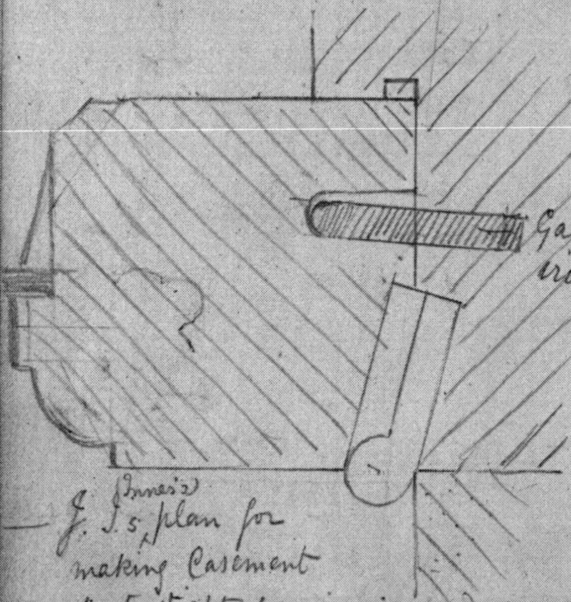

Innes's
J. I's plan for
making Casement
water tight. (opening inwards)

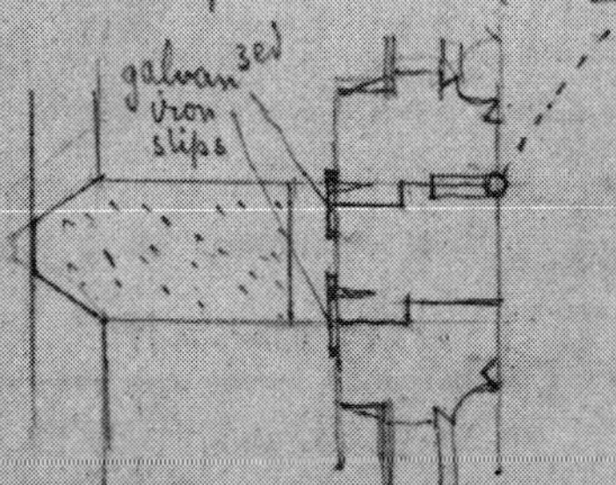

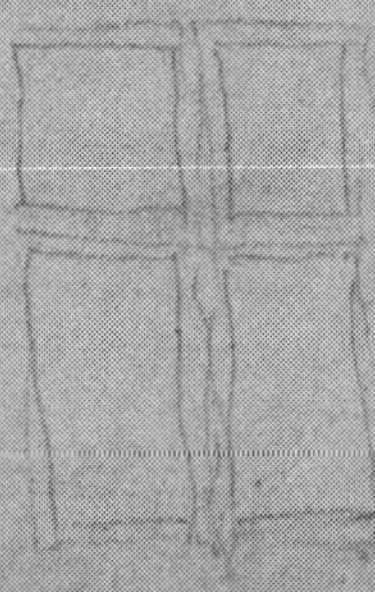

Casement in transomed
window. light above
falling inwards – (Section)

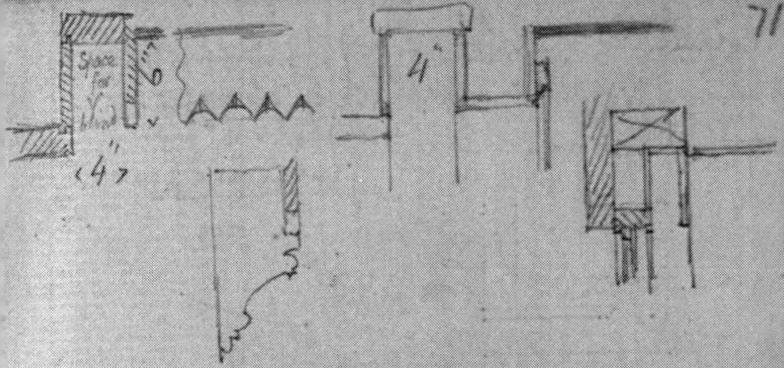

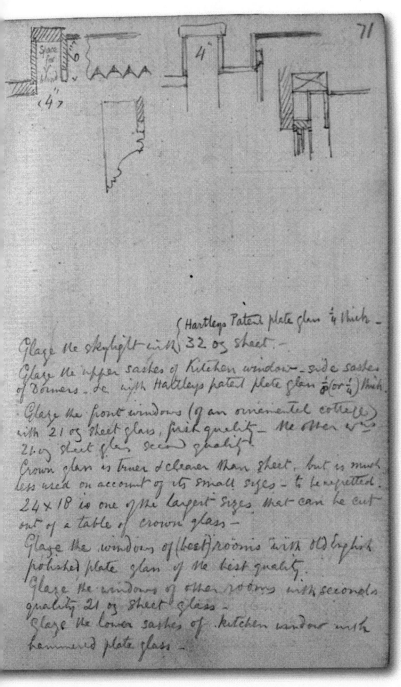

Glaze the skylight with { Hartleys Patent plate glass ¼ thick –
{ 32 oz sheet. –

Glaze the upper sashes of kitchen window – side sashes of Dormers &c with Hartleys patent plate glass ⅛ (or ¼) thick.

Glaze the front windows (of an ornamental cottage) with 21 oz sheet glass, first quality – the other w^ns 21 oz sheet glass second quality.

Crown glass is truer & clearer than sheet, but is much less used on account of its small sizes – to be regretted.

24 x 18 is one of the largest sizes that can be cut out of a table of crown glass –

Glaze the windows of (best) rooms with old English polished plate glass of the best quality.

Glaze the windows of other rooms with seconds quality 21 oz sheet glass.

Glaze the lower sashes of kitchen window with hammered plate glass –

Tile floors. "Wood may be readily replaced with mosaic – nail fillets to the joists at 3 in from the upper surface – saw the fl. boards into short lengths & fit them in between the joists upon the fillets – concrete may then be filled in flush with the upper face of the joist, & faced with the usual thin coat of cement. The tiles & cement will occupy about the same space as the floor boards they replace. Tiles laid on boards witht. concrete are certain to become loose within a few weeks.

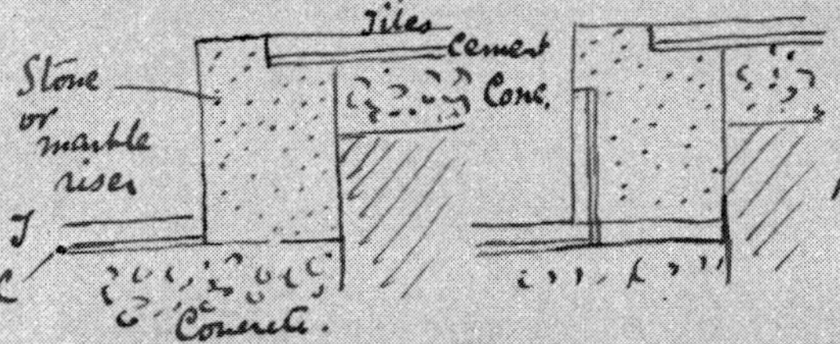

Steps may be fitted in this manner

Skirting boards &c shd be removed & replaced resting on the tiles; a better appearance than when the cut joints show.

Font – "Caen stone – 2 pieces – bowl lined with 7 lb lead – 1 in. lead waste pipe with brass plug & chain" – "catch pit to be provided under concrete bed for water" [why not a drain?] "Font to stand on a solid bed of concre carried up from 18 in below floor."

Ht. of F. from standing or officiating step – 3-10.

All the dimensions seem rather large.

Brass inscriptn. plate to the memy. of — (to whom the F is erected) on centre of lower step.

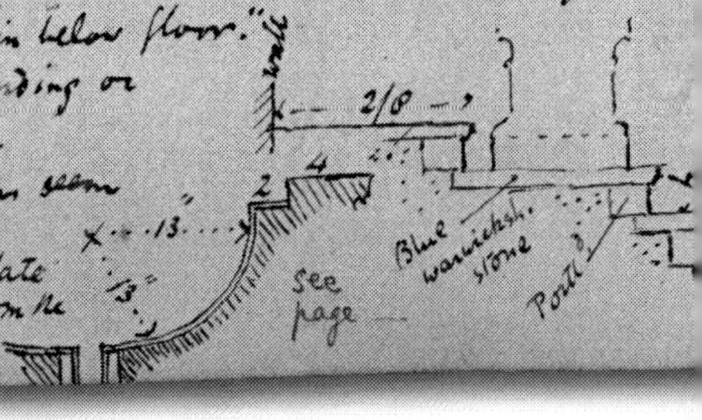

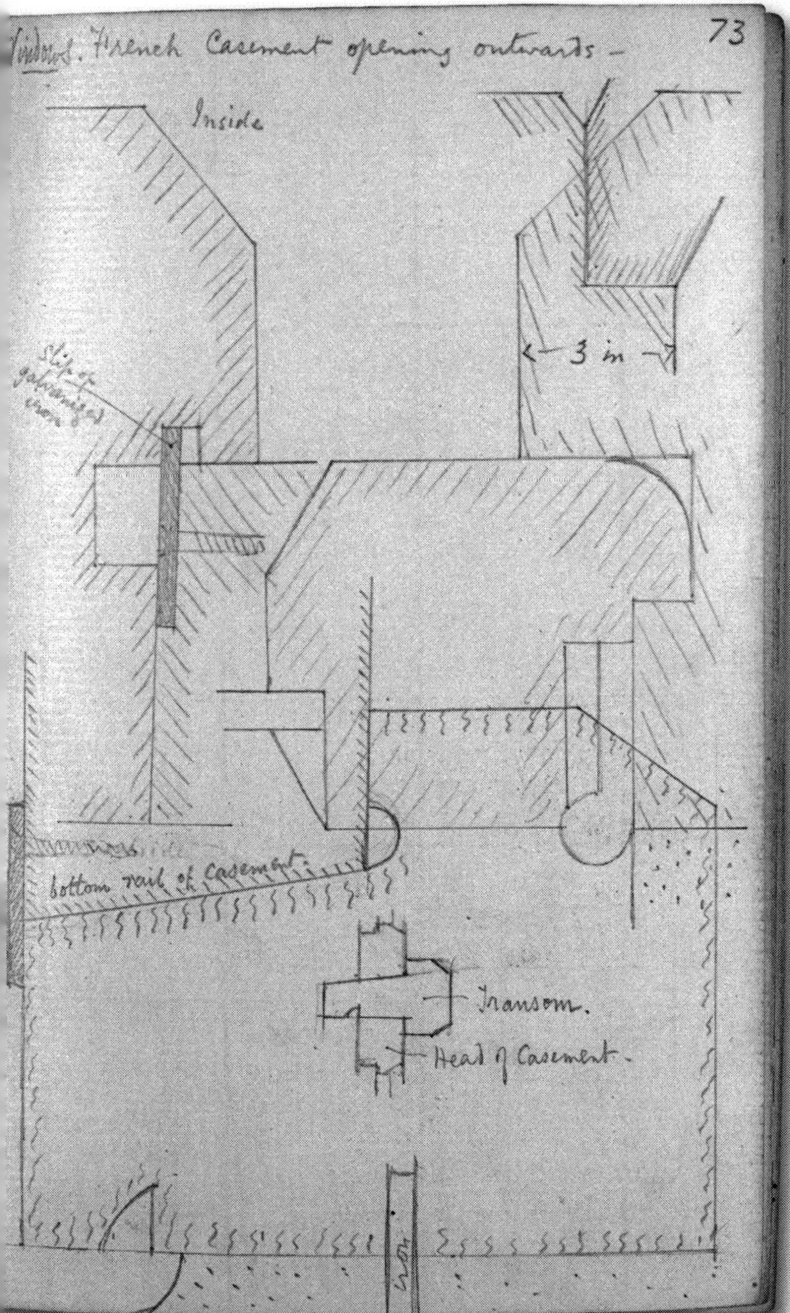
Windows. French Casement opening outwards –
73
Inside
3 in
bottom rail of casement.
Transom.
Head of Casement.

The ordinary sink trap with a dipstone is often a delusion, as the least jar will crack cemt. round top. Use Siphon bends. ~~[illegible]~~ & 885 / 485

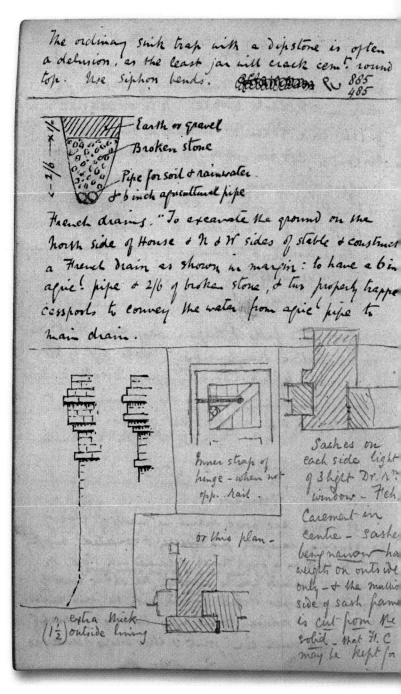

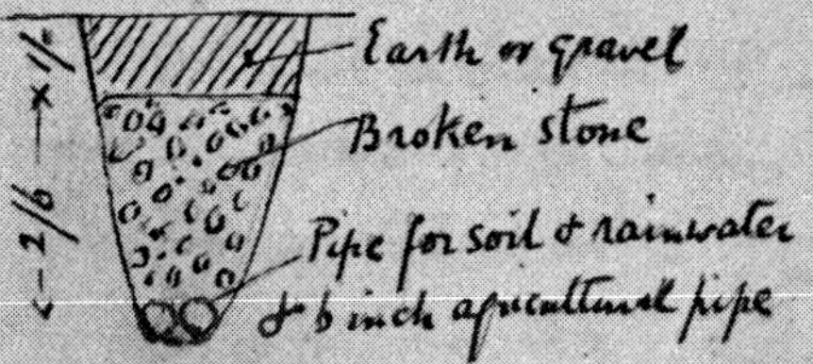

French drains. "To excavate the ground on the North side of House & N & W sides of stable & construct a French drain as shown in margin: to have a 6 in agricl. pipe & 2/6 of broken stone, & two properly trapped cesspools to convey the water from agricl. pipe to main drain.

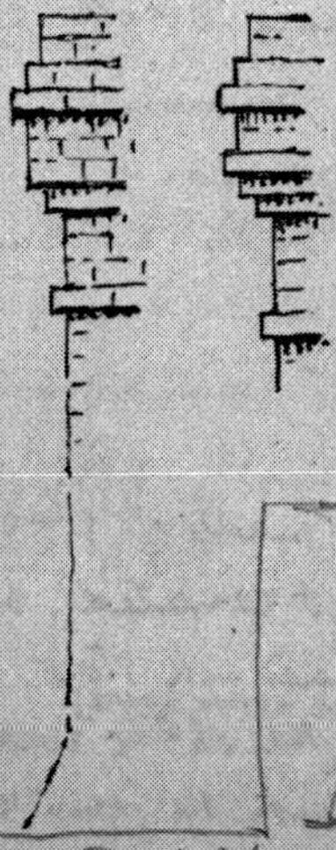

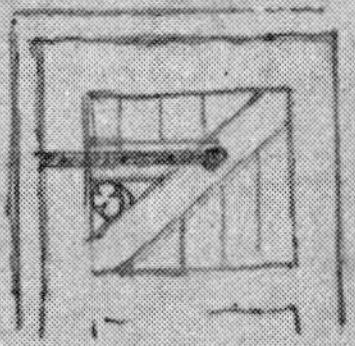

Inner strap of hinge – when not opp. rail.

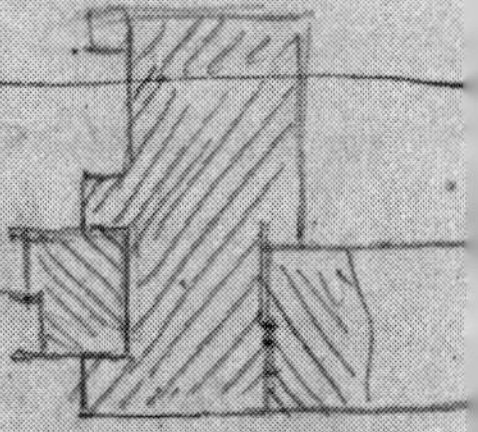

Sashes on each side light of 3 light Dr. Rm. window – Fch. Casement in centre – Sashes being narrow have weight on outside only – & the mullion side of sash frame is cut from the solid – that Fr. C may be kept for

or this plan –

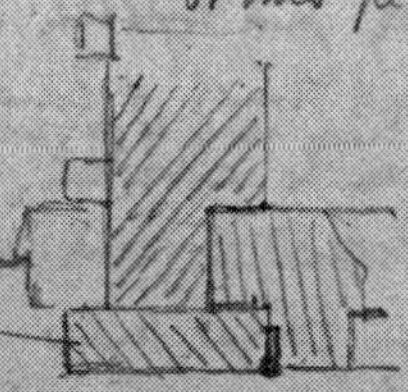

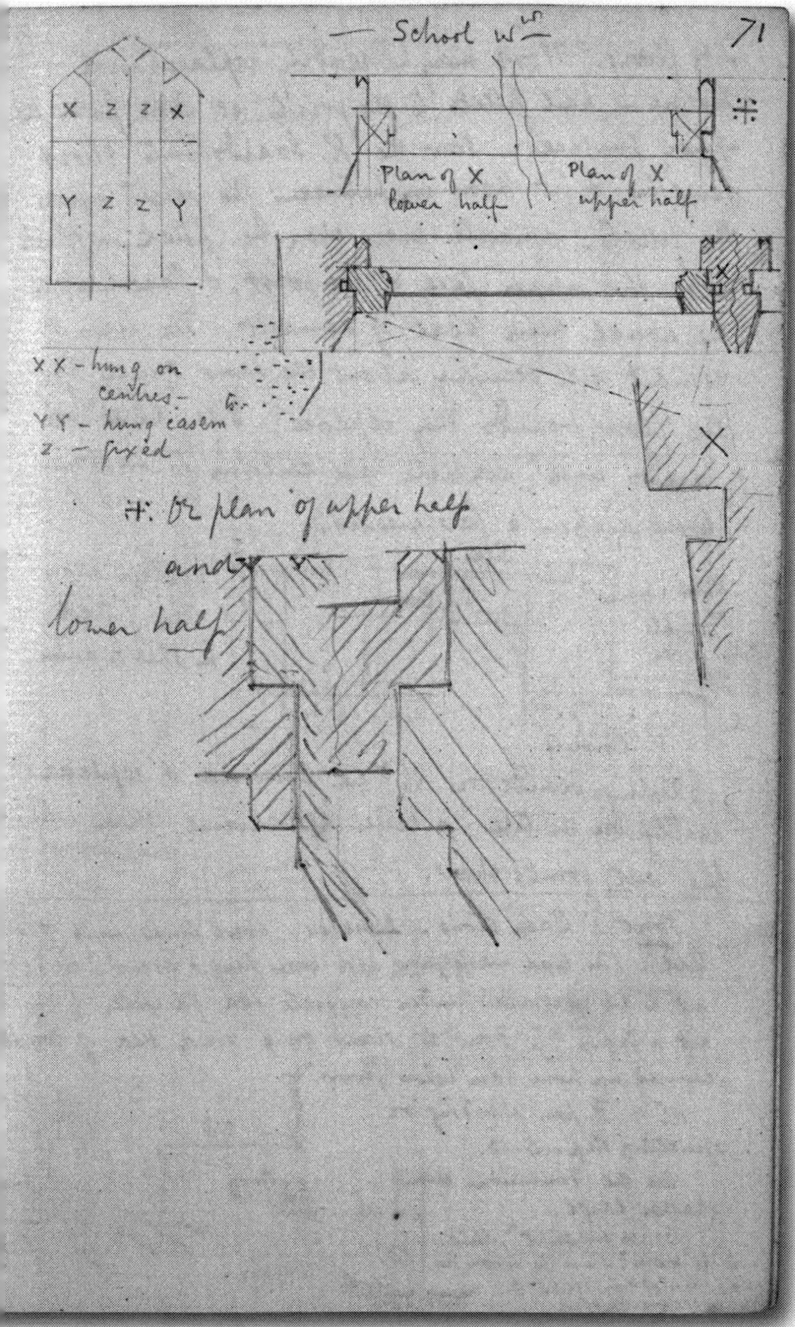
School wdw
71
X Z Z X
Y Z Z Y
Plan of X
lower half
Plan of X
upper half
X X – hung on
centres –
Y Y – hung casem
z – fixed
#. Or plan of upper half
and
lower half
X

pp. 072ii – 073ii

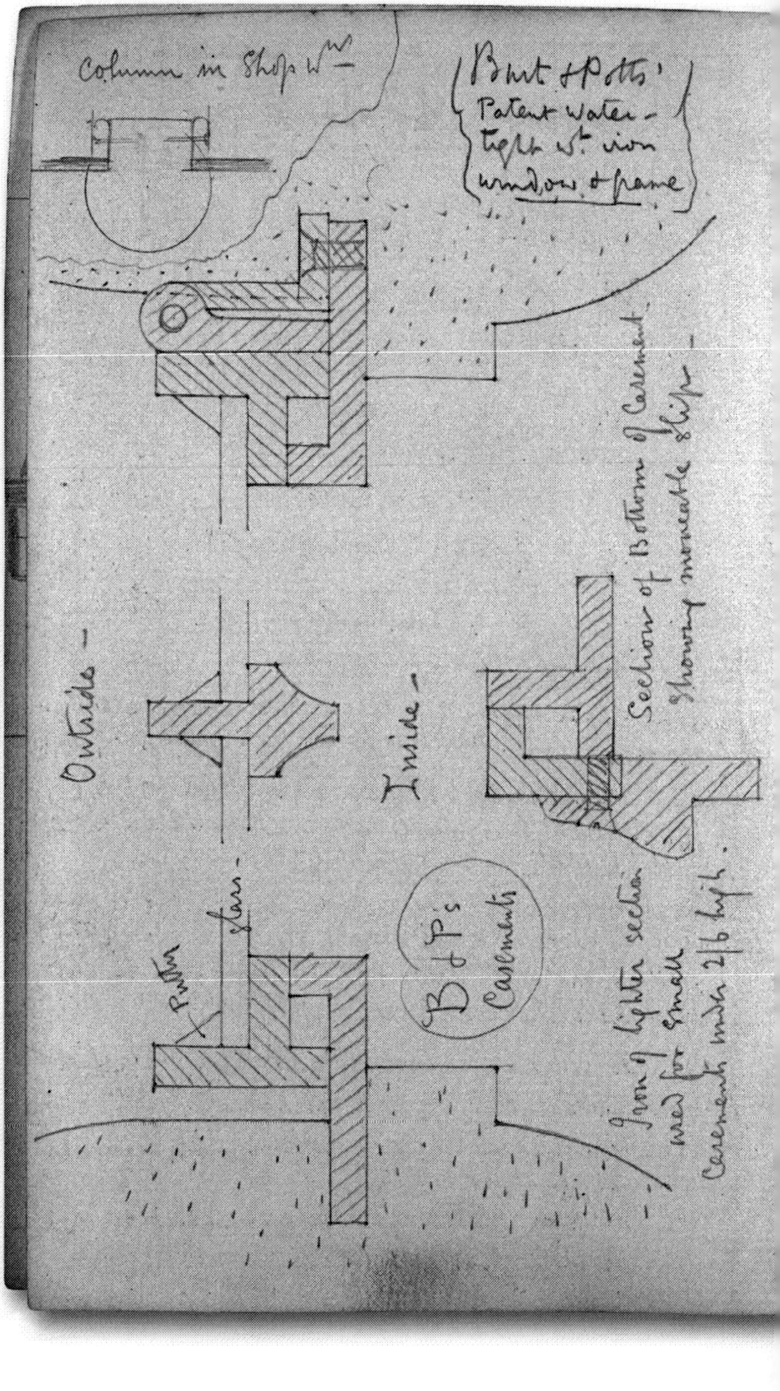

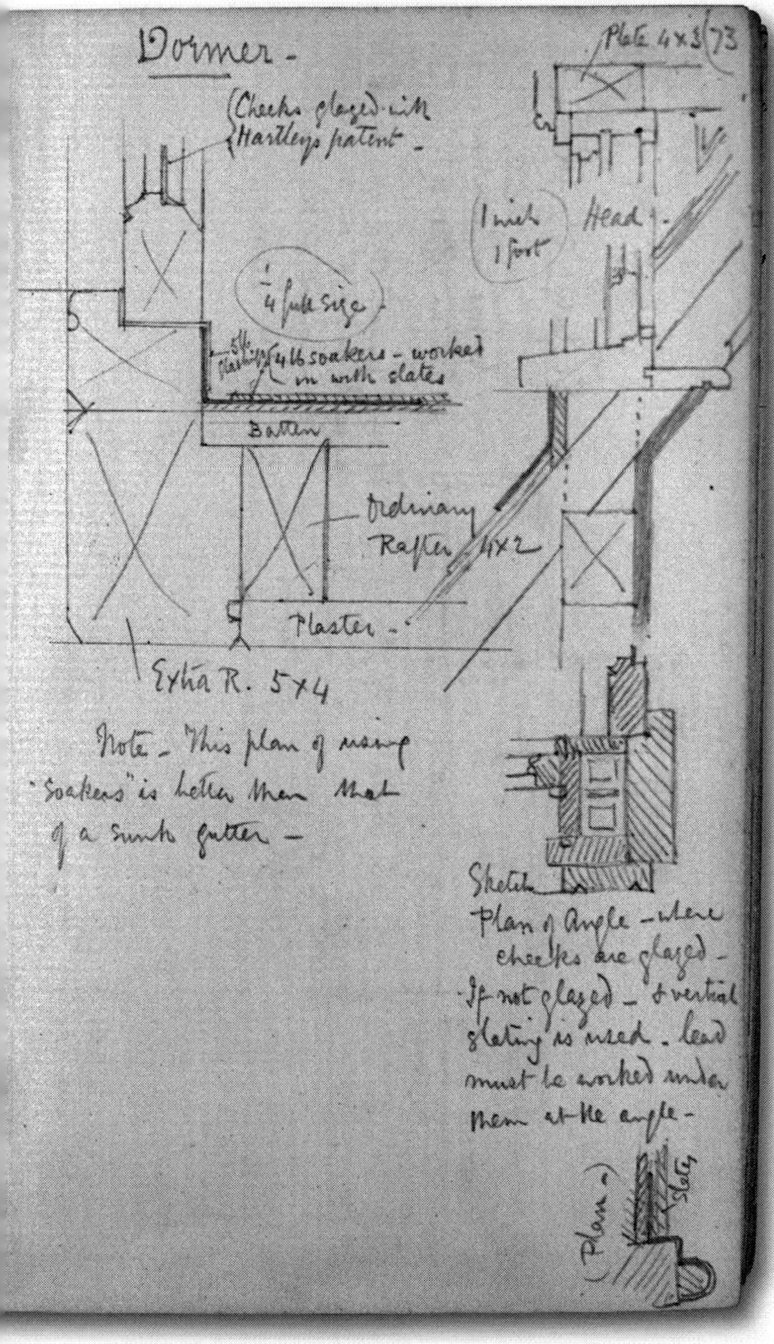
Dormer -
Plate 4x3
73
Cheeks glazed with
Hartley's patent -
1 inch
1 foot
Head -
1/4 full size
4 lb soakers - worked
in with slates
Batten
Ordinary
Rafter 4x2
Plaster -
Extra R. 5x4
Note - This plan of using
"Soakers" is better than that
of a sunk gutter -
Sketch
Plan of Angle - where
cheeks are glazed -
If not glazed - & vertical
slating is used - lead
must be worked under
them at the angle -
(Plan -)
Slates

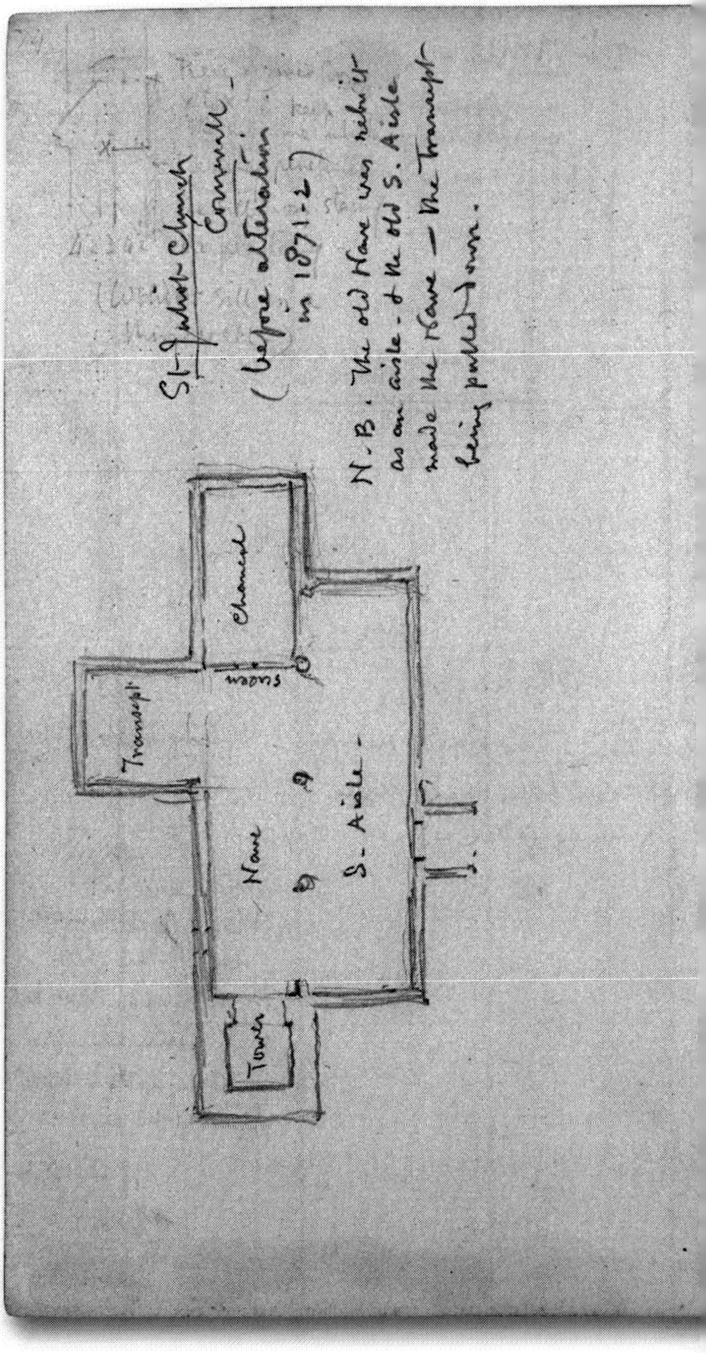
St Juliot Church
Cornwall –
(before alteration
in 1871-2)
N.B. The old Nave was rebuilt
as an aisle – & the old S. Aisle
made the Nave – the Transept
being pulled down.
Transept
Tower
Nave
Chancel
screen
S. Aisle –

26

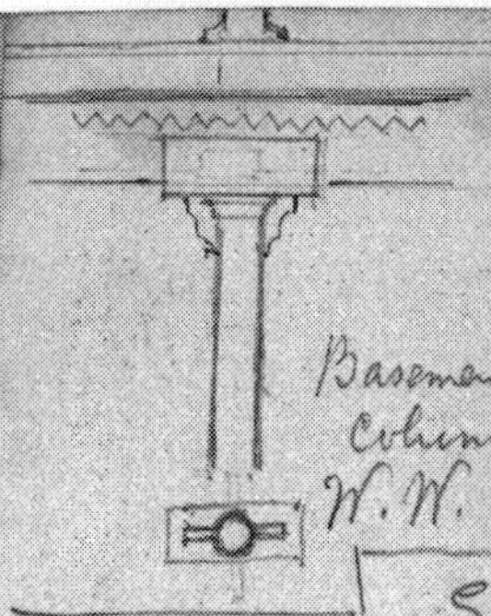

Basement floor Columns – W. W. Chapel –

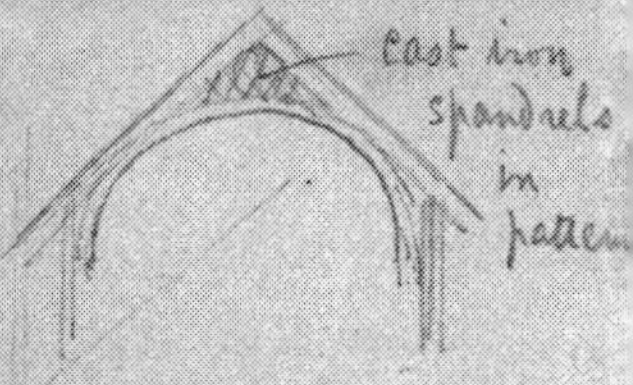

Sliding Doors –

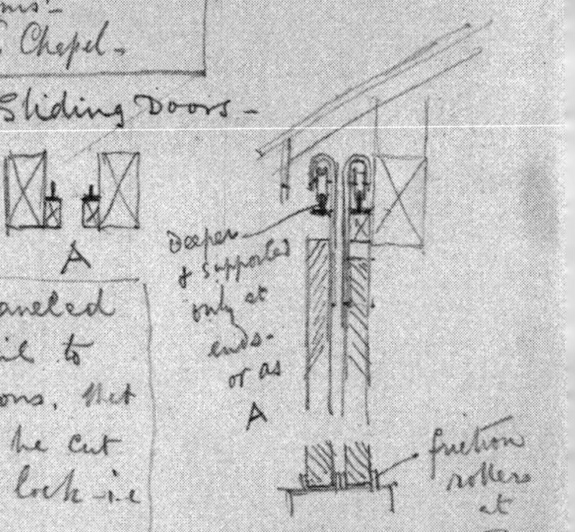

Mem concerning paneled Doors – Lock rail to have double tenons, that the tenon may not be cut off by mortice for lock – i.e

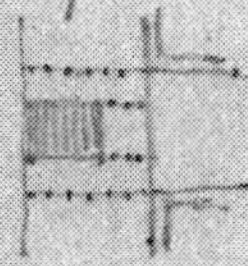

Sl – House –

New flues cut in & carried up in old walls, new recess for housemaids sink &c, built in brickwork in cement.

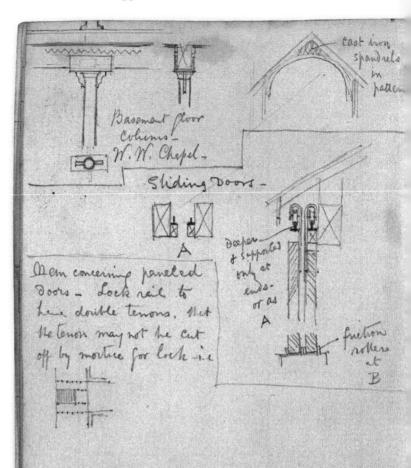

(78)

Floors – &c. –

Concrete (cem^t.) (4 in. thick, a conv^t. thickness: finished with a steel trowel.) Cheaper than paved, but if in a damp situation the moisture condenses in drops upon its surface. At St. House, concrete is used for coach house – &c – asphalte for ~~Stable~~ kitchen yard & coach house yard – the outer margin being formed thus "9" with a Purbeck channel, delivering at one end into sink & cesspool connected with drain –

Coach-house doors 1/8 scale

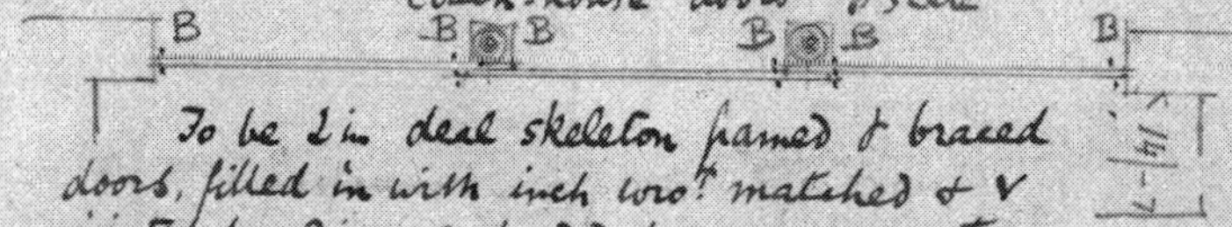

To be 2 in deal skeleton framed & braced doors, filled in with inch wro^t. matched & V jointed boarding, suspended by means of strong wrought iron straps & wheels running on a piece of 3" T iron bolted & blocked out from wall & beam to be guided at bottom by means of w^t. iron guides on a ∧ iron bar. Two of the doors to be fastened by means of ¾ strong wro^t. iron bolts at top & bottom: the other to have a strong galvanized hasp, padlock & staple.

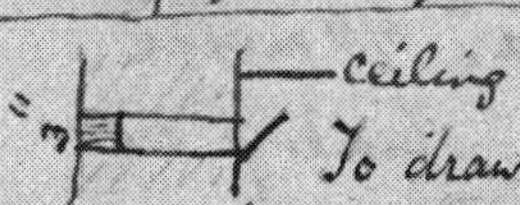

To draw openings in the old wall over each horse's head in stalls & 1 in middle of each loose box as in margin. To have terra cotta air brick 9 x 3 on outside of each, & 3/4 hopper internally.

To sink a well in yard 3 ft. internal dia. (3/6 pps. better) & 15 feet deep – steined with a lining of ½ brick – three times in the whole height a foot vertically to be built in cement – to be domed at top with ½ brick arch – leaving a man-hole in centre 2 ft in diameter – carried up in half brick to ~~the~~ level of paving, & covered with a

Purbeck paving stone 3 feet square, with iron ring let in & screwed at the back on to an iron plate."

Provide & fix ... jack pump – – fastened to piece of — stone – (in well?) – – –

Spec^n from memory –

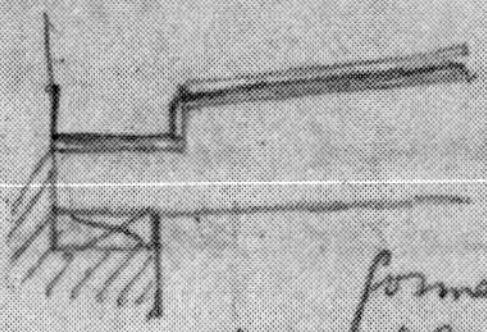

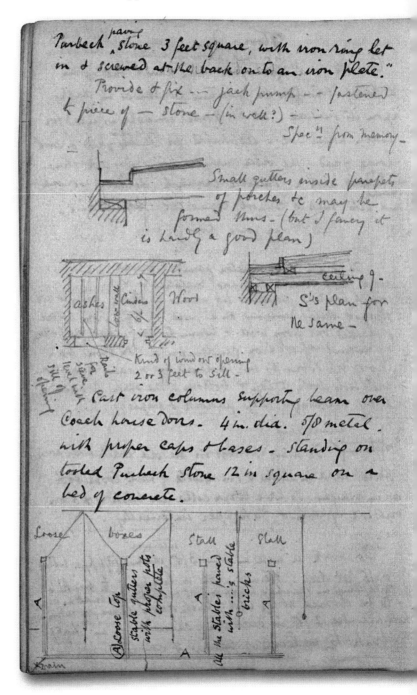

Small gutters inside parapets of porches &c may be formed thus – (but I fancy it is hardly a good plan)

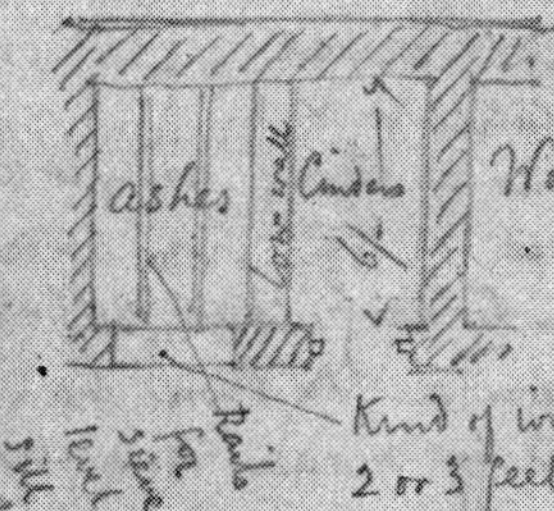

S's plan for the same –

Cast iron columns supporting beam over Coach house doors – 4 in. dia. 5/8 metal – with proper caps & bases – standing on tooled Purbeck stone 12 in square on a bed of concrete.

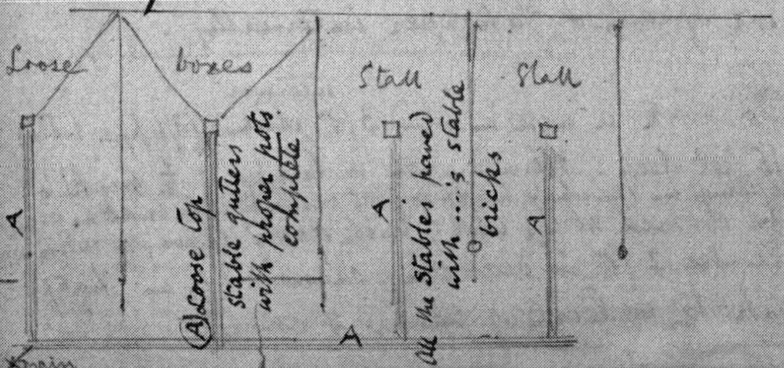

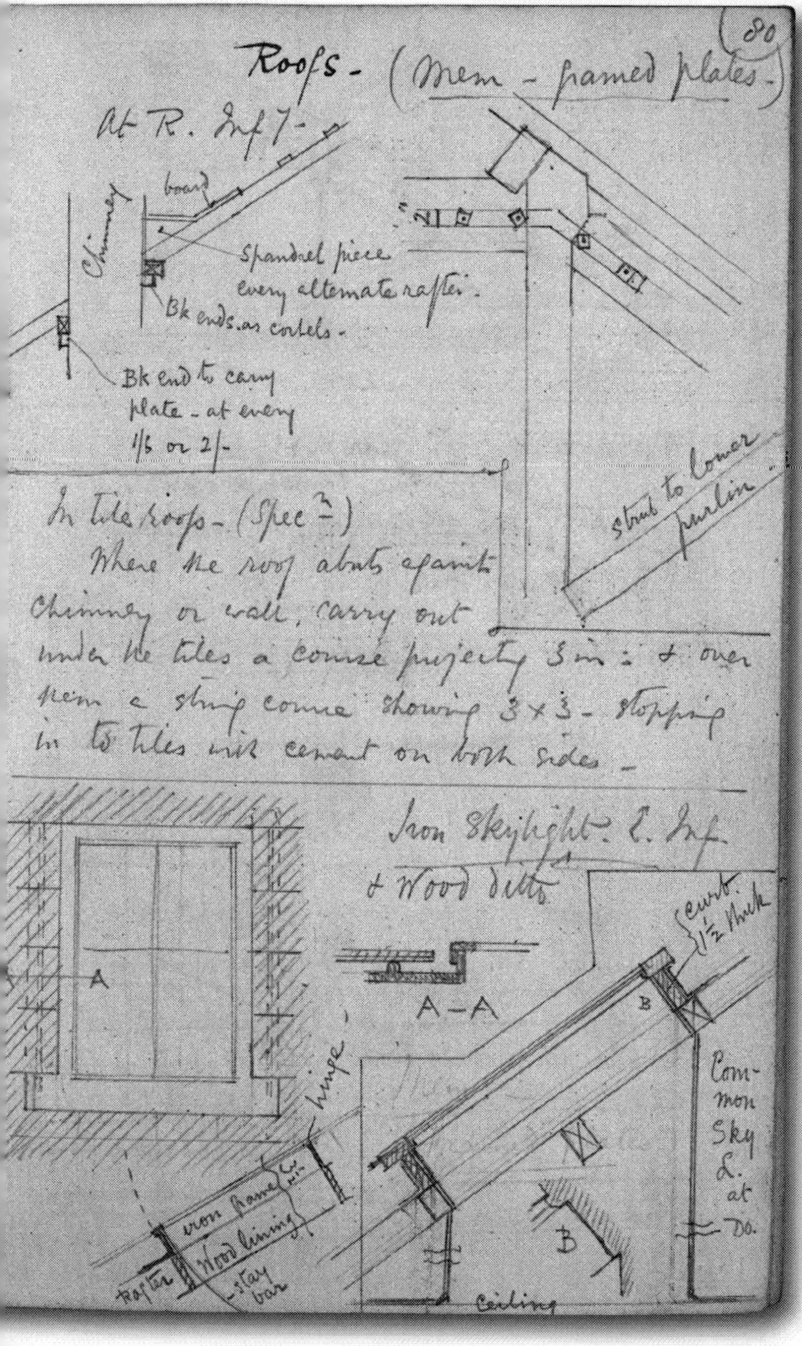
80
Roofs - (Mem - framed plates -)
At R. Inf7 -
board
Chimney
Spandrel piece
every alternate rafter.
Bk ends. as corbels -
Bk end to carry
plate - at every
1/6 or 2/-
strut to lower
purlin
In tile roofs - (Spec 3)
Where the roof abuts against
Chimney or wall, carry out
under the tiles a course projecting 3 in: & over
them a string course showing 3 x 3 - stopping
in to tiles with cement on both sides -
Iron Skylight - E. Inf
& Wood ditto
cemt.
1½ thick
A
A-A
B
hinge
Common
Sky
L.
at
Do.
iron frame
Wood lining
rafter
stay bar
Ceiling

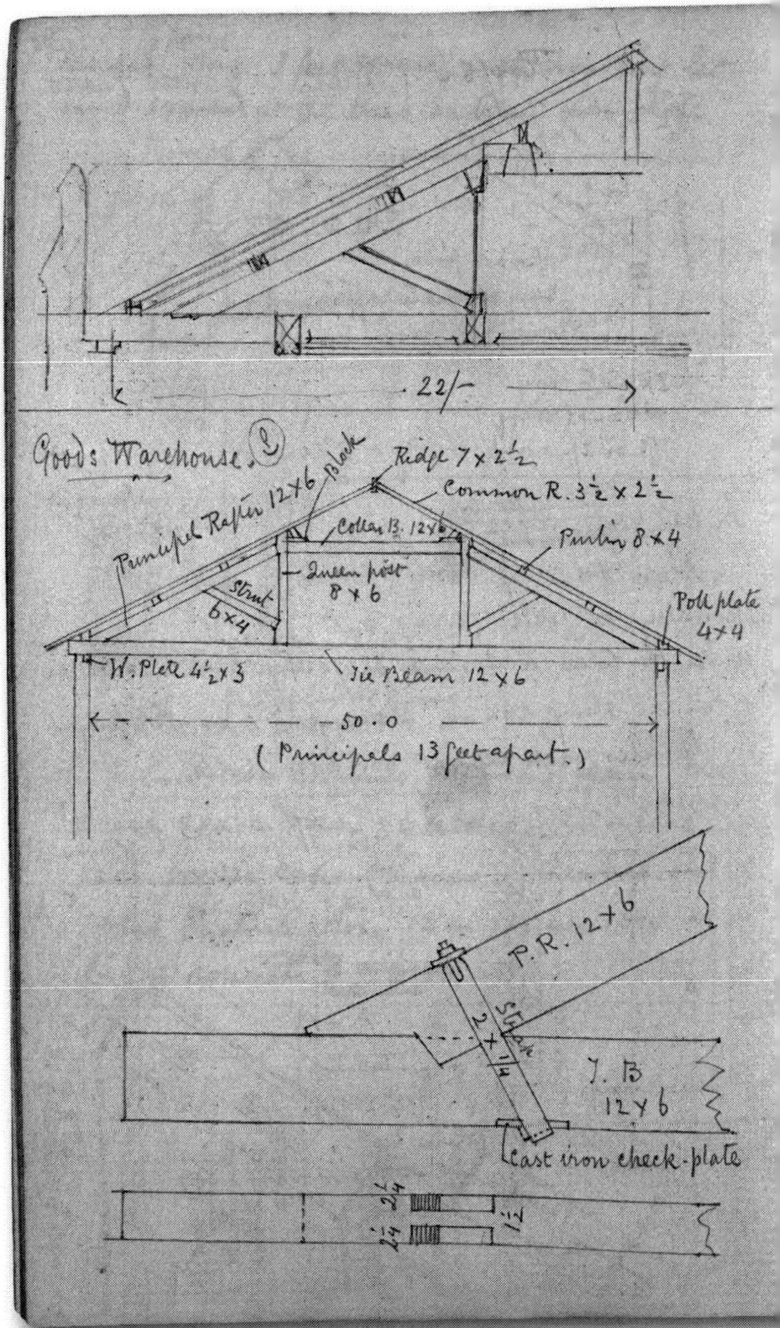
22/-
Goods Warehouse. 2
Ridge 7 x 2½
Principal Rafter 12 x 6
Block
Common R. 3½ x 2½
Collar B. 12 x 6
Purlin 8 x 4
Queen post 8 x 6
Strut 6 x 4
Poll plate 4 x 4
W. Plate 4½ x 3
Tie Beam 12 x 6
50 . 0
(Principals 13 feet apart.)
P.R. 12 x 6
Strap
2 x ¼
T. B 12 x 6
Cast iron check-plate
2¼
2¼
1½

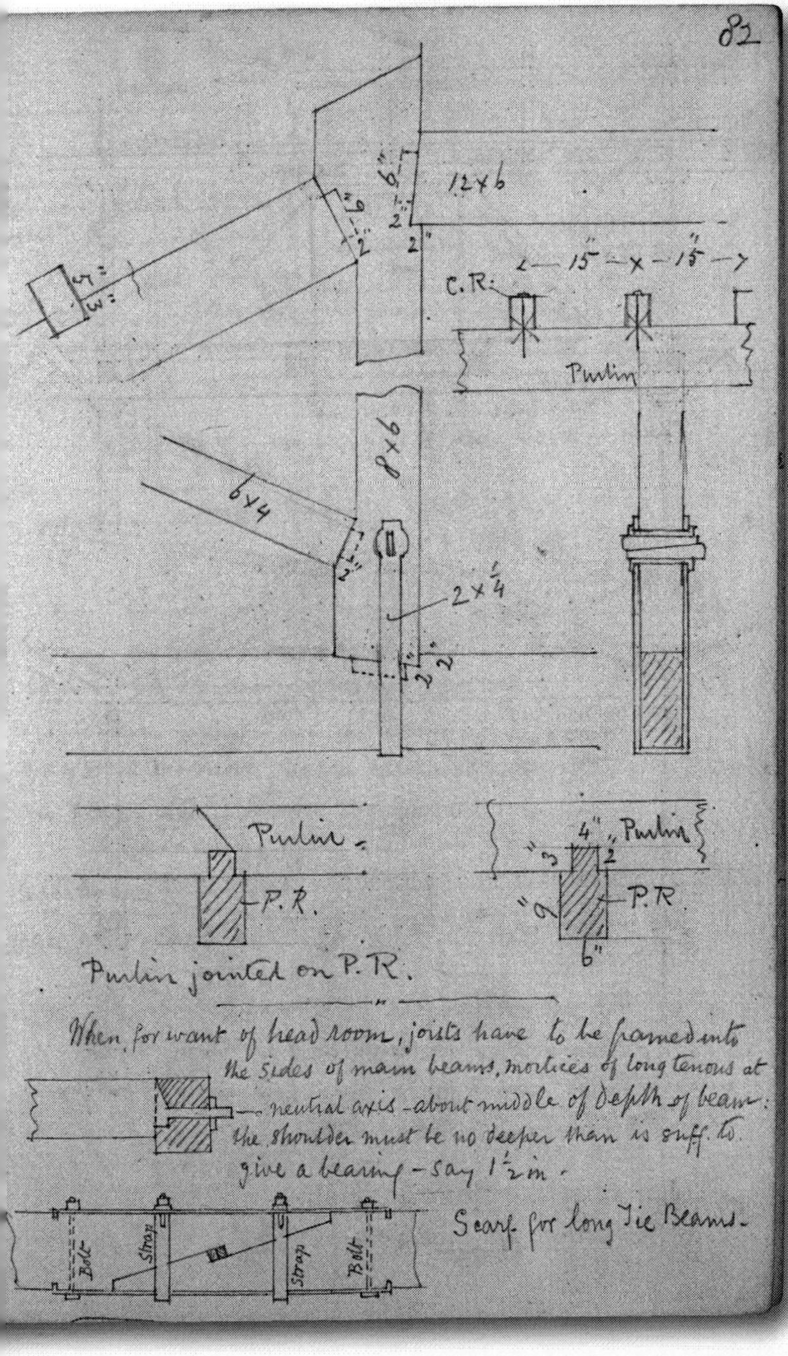
82
12 × 6
C.R.
15" × 15"
Purlin
8 × 6
6 × 4
2 × ¼
Purlin.
P.R.
Purlin jointed on P.R.
4" Purlin
P.R
6"
When, for want of head room, joists have to be framed into the sides of main beams, mortices of long tenons at — neutral axis – about middle of depth of beam: the shoulder must be no deeper than is suff. to give a bearing – say 1½ in.
Scarf for long Tie Beams.
Bolt
Strap
Strap
Bolt

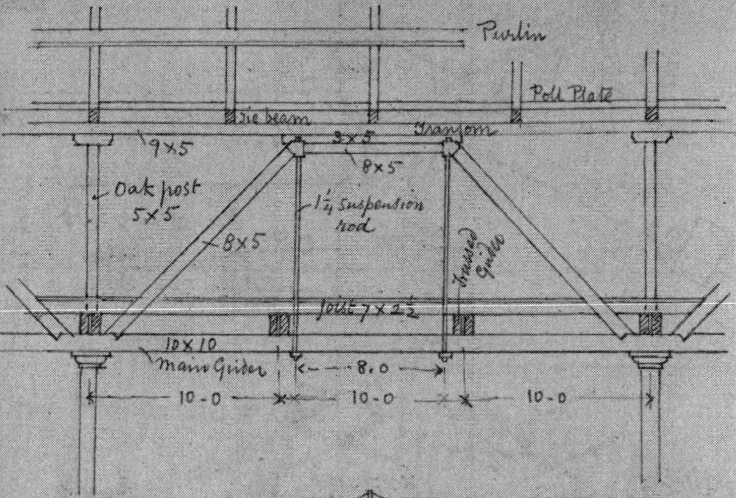

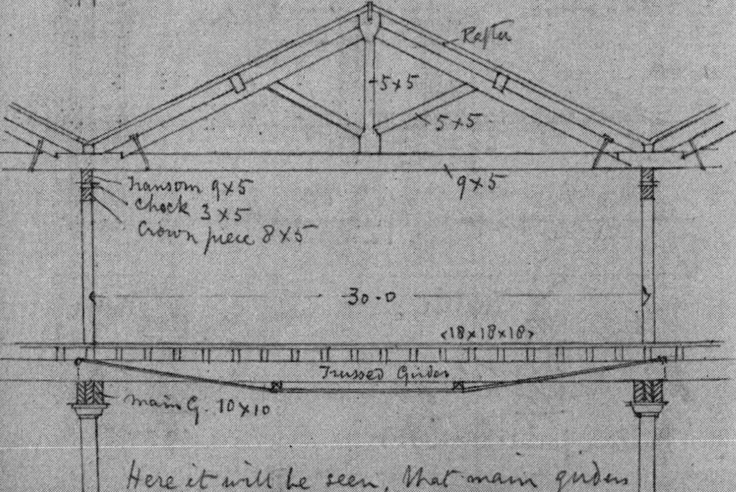

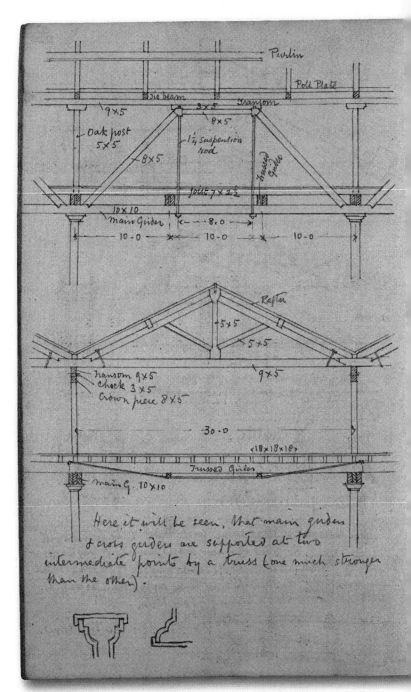

Here it will be seen, that main girders & cross girders are supported at two intermediate points by a truss (one much stronger than the other).

84

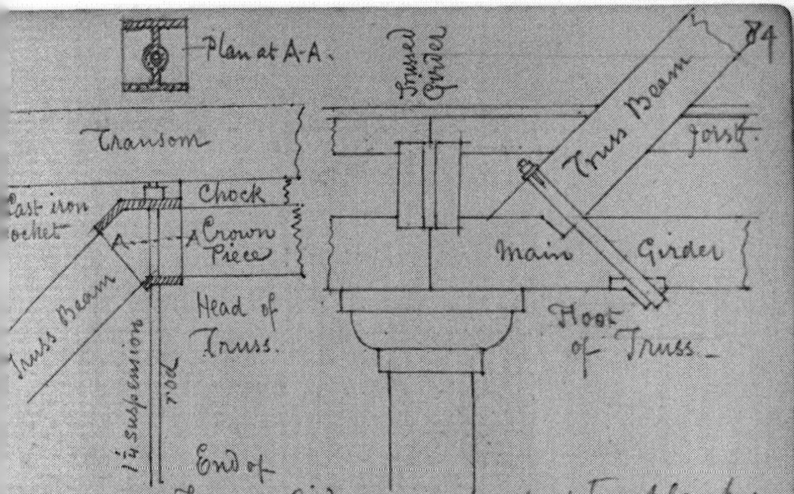

Trussed Girder – made up of two planks 11×3, with the tension rod 1¼×1¼, between them – the head of each girder

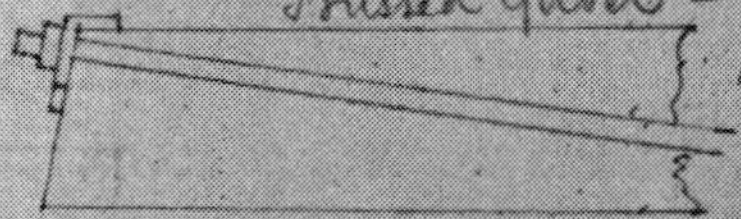

having a cast iron washer, which has a square bearing on the end of the girder –

Main girder – 10×10 – made up of a centre piece 10×4, & 2 outside pieces each 10×3 – combined into one beam by 3 straps 7/6 apart.

A beam may often be built up, by careful selection of sawn deals or planks, which shall be stronger than any whole balk of equal dimensions –

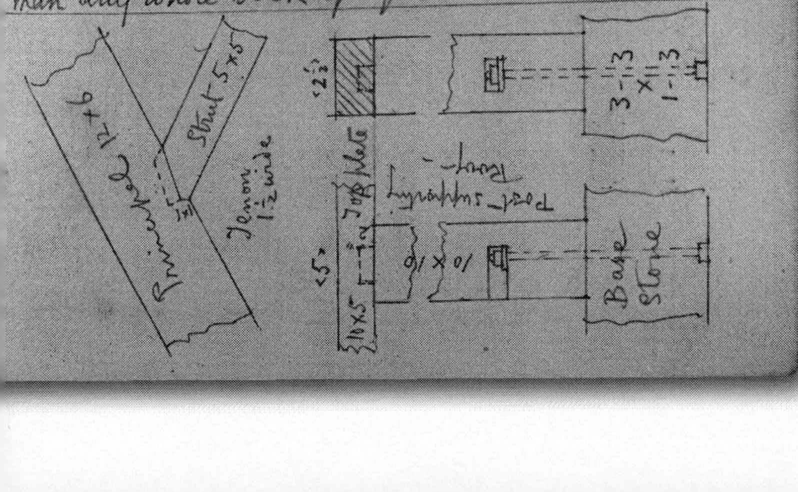

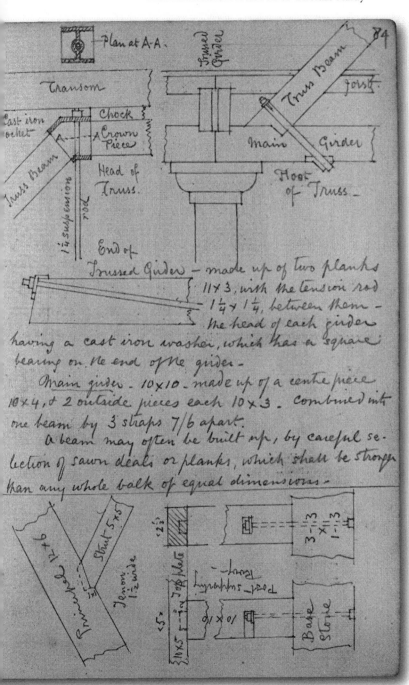

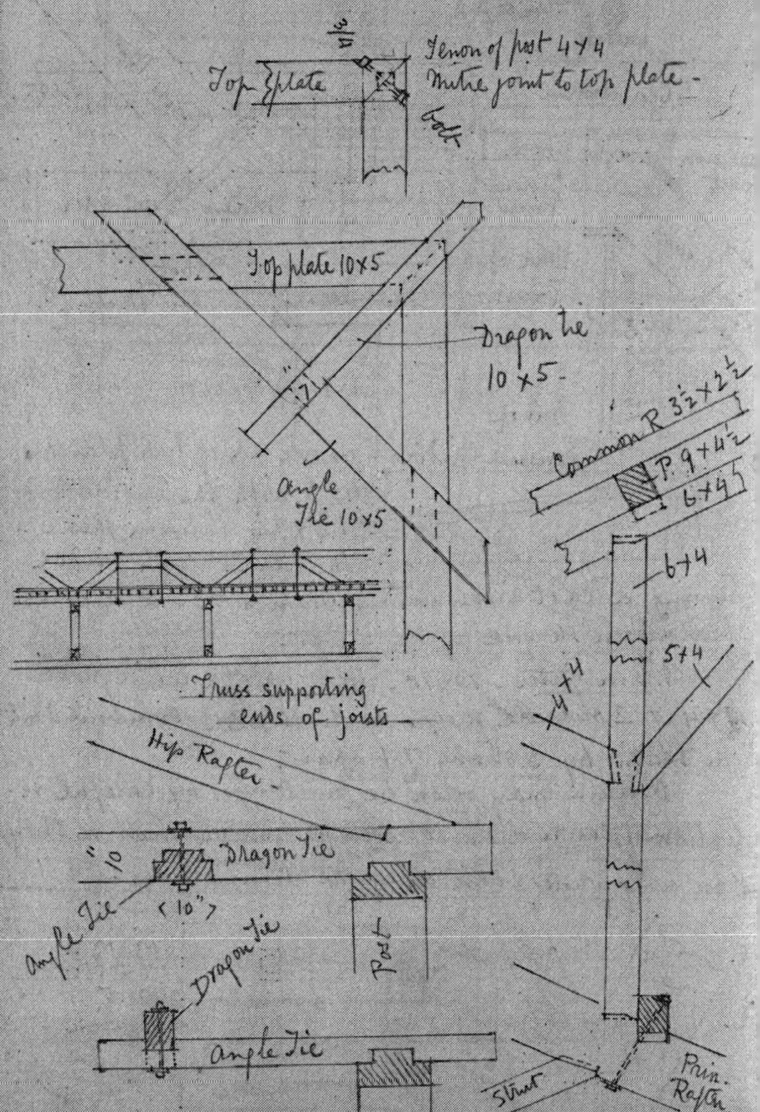

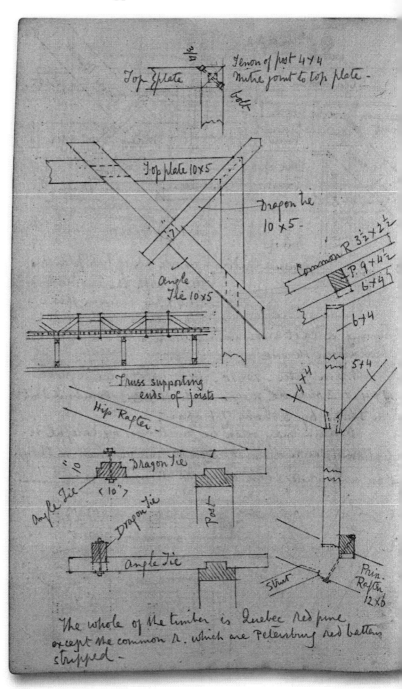

The whole of the timber is Quebec red pine except the common R. which are Petersburg red battens stripped –

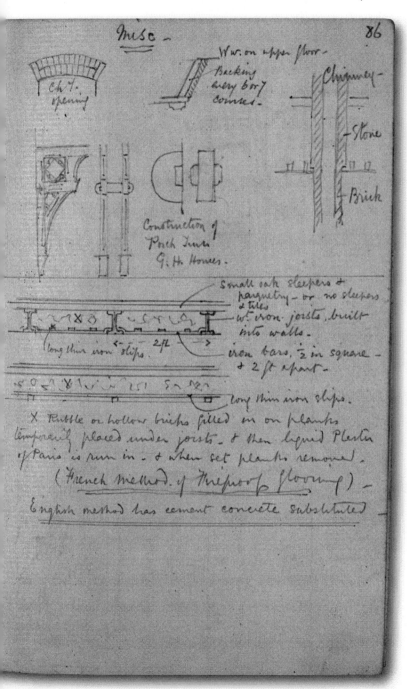

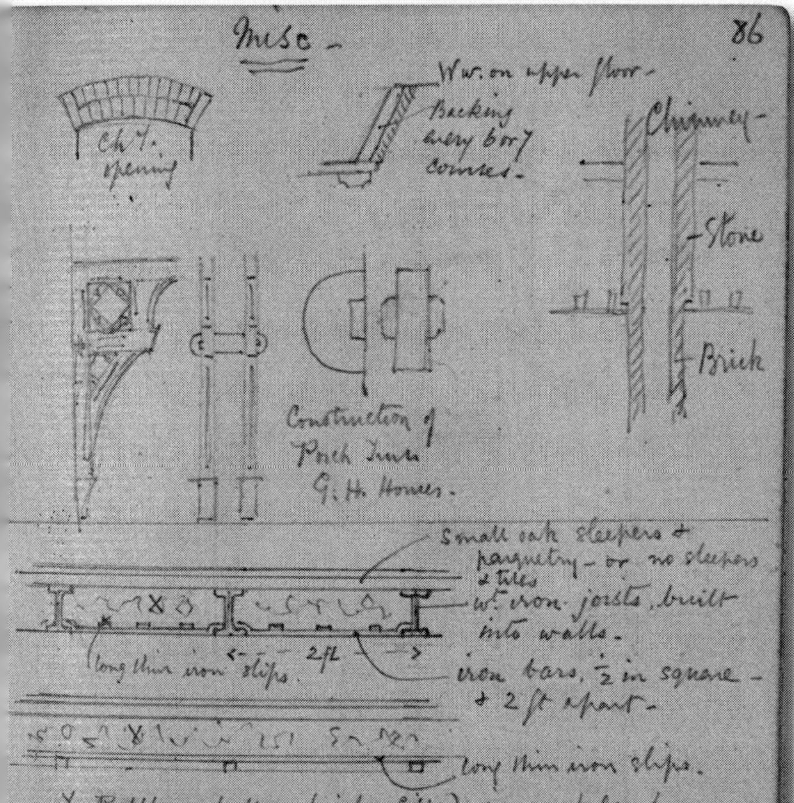
Misc –
86
Ch'y. opening
W.c. on upper floor –
Backing every 6 or 7 courses –
Chimney –
Stone
Brick
Construction of Porch Truss G. H. Houses.
Small oak sleepers & parquetry – or no sleepers & tiles
wt. iron joists, built into walls.
long thin iron slips.
2 ft
iron bars, ½ in square – & 2 ft apart –
long thin iron slips.
X Rubble or hollow bricks filled in on planks temporarily placed under joists – & then liquid Plaster of Paris is run in – & when set planks removed.
(French method of fireproof flooring) –
English method has cement concrete substituted –

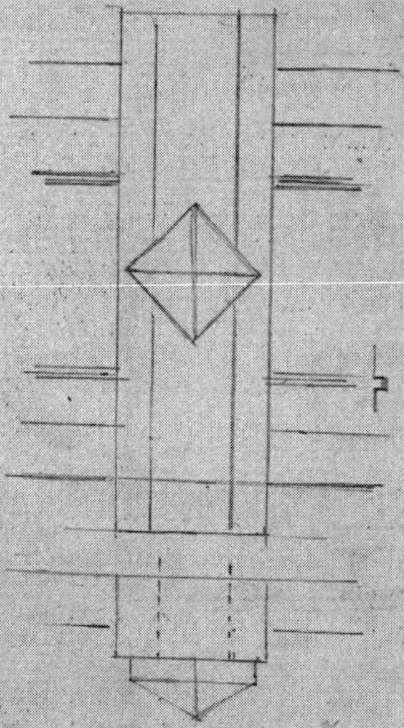

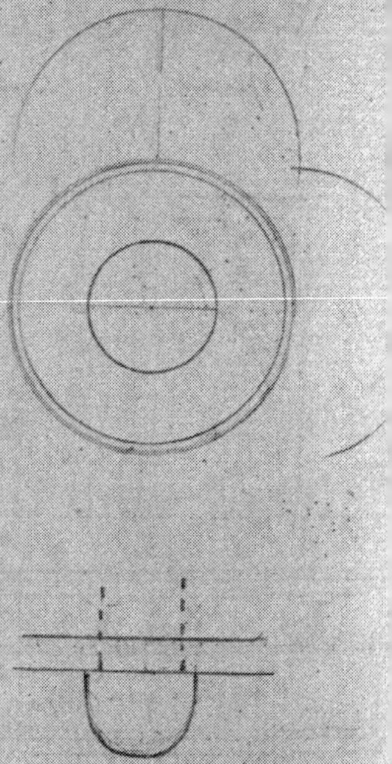

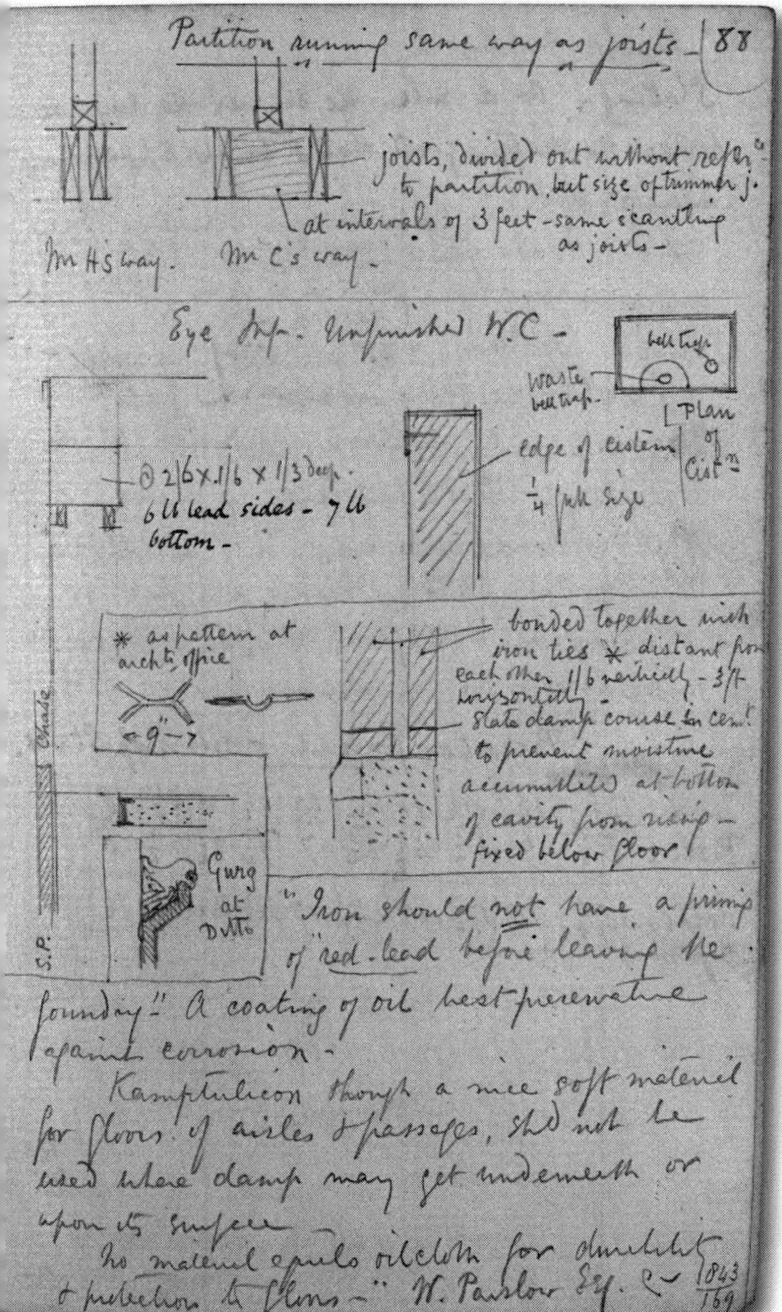

Partition running same way as joists – 88

joists, divided out without refer^ce to partition, but size of trimmer j.
at intervals of 3 feet – same scantling as joists –

Mr H's way. Mr C's way –

Eye Insp. – Unfinished W.C –

bell trap

waste bell trap.

Plan of Cist^n

edge of cistern

1/4 full size

@ 2/6 x 1/6 x 1/3 deep.
6 lb lead sides – 7 lb bottom –

* as pattern at archt's office

<– 9" –>

bonded together with iron ties * distant from each other 1/6 vertically – 3/7 horizontally –
Slate damp course in cem^t to prevent moisture accumulated at bottom of cavity from rising – fixed below floor

Chase

S.P.

Gurg at Ditto

"Iron should not have a priming of red-lead before leaving the foundry –" A coating of oil best preservative against corrosion –

Kamptulicon though a nice soft material for floors of aisles & passages, sh^d not be used where damp may get underneath or upon its surface –

No material equals oilcloth for durability & protection to floors –" W. Paislow Esq. ~ 1843/169

W. Paislow (continued) –

Slating – As a rule, the clearer the ring, the better the slate. Good slates, bright appearance; inferior, dull.

Fr. Nails for Stone Tiling should be of different lengths – from 2 to 4 in. galvanized iron. Battens about 1 x 2.

For slating – Surveyors will now pass none but zinc nails, on account of rust. $1\frac{1}{2}$ to 2 in. long – $1\frac{3}{4}$ the best length if made –

(S) R.W.P.s should never empty into a soil drain, for if the latter becomes choked from frost or otherwise, the R.W. forces the soil back into the house through the syphon traps &c.

Proportion for treads & risers of Stairs.

Tread =	$12\frac{1}{2}$	12	$11\frac{1}{2}$	11	$10\frac{1}{4}$	10	$9\frac{1}{2}$	9	$8\frac{1}{2}$	8
Riser =	$5\frac{7}{8}$	6	$6\frac{1}{4}$	$6\frac{1}{2}$	$6\frac{3}{4}$	7	$7\frac{1}{4}$	$7\frac{1}{2}$	$7\frac{3}{4}$	8
Total = (Progressive)	$18\frac{1}{4}$	18	$17\frac{3}{4}$	$17\frac{1}{2}$	$17\frac{1}{4}$	17	$16\frac{3}{4}$	$16\frac{1}{2}$	$16\frac{1}{4}$	16

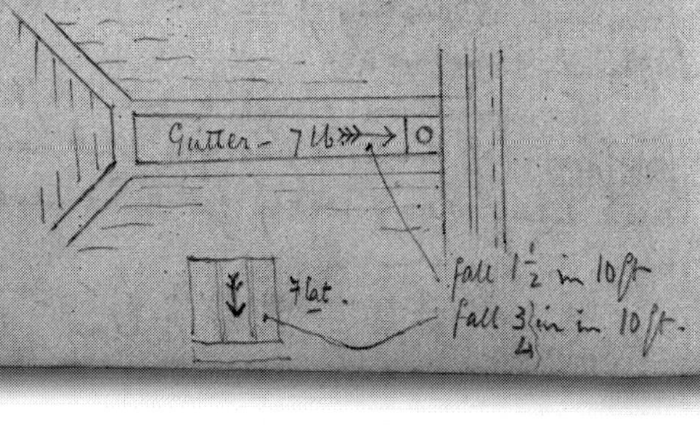

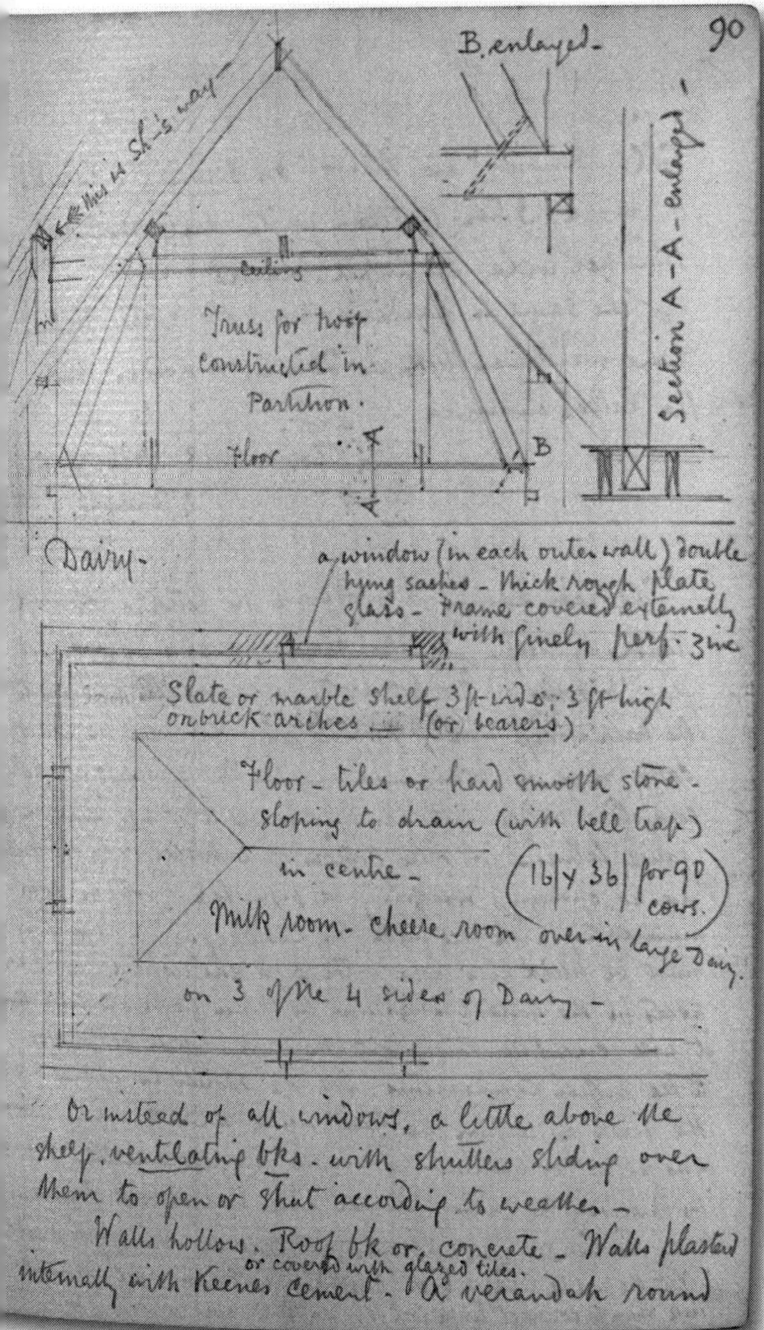
90
B, enlarged -
Section A - A - enlarged -
this is Sh's way -
Ceiling
Truss for roof
constructed in
Partition.
Floor
A
B
A
Dairy -
a window (in each outer wall) double
hung sashes - thick rough plate
glass - Frame covered externally
with finely perf. zinc
Slate or marble shelf 3 ft wide, 3 ft high
on brick arches (or bearers)
Floor - tiles or hard smooth stone -
sloping to drain (with bell trap)
in centre -
16 / x 36 / for 90
cows.
Milk room - cheese room over in large Dairy.
on 3 of the 4 sides of Dairy -
Or instead of all windows, a little above the
shelf, ventilating bks - with shutters sliding over
them to open or shut according to weather -
Walls hollow. Roof bk or concrete - Walls plastered
or covered with glazed tiles.
internally with Keenes Cement - A verandah round

outside would be desirable for shade &c, &
convenient for drying & airing the utensils.
GRC. Sawn slate shelf – on strong fir bearers,
& above, 3 tier of 1 inch white deal shelves
11 inches wide on proper bearers.
The same to Larder: (though the slate shelves
were narrower both in Dairy & Larder in
the latter instance.

Bath Room. { & Water Service of Dwelling,
Ap 28. 71

The less casing & woodwork the better – the bath
standing by itself. It shd always have a light hinged
flap or cover. For hot water, a gas heater attached to
the bath itself, will if properly made be found the least
costly mode of obtaining a supply. The simplest applicn.
consists of boiler with gas ring below it, & a zinc wire
gauze between it & the bottom of the boiler. In the boiler
are no openings, excepting a pipe top & bottom, communicating with the bath, wh. when required to be used
must be filled with cold water & the gas lighted: as the w.
heats in the boiler – fed as will be seen from the bath itself
it will circulate throughout the bath, & will soon rise
to the proper temperature. The top should be closed upon
the bath to retain the heat until ready for use. Where
gas is not convenient a small fire plate heating a boiler
in precisely the same manner will supply its place.
When the levels will permit it will be found preferable
to let the waste pipe of bath discharge into pan of W.C. or housemaid
sink than to connect with soil p. as trap may become dry if bath

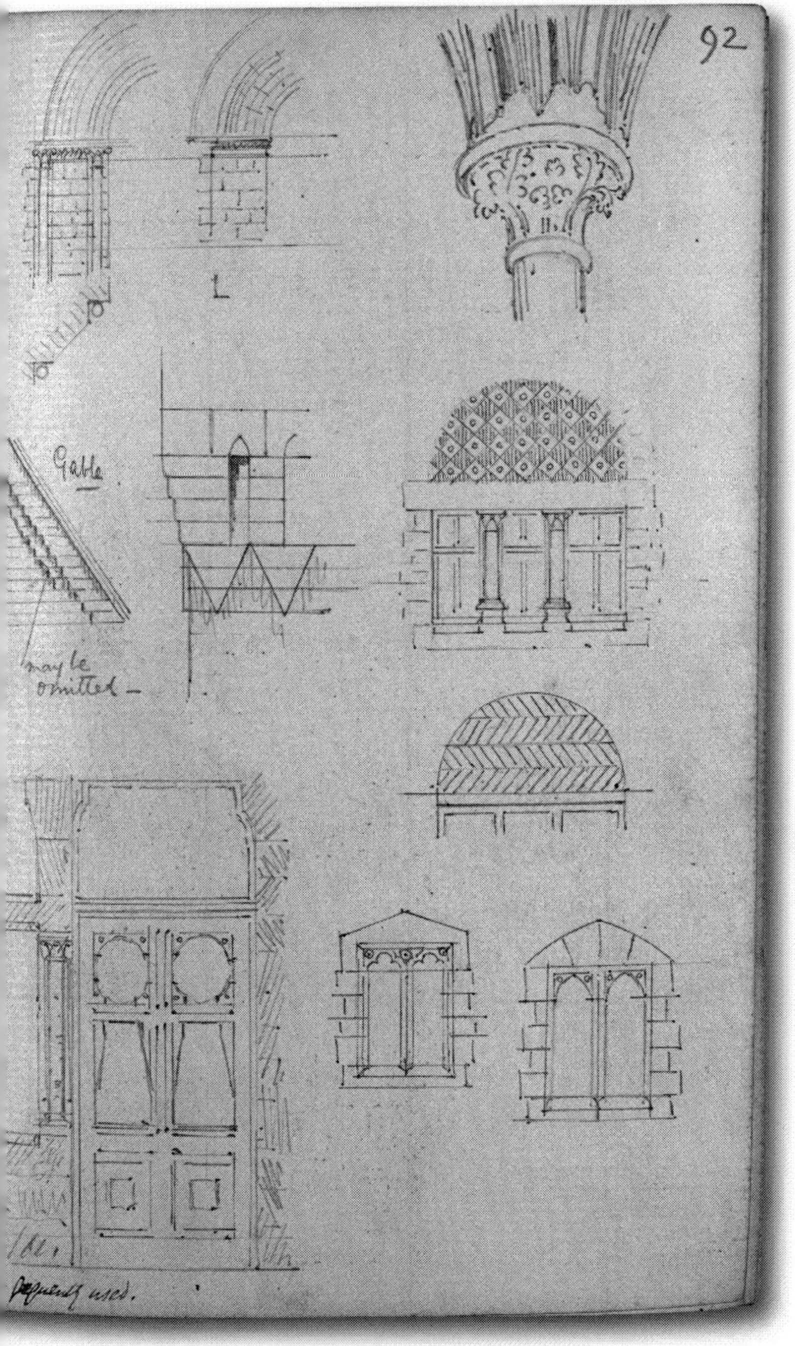
92
L
Gable
may be omitted —
frequently used.

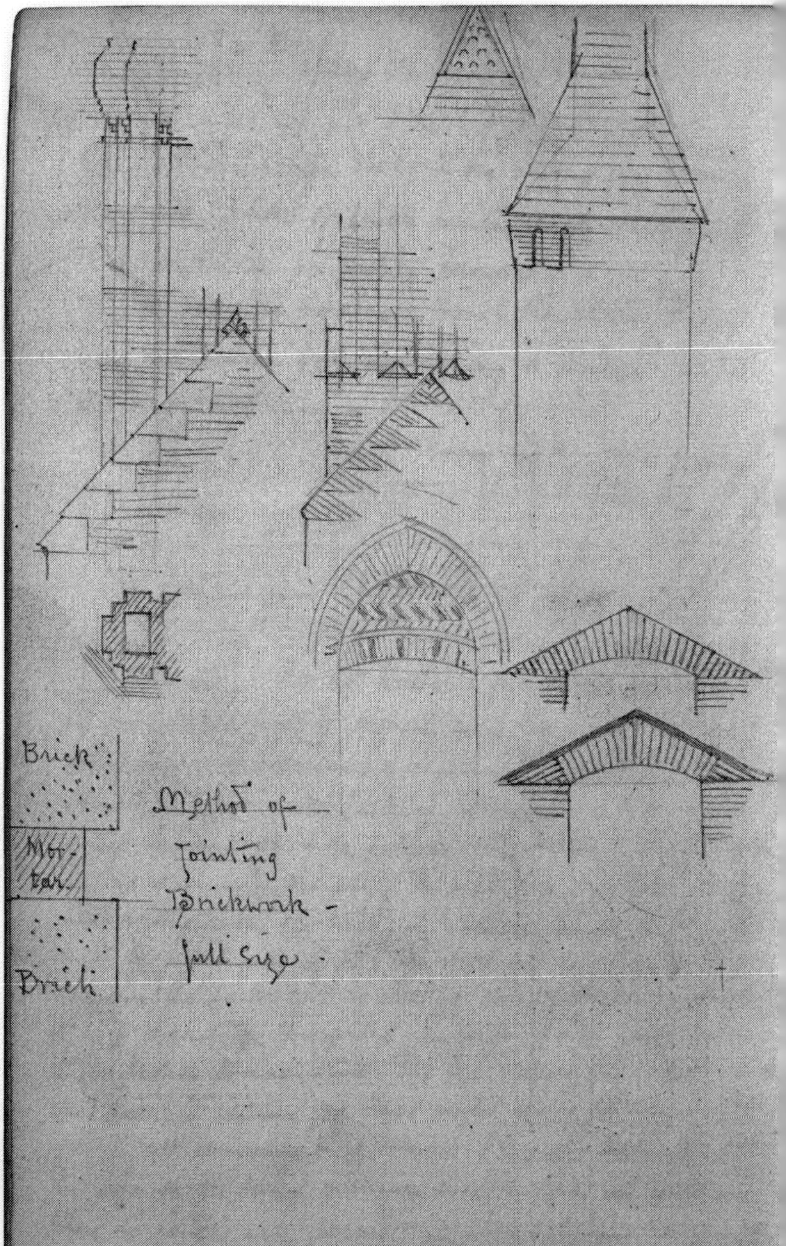
Brick
Mor-
tar.
Brick
Method of
Jointing
Brickwork -
full size.

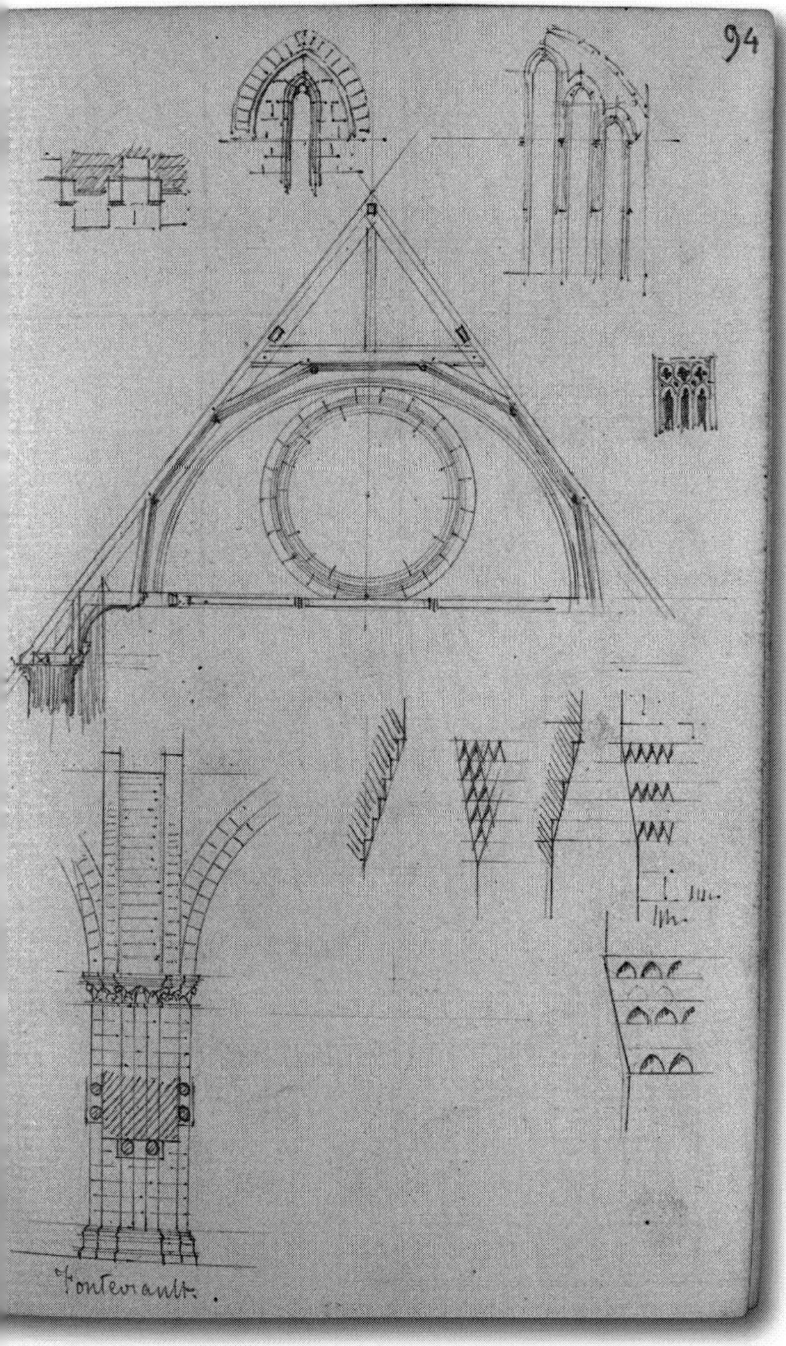
94
Fontevrault.

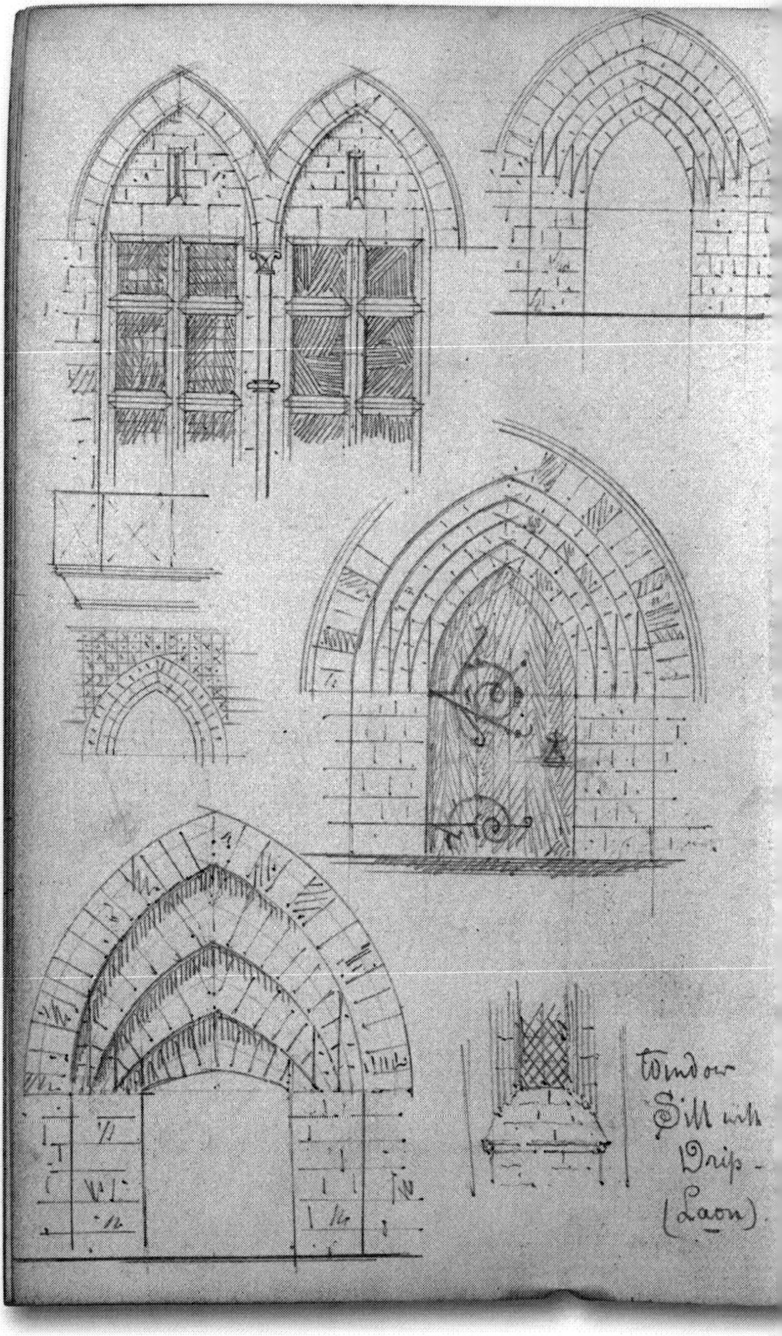
Window
Sill with
Drip -
(Laon).

96

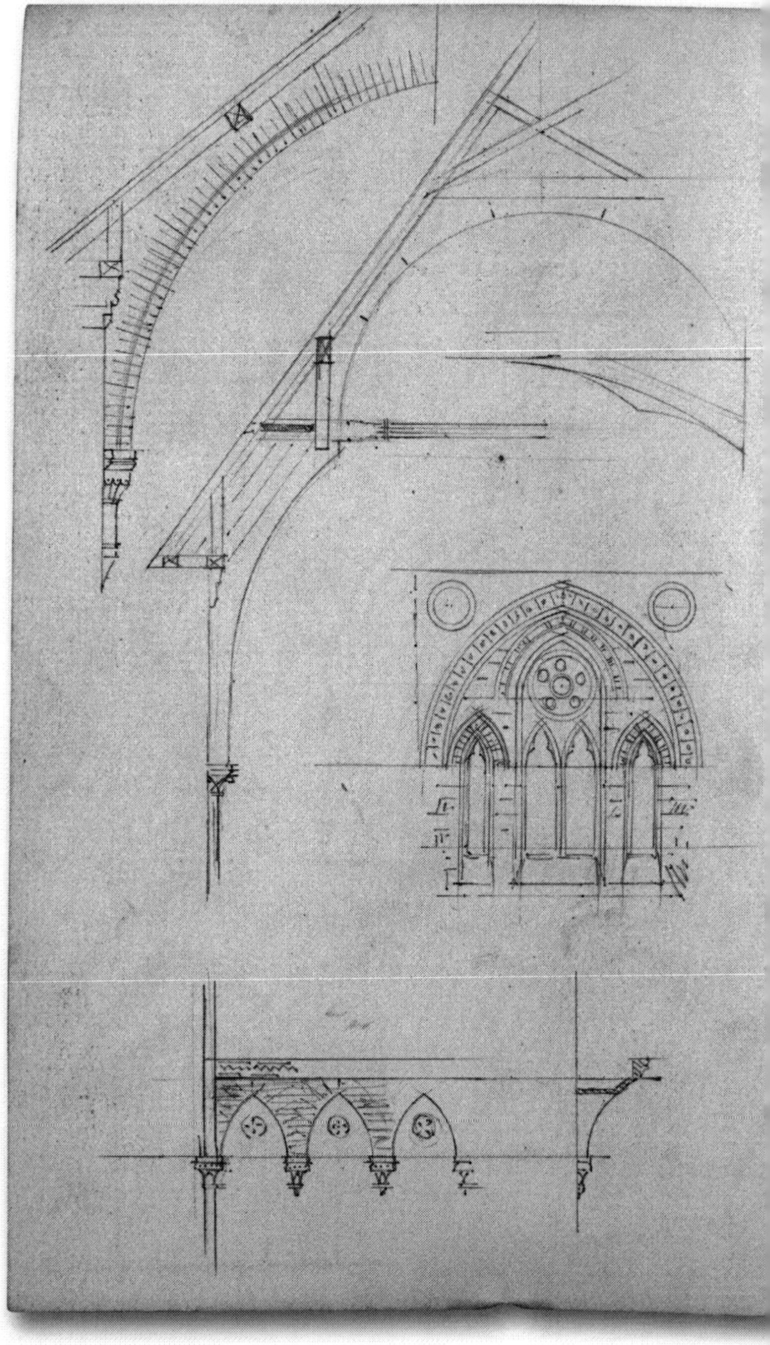

98

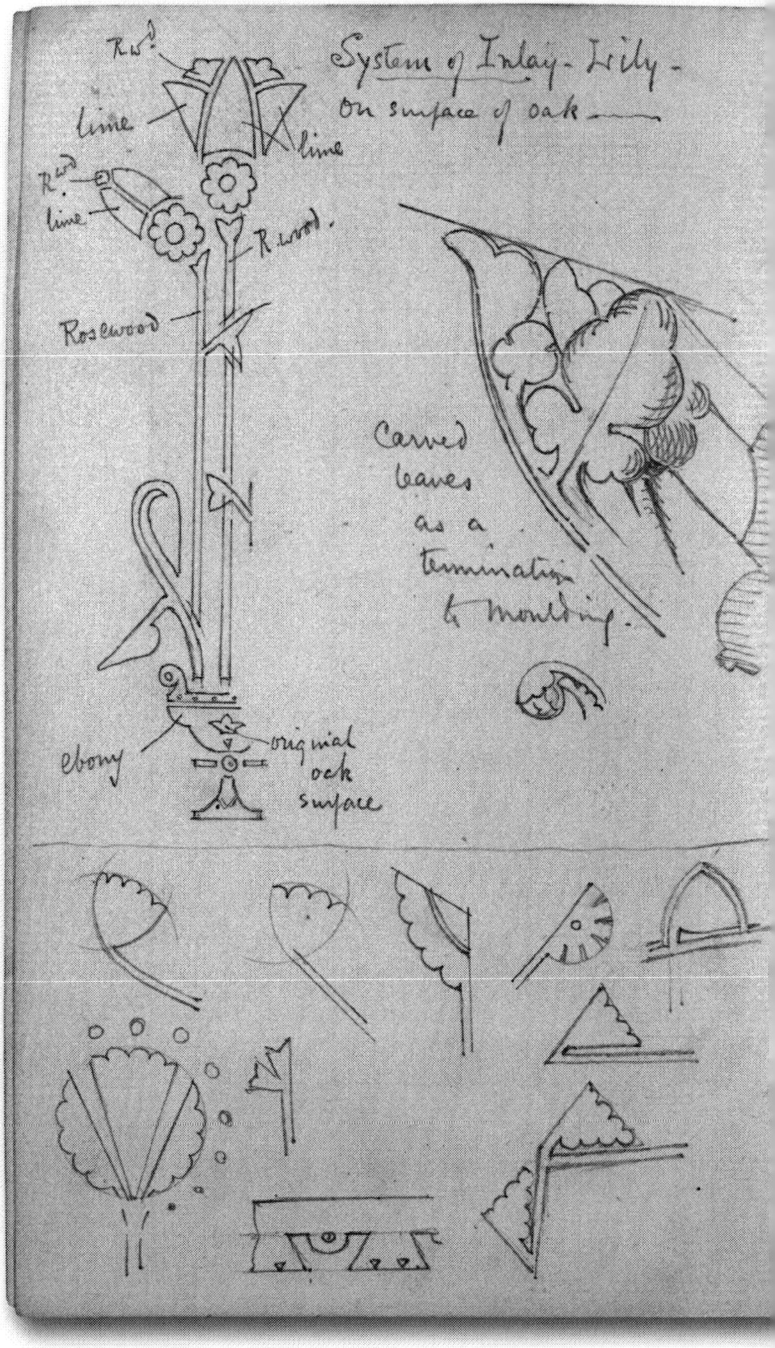
System of Inlay - Lily -
On surface of oak
R.w.
lime
lime
R.wd.
lime
R.wood.
Rosewood
ebony
original oak surface
Carved leaves as a termination to moulding.

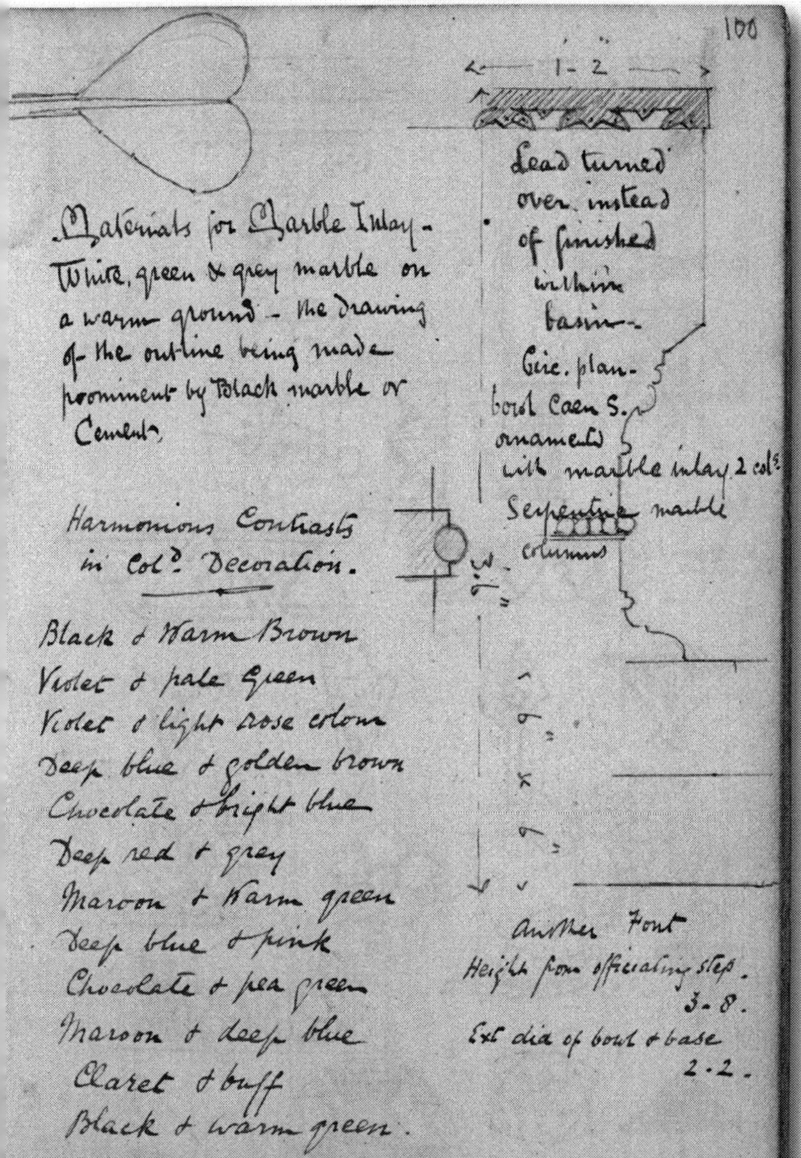

100

Materials for Marble Inlay –
White, green & grey marble on
a warm ground – the drawing
of the outline being made
prominent by Black marble or
Cement,

Harmonious Contrasts
in Col^d. Decoration.

Black & Warm Brown
Violet & pale Green
Violet & light rose colour
Deep blue & golden brown
Chocolate & bright blue
Deep red & grey
Maroon & Warm green
Deep blue & pink
Chocolate & pea green
Maroon & deep blue
Claret & buff
Black & warm green.

1-2

Lead turned
over instead
of finished
within
basin –
Circ. plan.
bowl Caen S.
ornaments
with marble inlay 2 col^s
Serpentine marble
columns

Another Font
Height from officiating step.
3 - 8.
Ext dia of bowl & base
2 - 2.

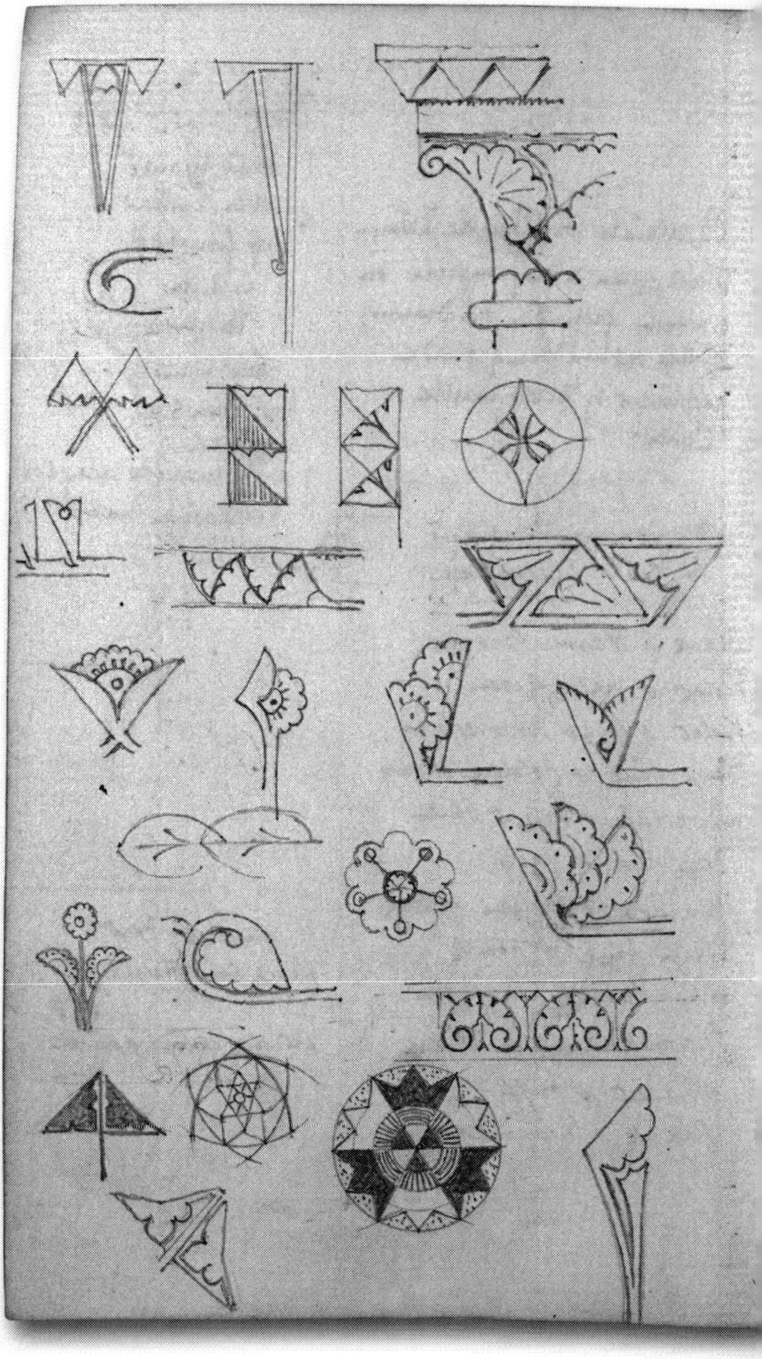

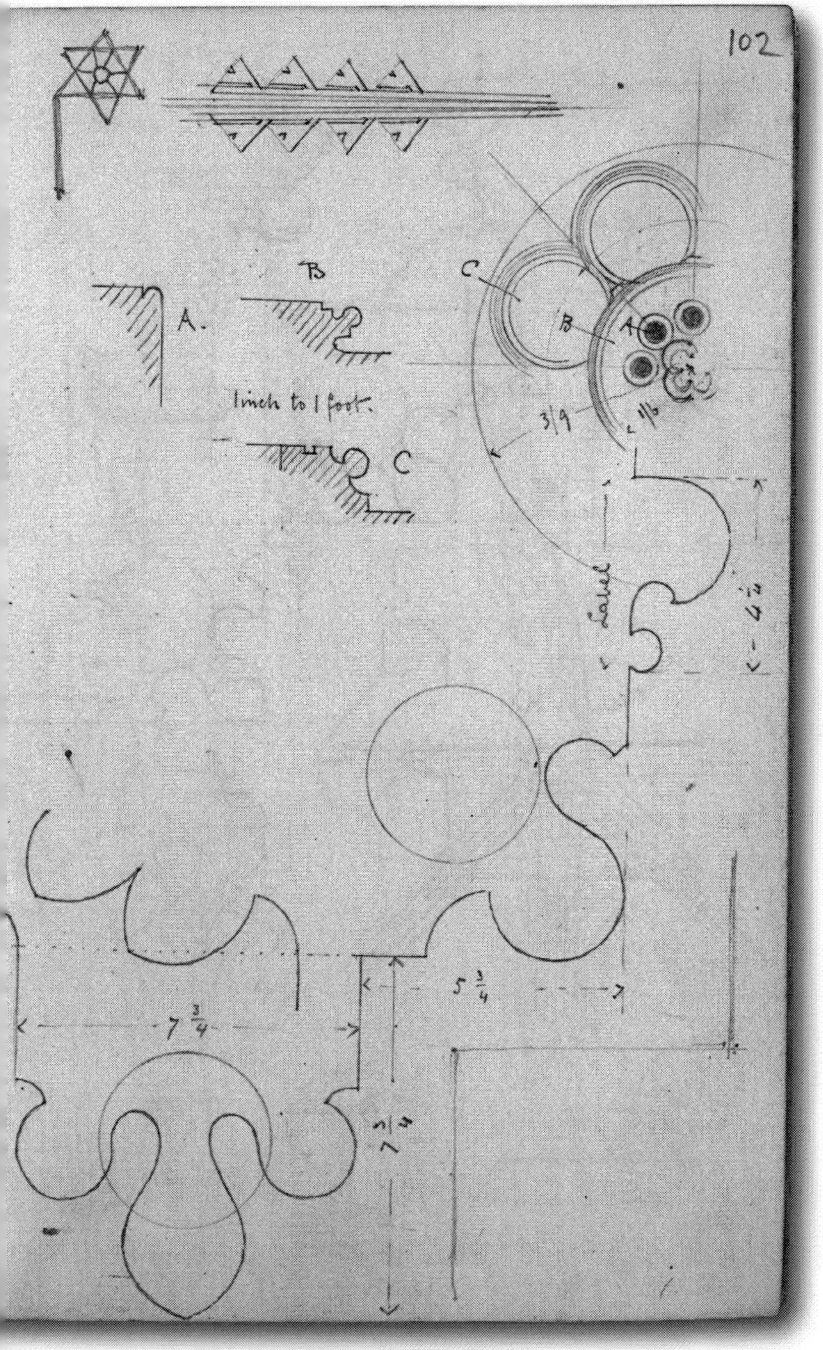
102
B
A.
1 inch to 1 foot.
C
C
B
A
3/9
5 3/4
7 3/4

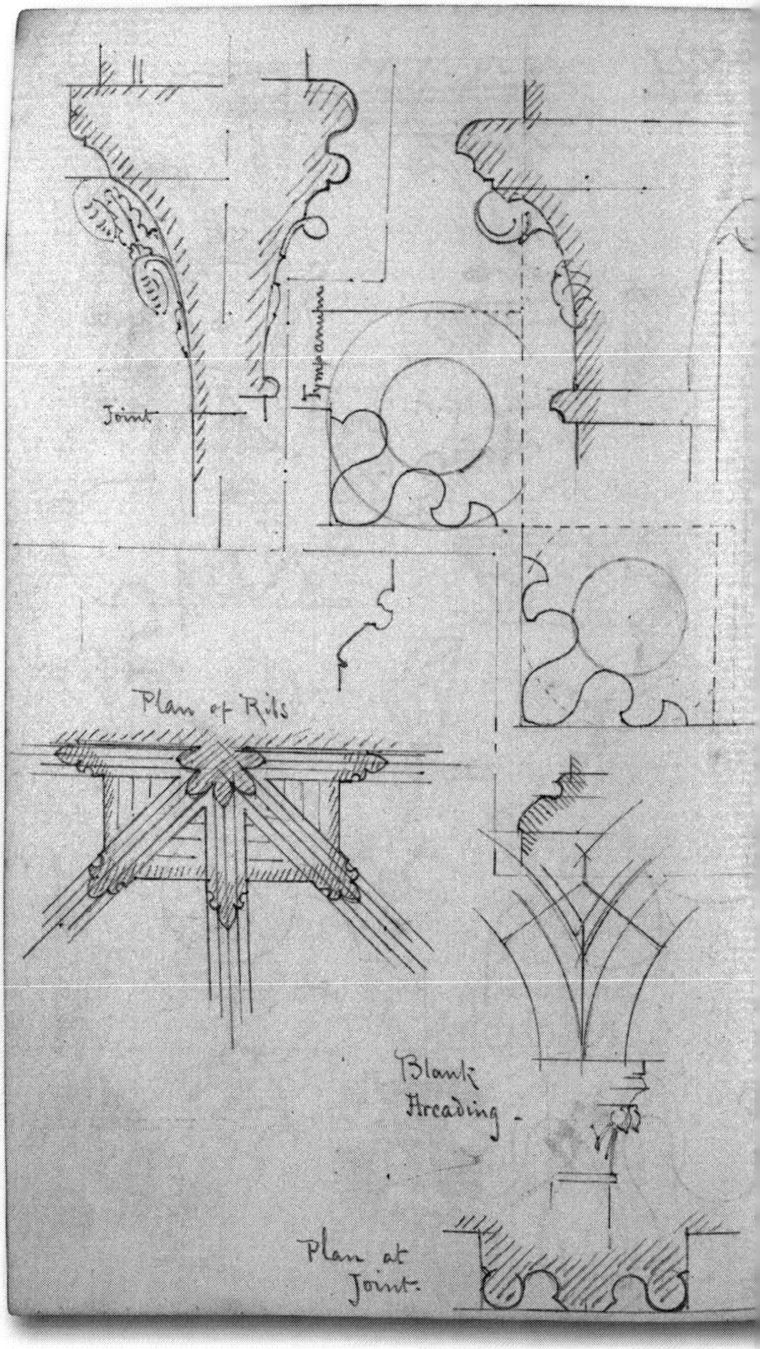
Joint
Tympanum
Plan of Ribs
Blank Arcading
Plan at Joint

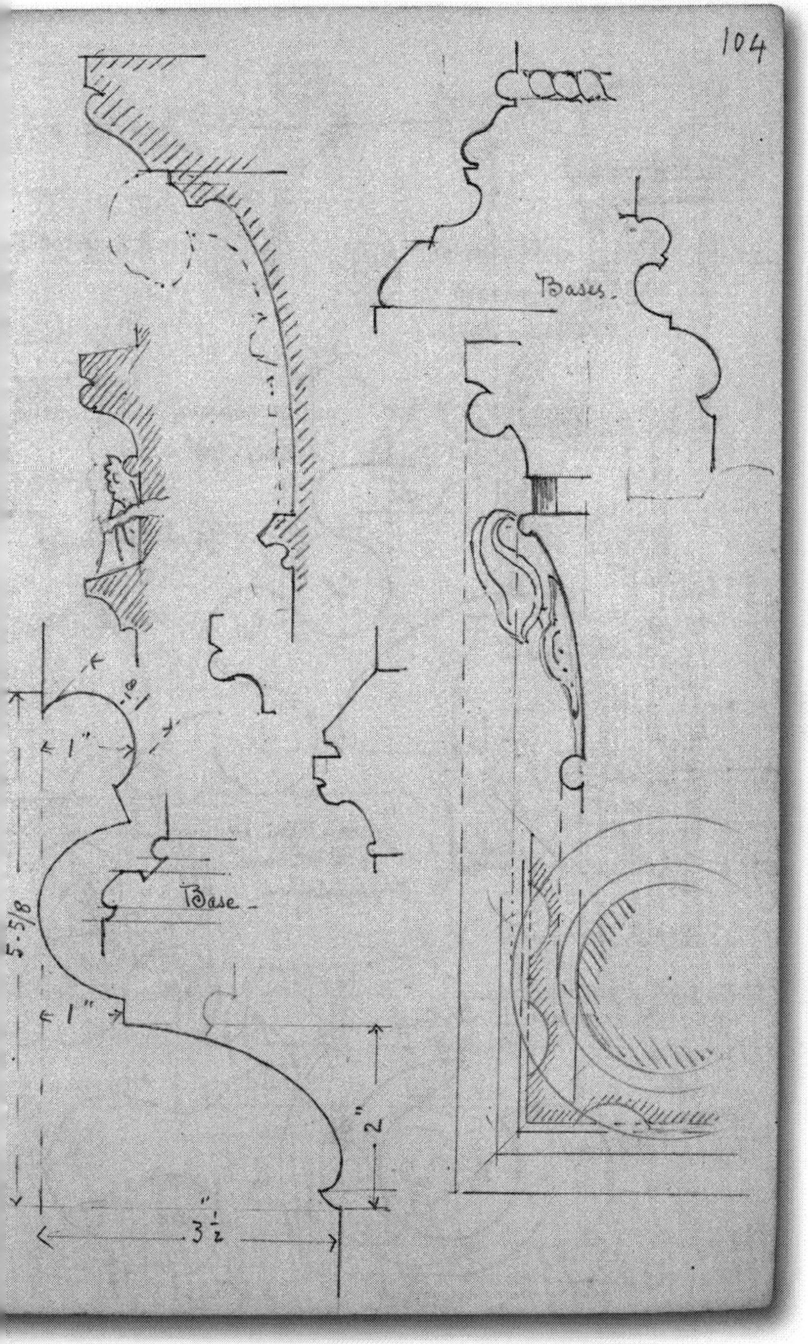
104
Bases
Base
1"
1"
5.5/8
2"
3 1/2

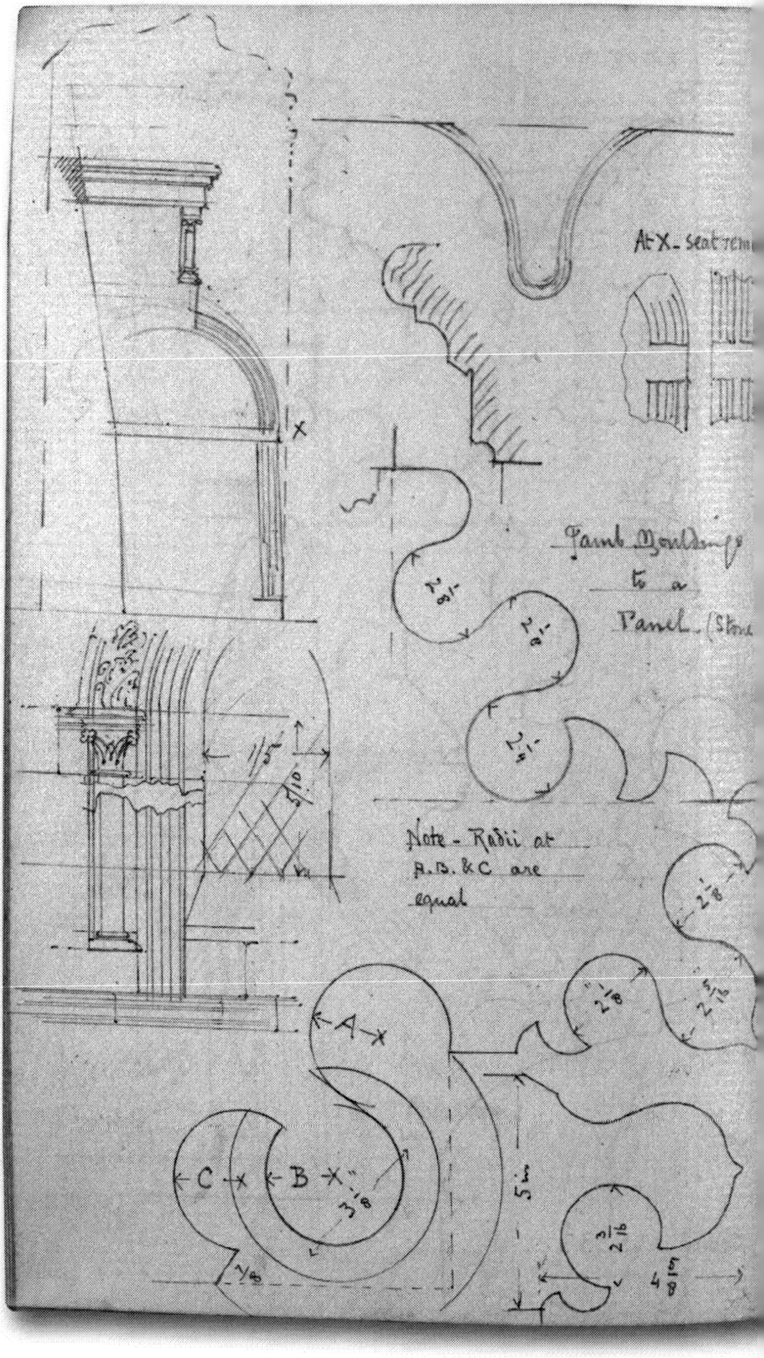
At X - seat ...
Jamb Mouldings
to a
Panel (Stone...
Note - Radii at
A. B. & C are
equal
A
B
C
X

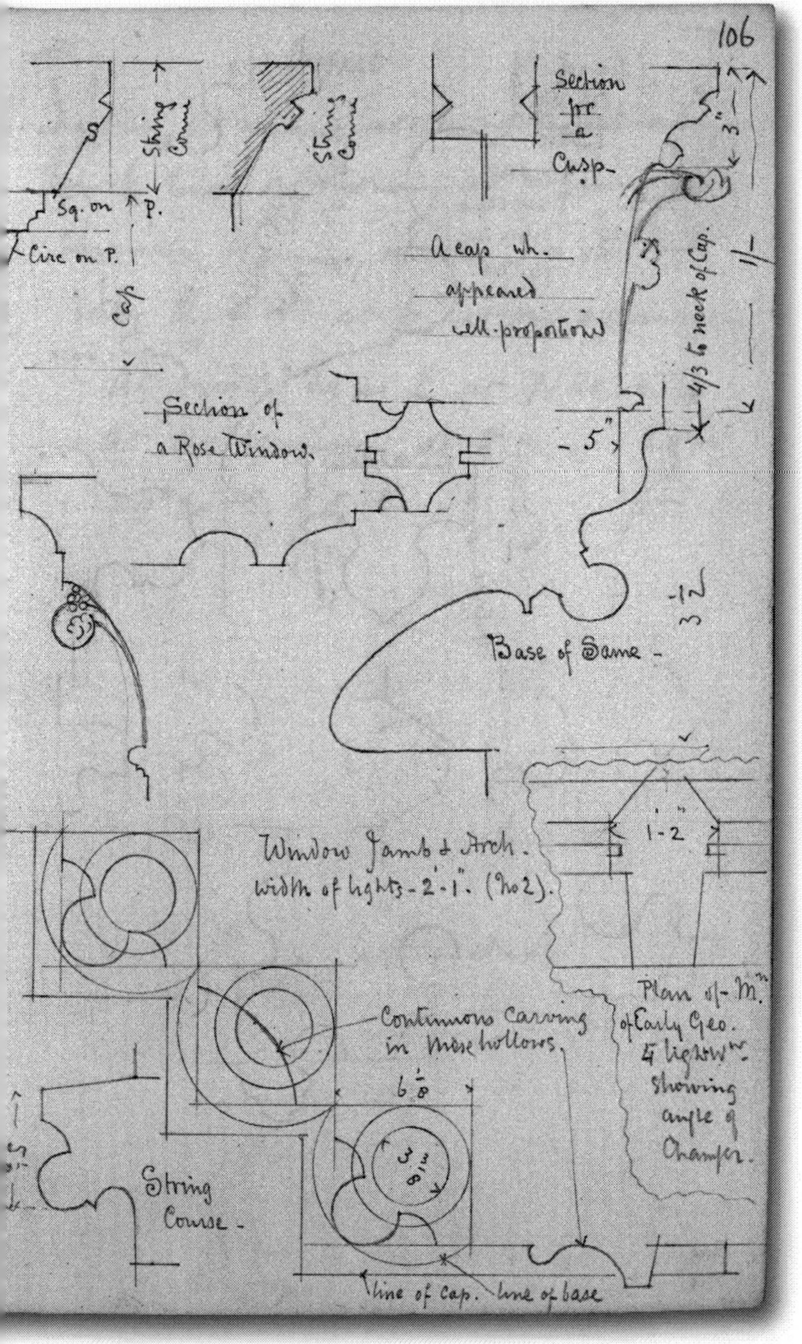
106
String Course
String Course
Sq. on P.
Circ on P.
Cap
Section for a Cusp.
A cap wh. appeared well-proportioned
4/3 to neck of Cap.
Section of a Rose Window.
5"
Base of Same -
Window Jamb & Arch.
width of lights - 2'-1". (No 2).
1'-2"
Plan of M[n] of Early Geo. 4 light w[w]. showing angle of Chamfer.
Continuous carving in these hollows.
6 1/8
3 3/8
String Course -
line of Cap.
line of base

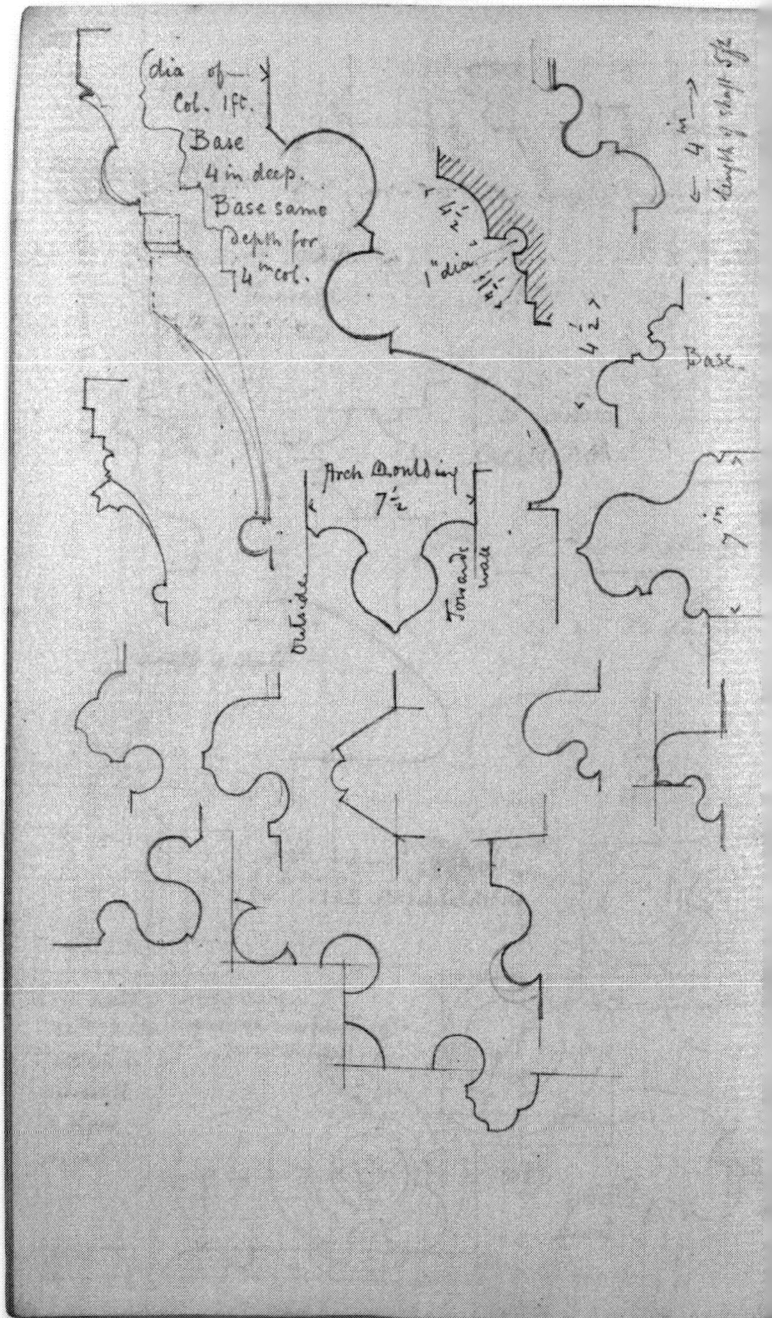
dia of Col. 1ft.
Base 4 in deep.
Base same depth for 4in col.
1" dia
Arch Moulding 7½
Outside
Towards wall
Base.
4 in
length of shaft 5ft
7 in

Aspect.

The sun is much farther north at any given time of morning or evening in summer than in winter – & is only due E. & W. at 6. at the equinoxes. – At mids.r he is E. at 7. 20. a.m. – At the equinoxes at 8. a.m. he is 24°20' S. of E.

pp. 109 – 110

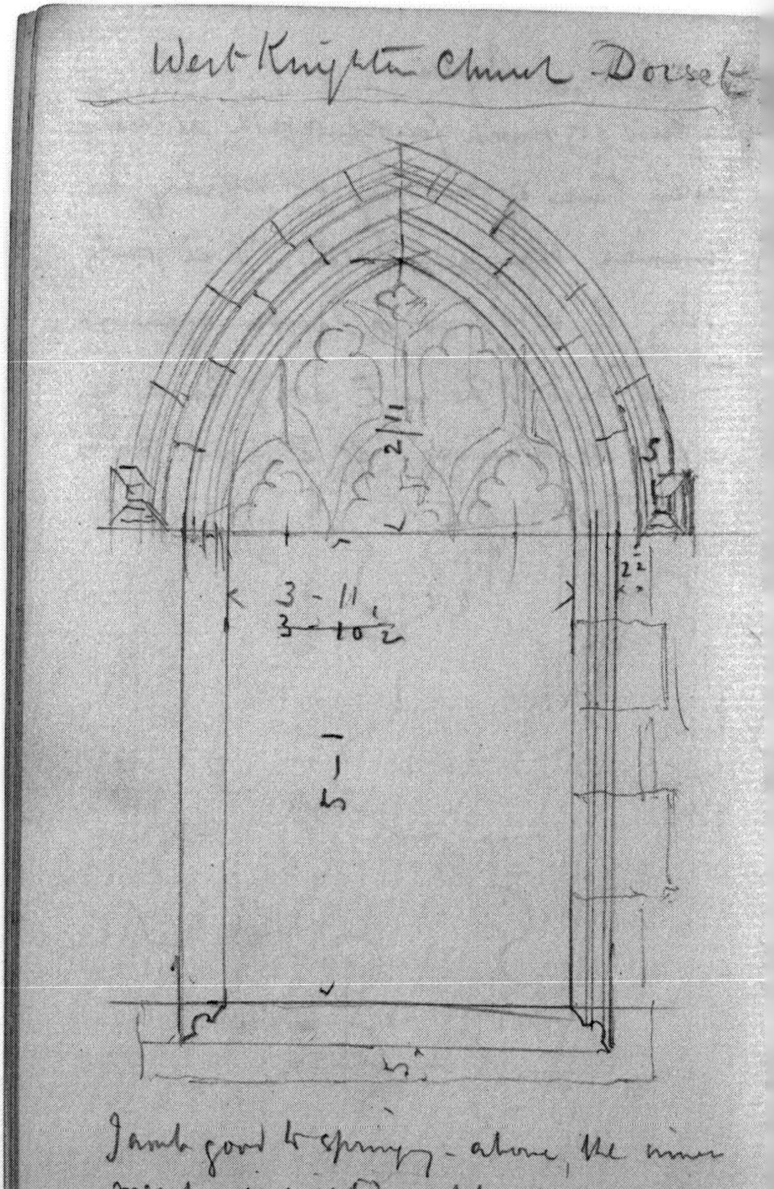
West Knighton Church - Dorset
3 - 11
3 - 10½
Jamb good to springing - above, the inner member is inserted roughly - evidently when tracery was taken out

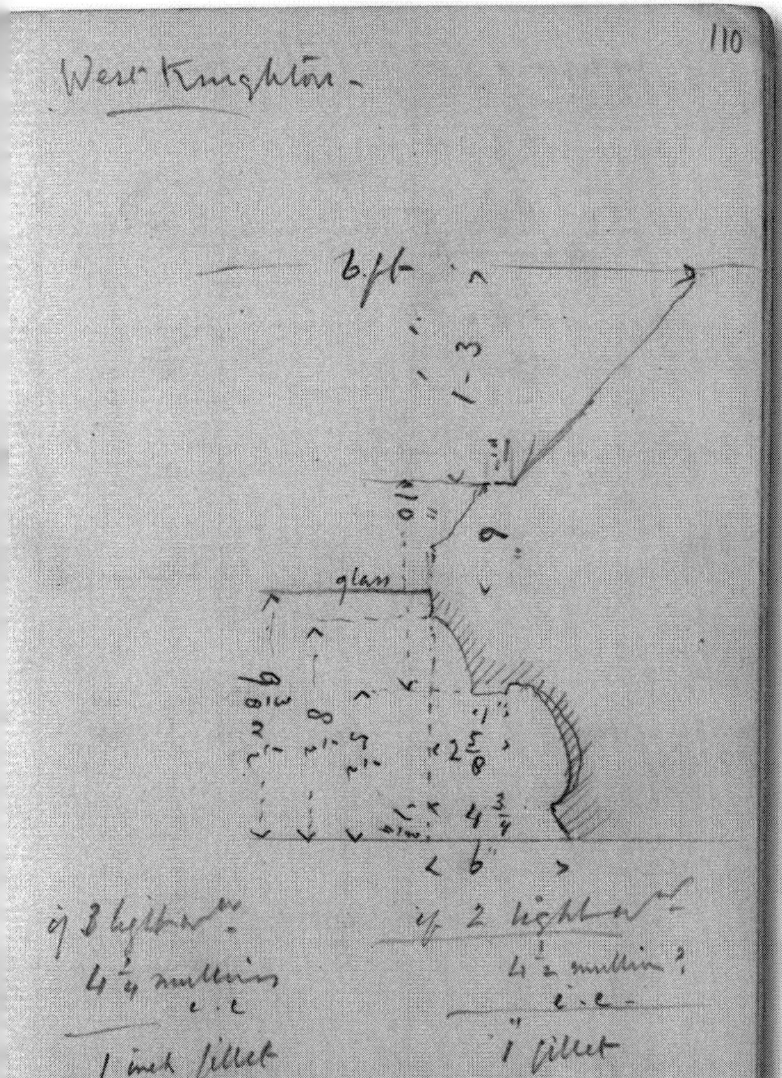
110
West Knighton
6 ft
glass
6"
if 3 lights
4 1/4 mullions
i.e.
1 inch fillet
1 5/8 hollow
1 5/8 hollow
4 1/4 x 2 =
say 1.0 3/4
if 2 lights
4 1/2 mullion?
i.e.
1" fillet
1 3/4 hollow
1 3/4 hollow
4 1/2
3 - 10 1/2
4 1/2
2) 3 . 6
1 . 9

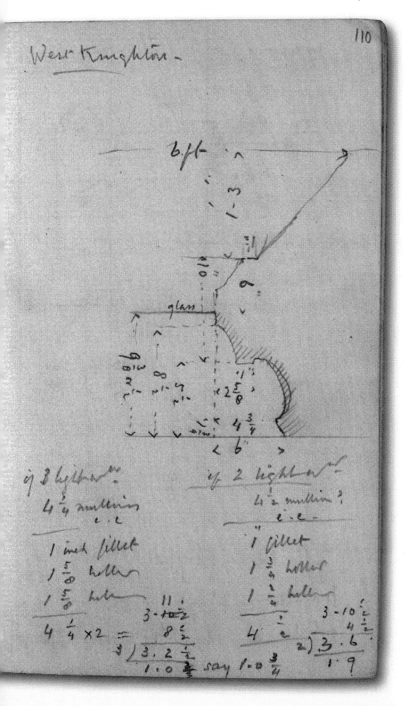

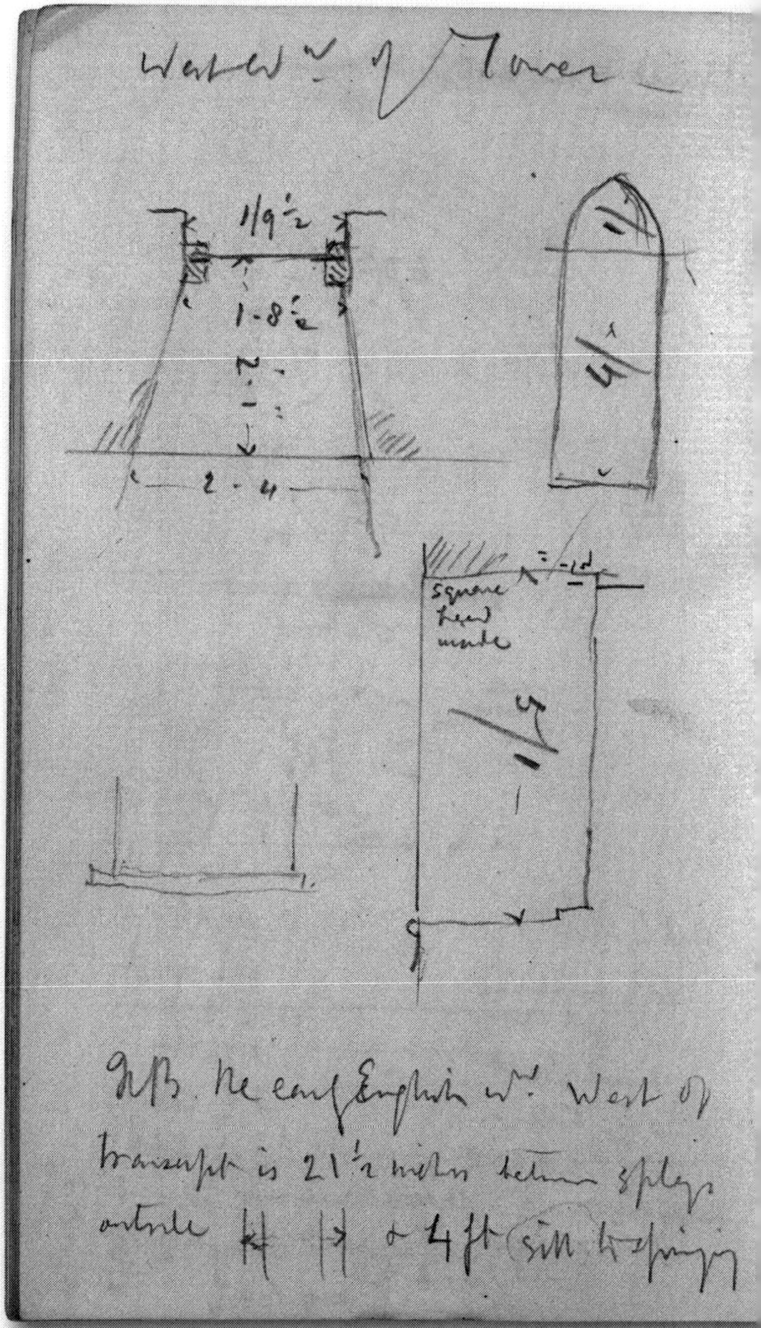
West wd of Tower
1/9½
1-8½
2-4
Square head inside
NB. The early English wd. West of
transept is 2 1½ inches between splays
outside & 4 ft (sill to springing

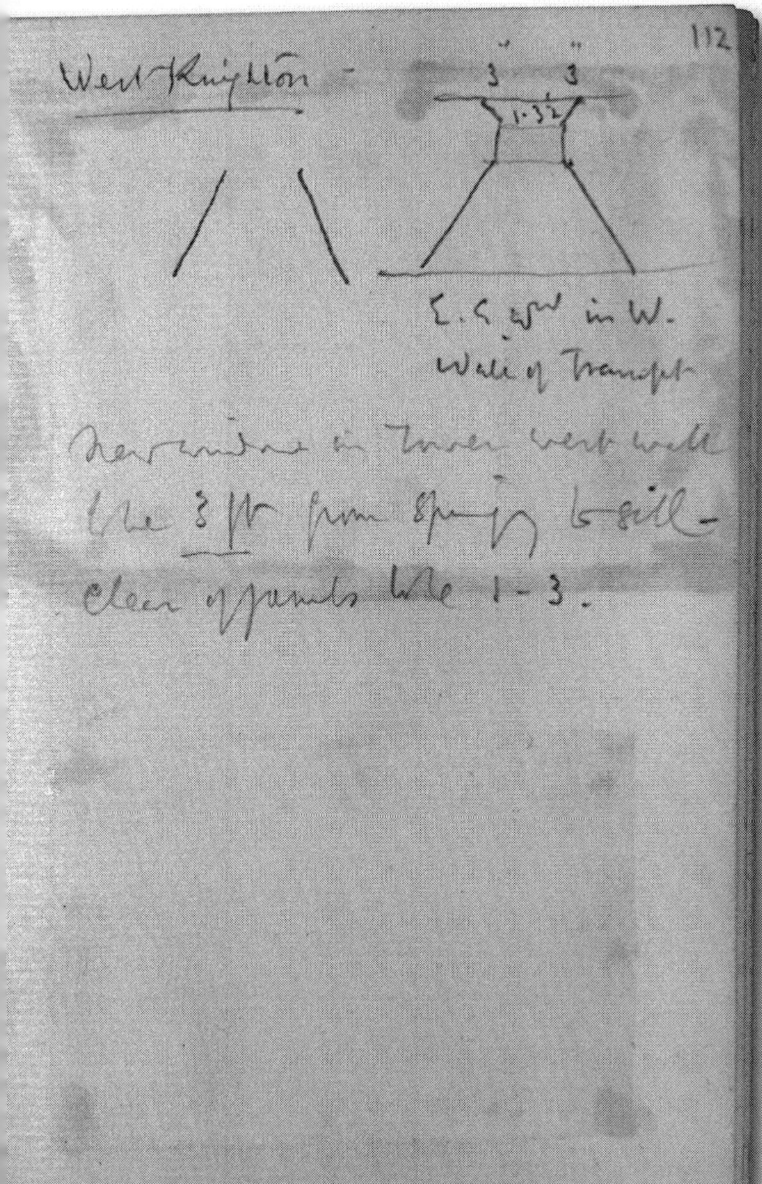
112
West Knighton
3" 3"
1·3½
E.S. wind in W. Wall of Transept
New window in Tower west wall
like 8 ft from springing to sill —
Clear of panels like 1–3.

Glastonbury Abbey · March '61.

1863

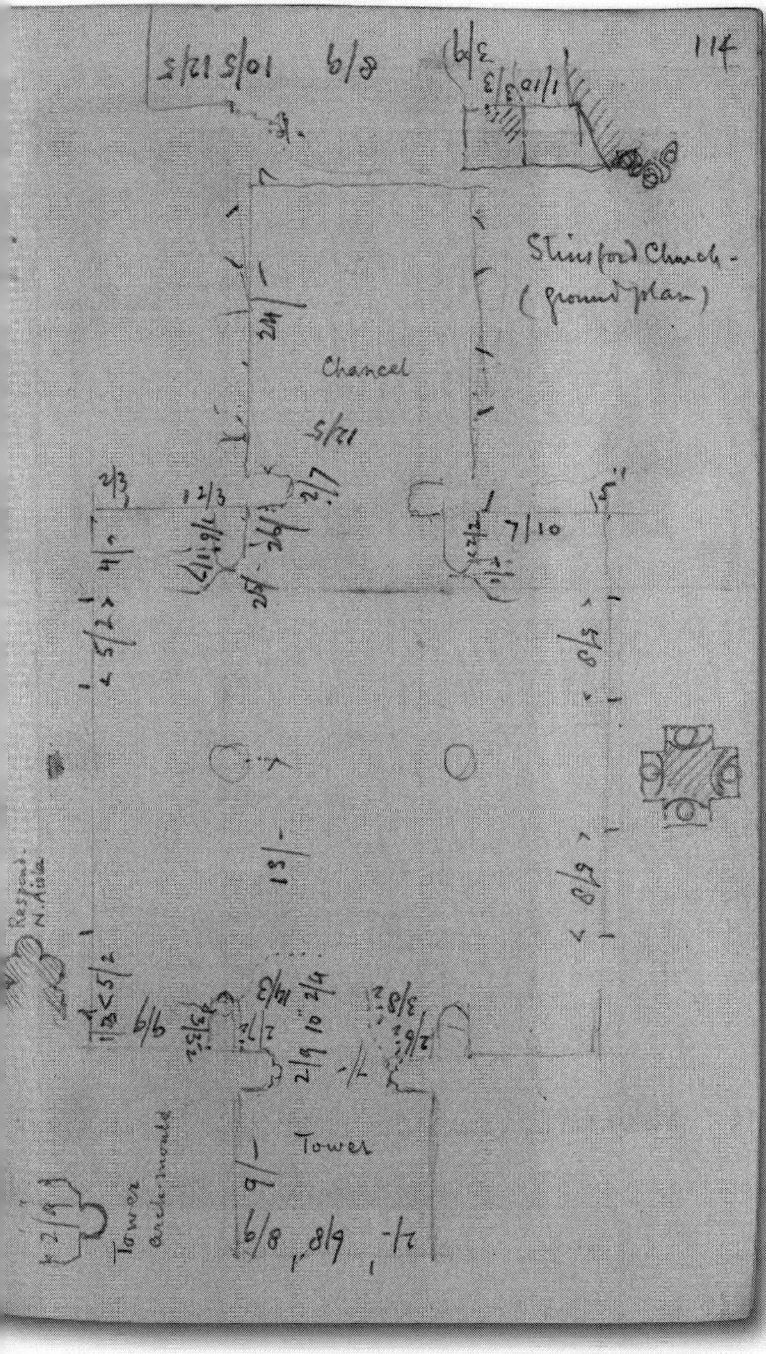
114
Stinsford Church -
(ground plan)
Chancel
Tower
Respond. N. Aisle
Tower Arch-mould

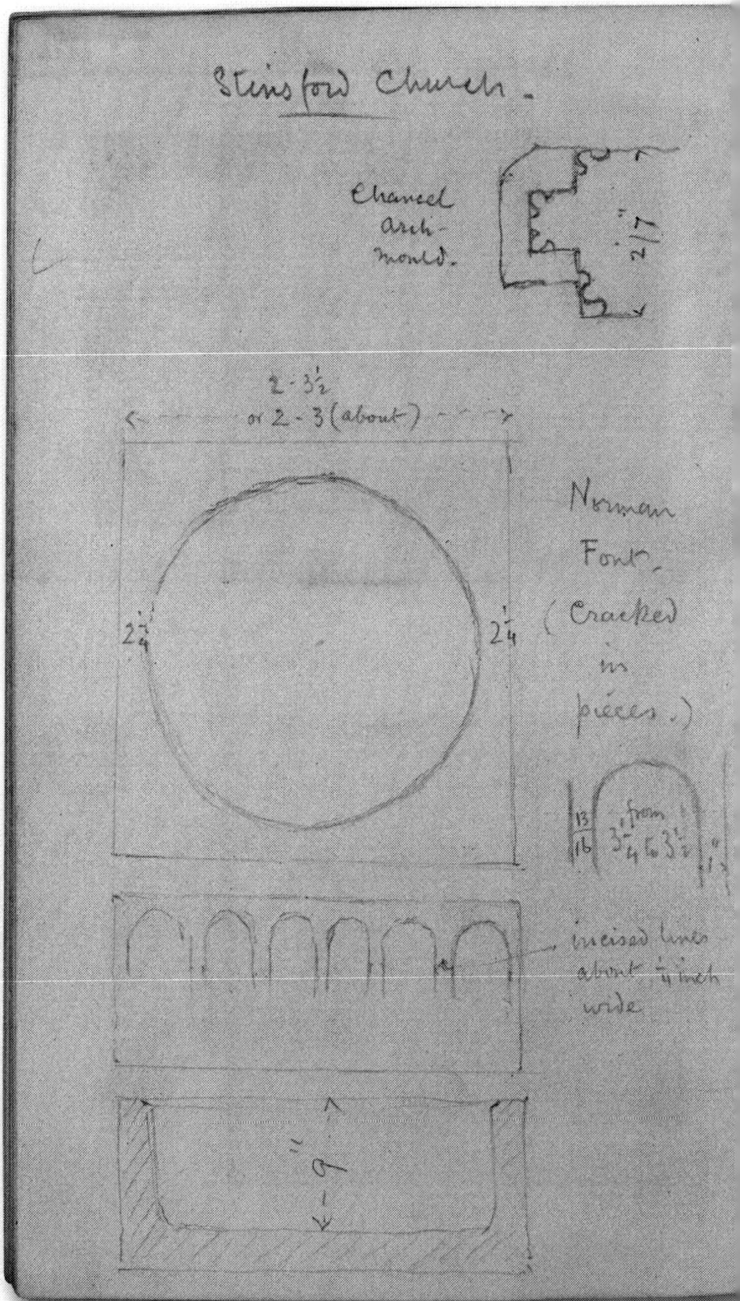
Stinsford Church.
Chancel arch mould.
2 - 3½
or 2 - 3 (about)
2¼
2¼
Norman Font.
(Cracked in pieces.)
incised lines about ¼ inch wide

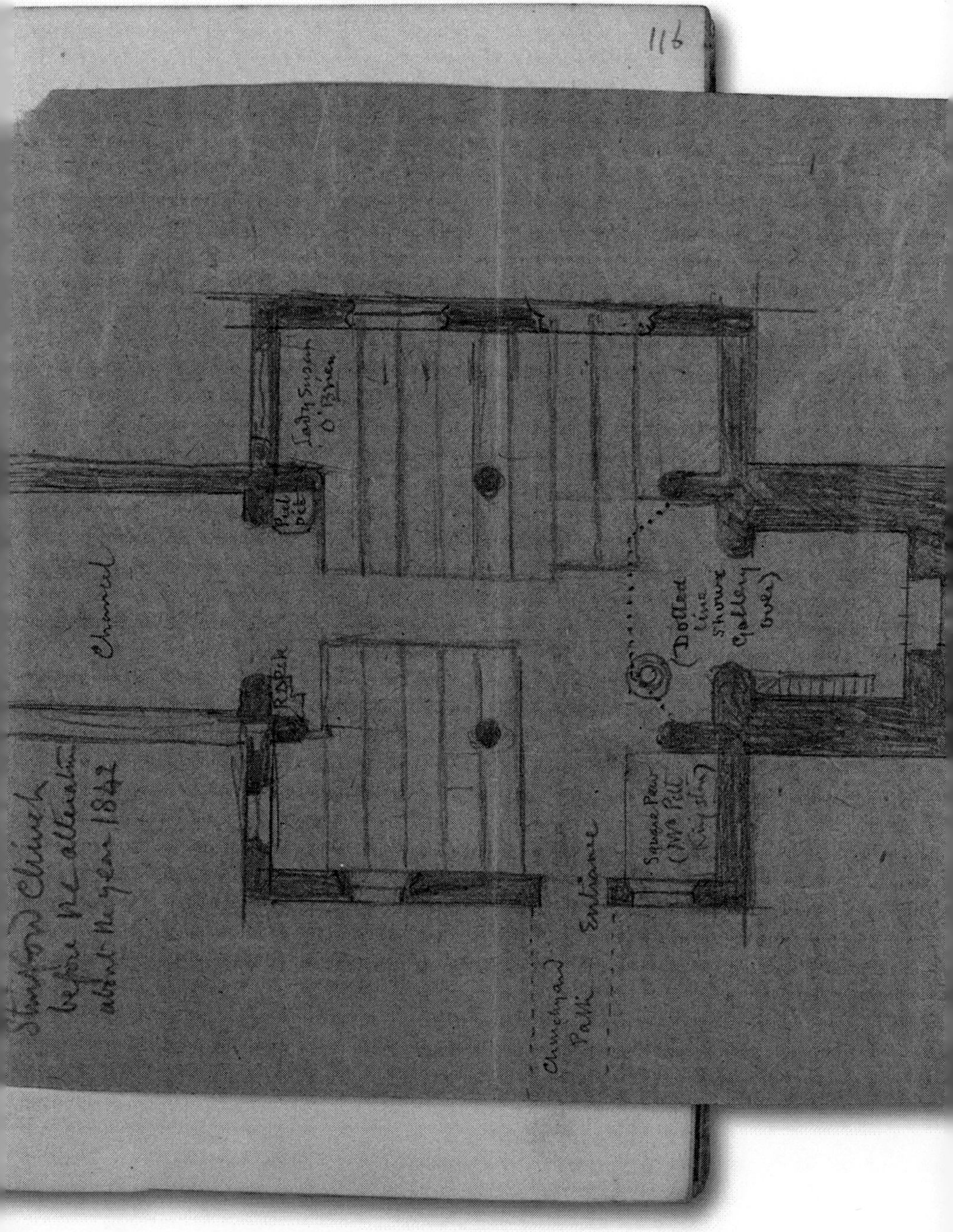
116
Stinsford Church before the alteration about the year 1842
Chancel
Lady Susan O'Brien
Pulpit
R Desk
Dotted line shows gallery over
Square Pew (Mr Pitt) (Kingston)
Entrance
Churchyard Path

Stinsford Church

Stinsford –

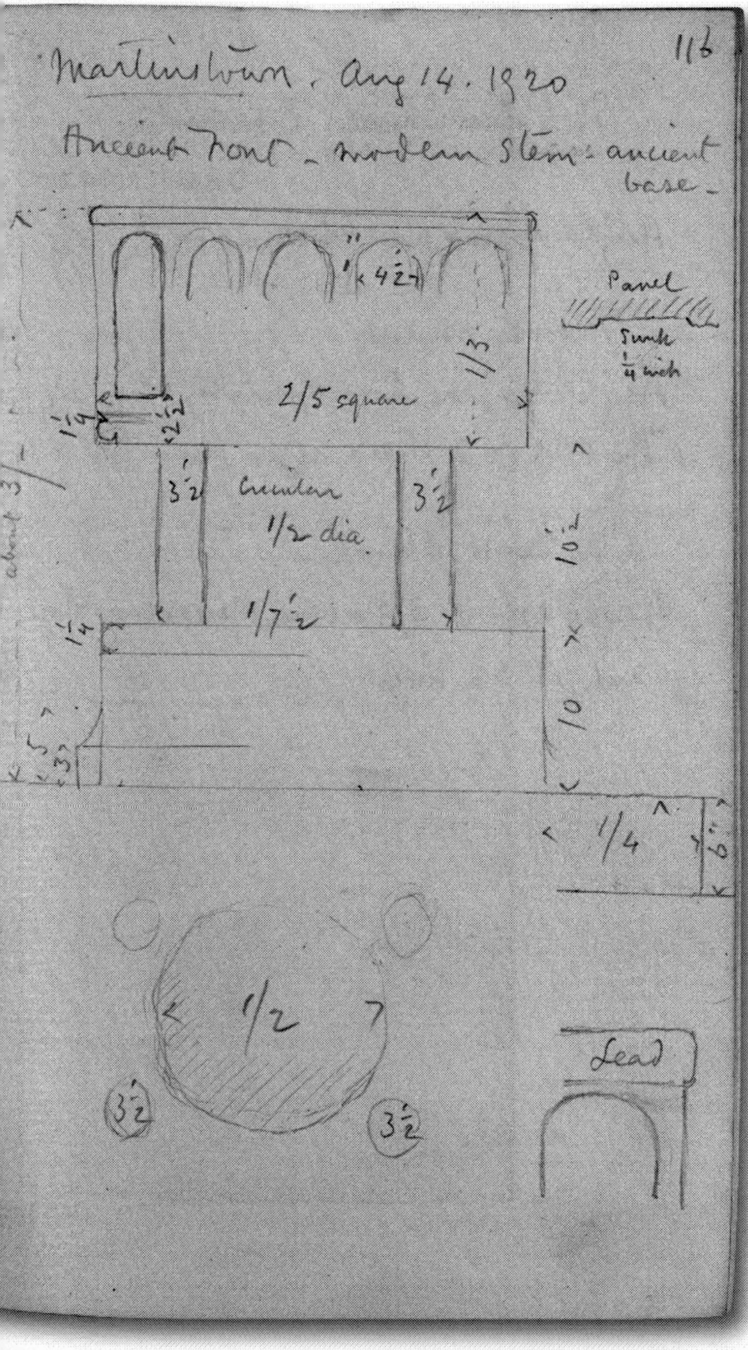
116
Martinstown. Aug 14. 1920
Ancient Font – modern stem: ancient base –
4½
Panel
Sunk ¼ inch
1/3
2/5 square
1¼
2½
3½
Circular 1/2 dia
3½
10½
about 3'
1/7½
1¼
10
3½
1/4
6"
1/2
Lead
3½
3½

St Peters Church Dorchester
Sept 1920
Height of font from floor, no step - 3/9

Trinity church -
Height of font from officiating step 3/4 -
(The step is 2 steps above floor.)

All Saints Church -
Height of font 3/3 above officiating step -
which is 3½ high

118

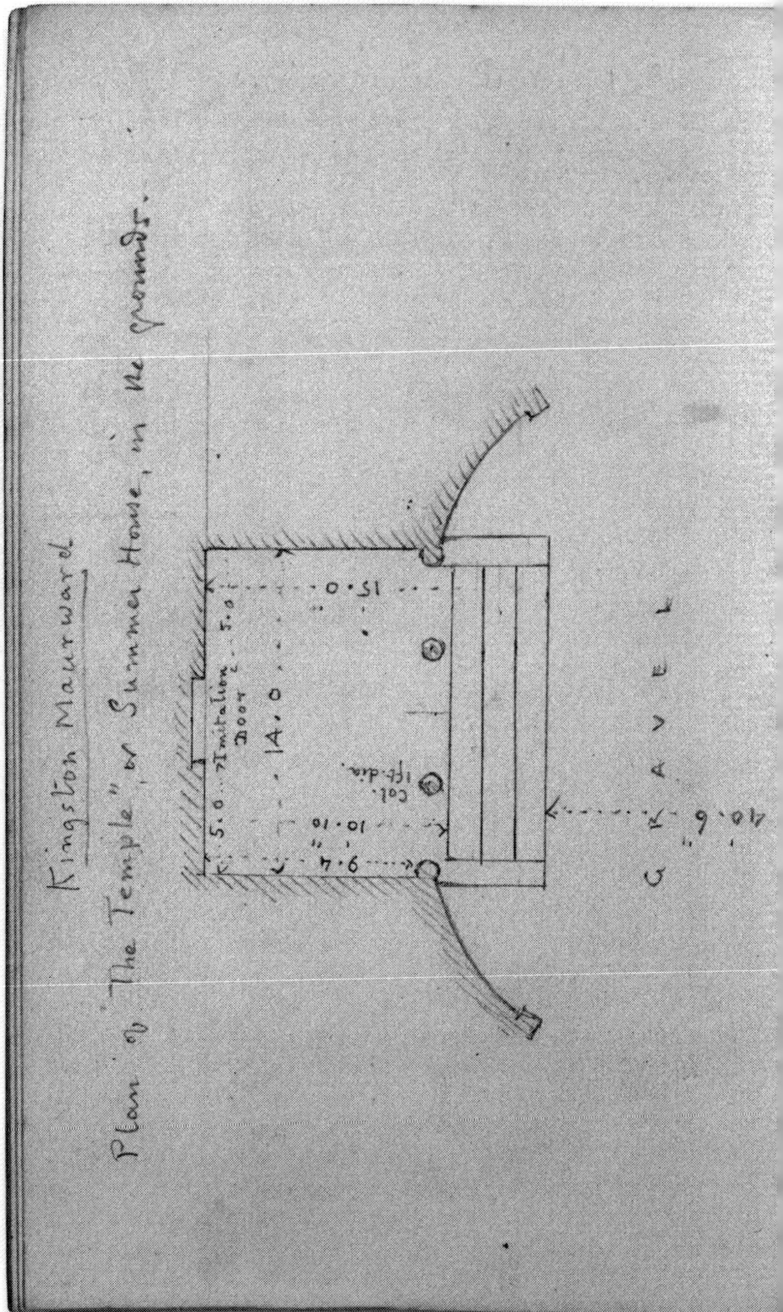
Kingston Maurward
Plan of "The Temple" or Summer House, in the grounds.
15.0
5.0
Imitation Door
5.0
14.0
Col. 1ft. dia.
10.10
9.4
GRAVEL
40.6

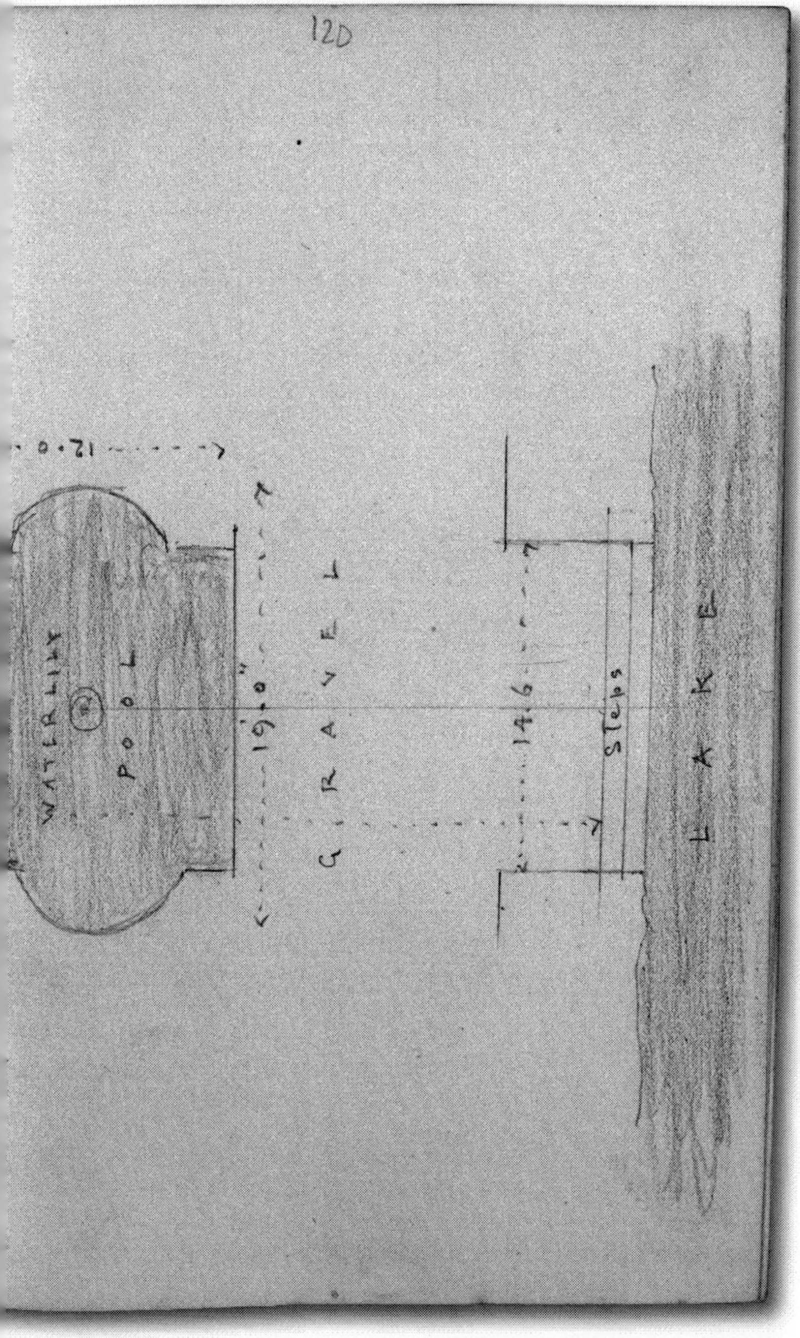
12D
12.0
WATER LILY
POOL
19.0
GRAVEL
14.6
Steps
LAKE

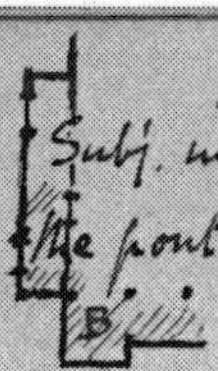

Subj. incised over exterior arch of D. ways & along
the font. Porch. plain groining, on st. corbels.
B Bapt^y. (font in centre) E. end of S. aisle. (@ 16/- sq.

Prin. Entrance = W. porch or narthex. 3 arches towards the street, ~~[illegible]~~ & over them as above: two side ones pierced with doorways – sq. headed – each arch filled with a sculptured subj. Nave 78 × 24 – entered by door in centre of W. end. Aisles 10 ft wide. Tower North side of N. aisle. lowest stage forming Porch

Above nave arcade & under ~~[illegible]~~ clearstory windows – (between two string courses) a triforium space – enriched by paintings in distemper on bk. wk. North from Old – South side from New Test – Groined in bk ribs in stone – springing from red stone vaulting shafts carved caps. Chancel A. goes up to the point of groining – springing from caps on a line with those of vaulting. At W. end of Nave at the level of the triforium is a projecting gallery carried on bold corbelling for access to N. aisle roof – a circular staircase leading from porch to this, & continued up to Nave roof, terminating with sq. turret attached to S. side of W. gable in which hangs a small bell, to be used till the tower is built. Above W. gallery are 2 large deeply recessed 2 light windows. Above these a large circ. window, with plate tracery, lights the roof over the groining. Chancel 42 × 23 – apsidal E. end – vaulting a continuation of that of Nave. Clearstory pierced with 11 lancet w^ns. below these the triforium – level with that of nave – lighted by 7 – 2 light w^ns. & presenting an arcade of towards chancel – on red stone columns. carved c's. Below this the walls of the ~~[illegible]~~ sacrarium is plastered for coloured decoration – upper part = painting of the Passion – lower diaper. Sacr. is 6 steps above nave. Sedilia & credence on S. side – 4 arched recesses [in juxta]

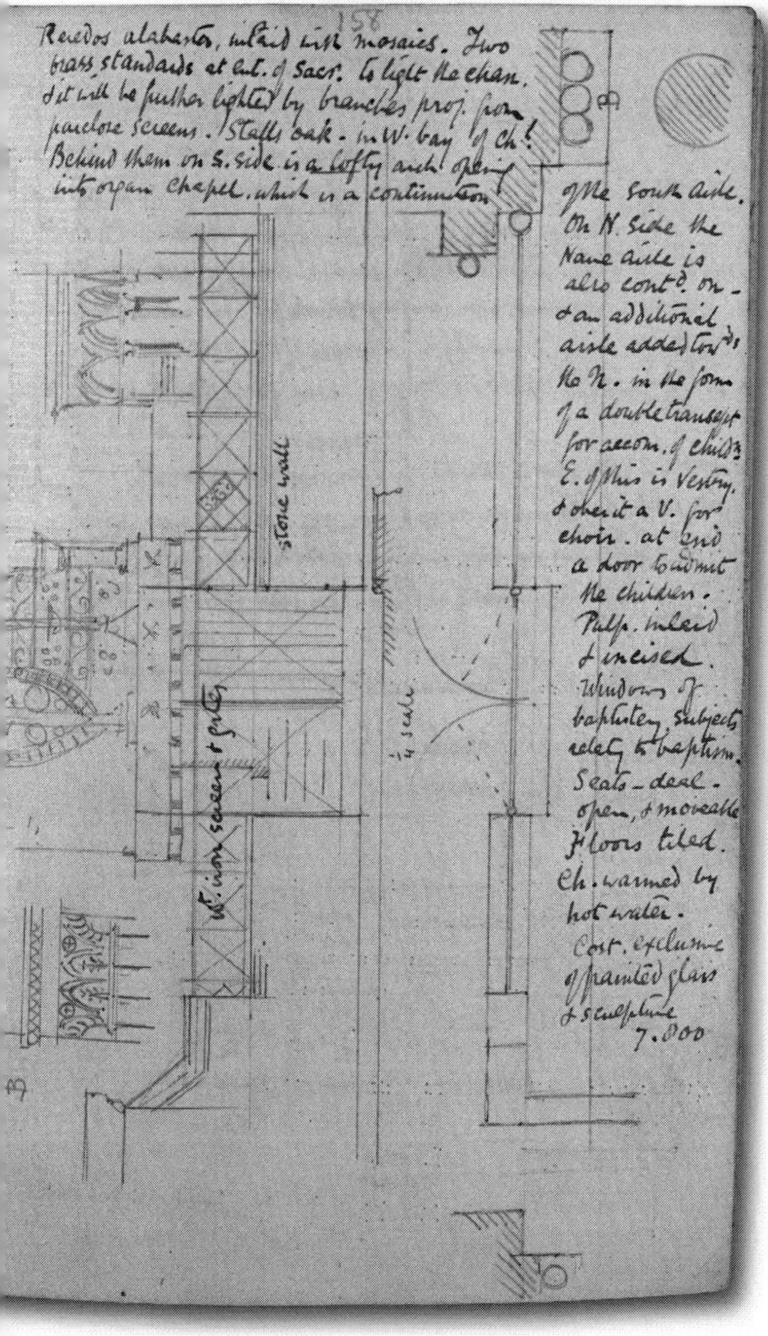
158

Reredos alabaster, inlaid with mosaics. Two brass standards at ent. of Sacr. to light the chan. & it will be further lighted by branches proj. from parclose screens. Stalls oak - in W. bay of Ch! Behind them on S. side is a lofty arch opening into organ chapel, which is a continuation of the south aisle. On N. side the Nave aisle is also contd. on - & an additional aisle added towds the N. in the form of a double transept for accom. of child[ren]. E. of this is Vestry, & over it a V. for choir. at end a door to admit the children. Pulp. inlaid & incised. Windows of baptistery, subjects relating to baptism. Seats - deal - open, & moveable. Floors tiled. Ch. warmed by hot water. Cost. exclusive of painted glass & sculpture 7.000

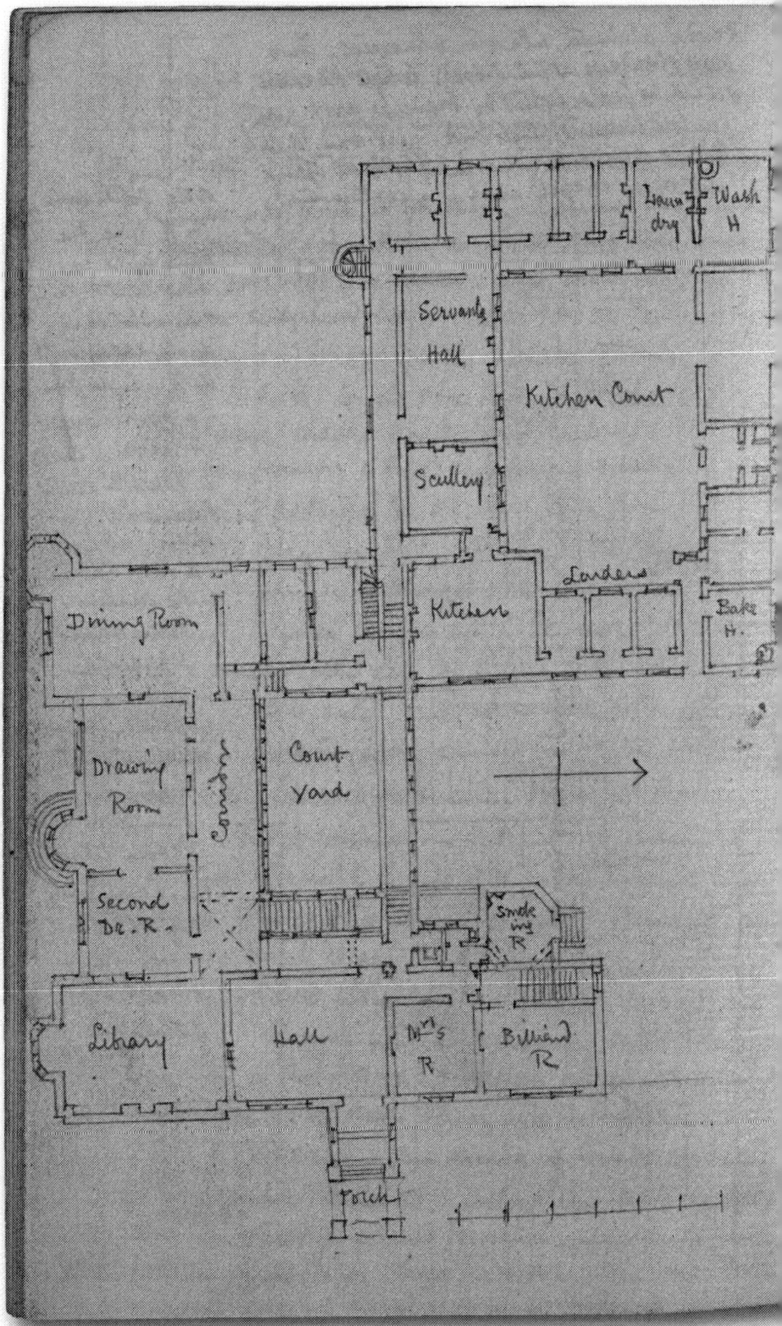
Laundry
Wash H
Servants Hall
Kitchen Court
Scullery
Larders
Kitchen
Bake H.
Dining Room
Drawing Room
Corridor
Court Yard
Second Dr. R.
Smoking R
Library
Hall
Mrs R
Billiard R
Porch

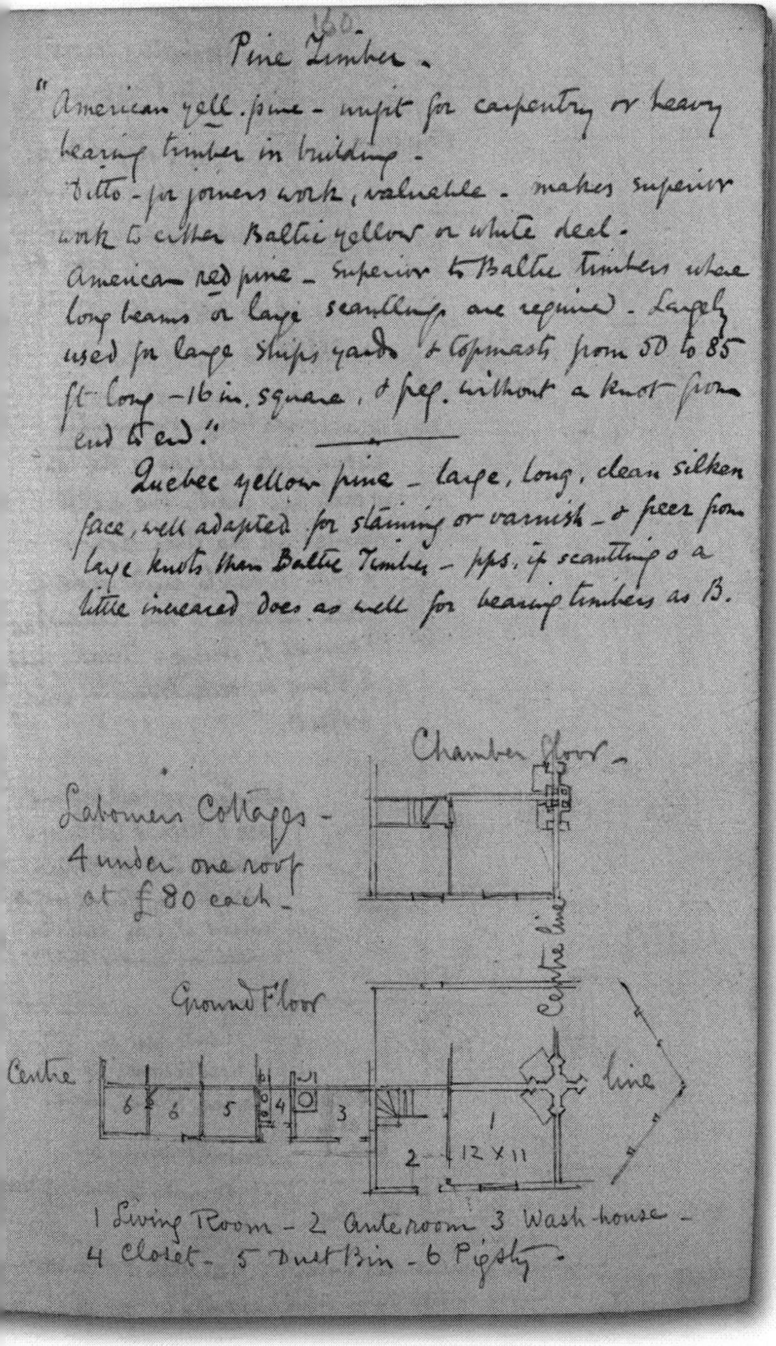

160.

Pine Timber.

"American yell. pine – unfit for carpentry or heavy bearing timber in building.
Ditto – for joiners work, valuable – makes superior work to either Baltic yellow or white deal.
American red pine – superior to Baltic timbers where long beams or large scantlings are required. Largely used for large ships yards & topmasts from 50 to 85 ft long – 16 in. square, & freq. without a knot from end to end."

Quebec yellow pine – large, long, clean silken face, well adapted for staining or varnish – & freer from large knots than Baltic Timber – pps. if scantlings a little increased does as well for bearing timbers as B.

Labourers Cottages – 4 under one roof at £80 each –

1 Living Room – 2 Anteroom 3 Wash-house – 4 Closet – 5 Dust Bin – 6 Pigsty –

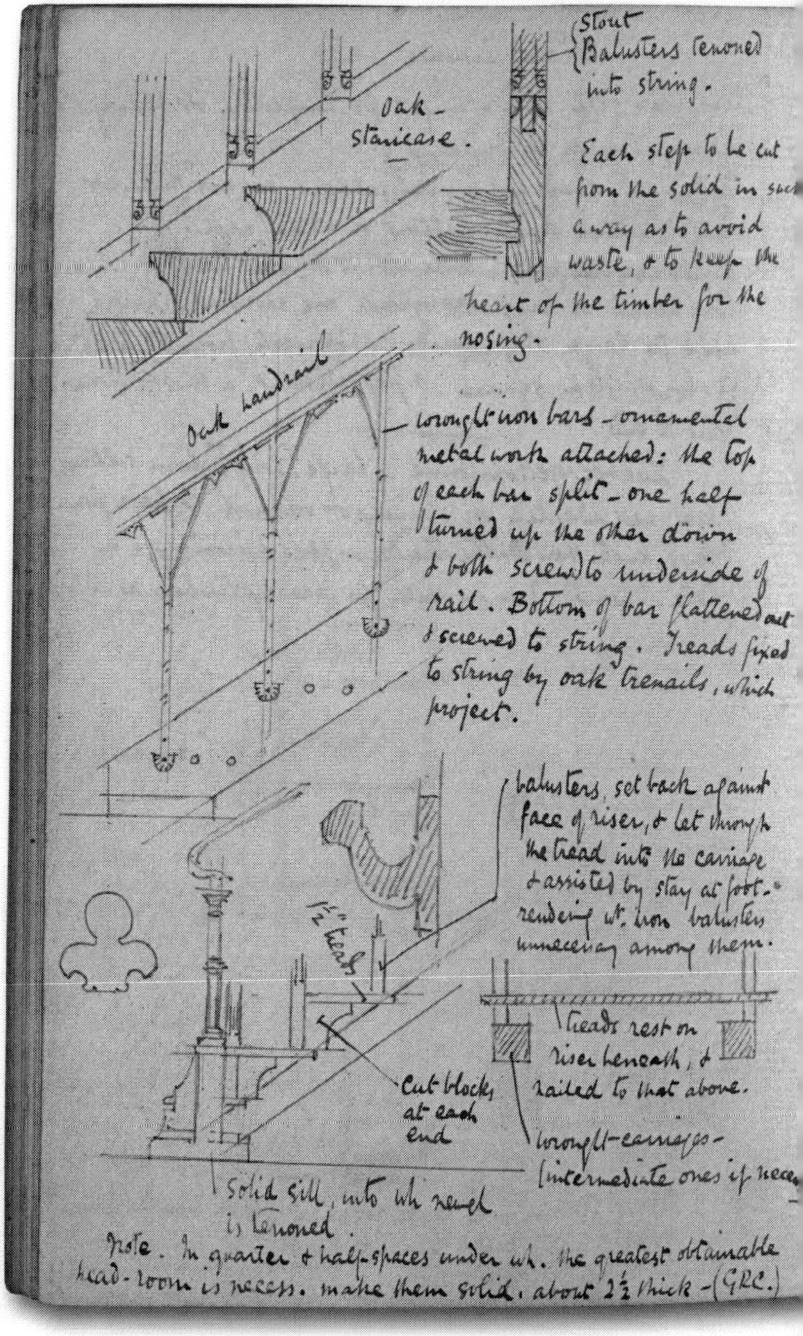
Stout Balusters tenoned into string.
Oak-staircase.
Each step to be cut from the solid in such a way as to avoid waste, & to keep the heart of the timber for the nosing.
Oak handrail
wrought iron bars - ornamental metal work attached: the top of each bar split - one half turned up the other down & both screwed to underside of rail. Bottom of bar flattened out & screwed to string. Treads fixed to string by oak trenails, which project.
balusters, set back against face of riser, & let through the tread into the carriage & assisted by stay at foot - rendering wt. iron balusters unnecessary among them.
1½" tread
Treads rest on riser beneath, & nailed to that above.
Cut blocks at each end
wrought-carriages - intermediate ones if necess
Solid sill, into wh newel is tenoned.
Note. In quarter & half-spaces under wh. the greatest obtainable head-room is necess. make them solid. about 2½ thick - (GRC.)

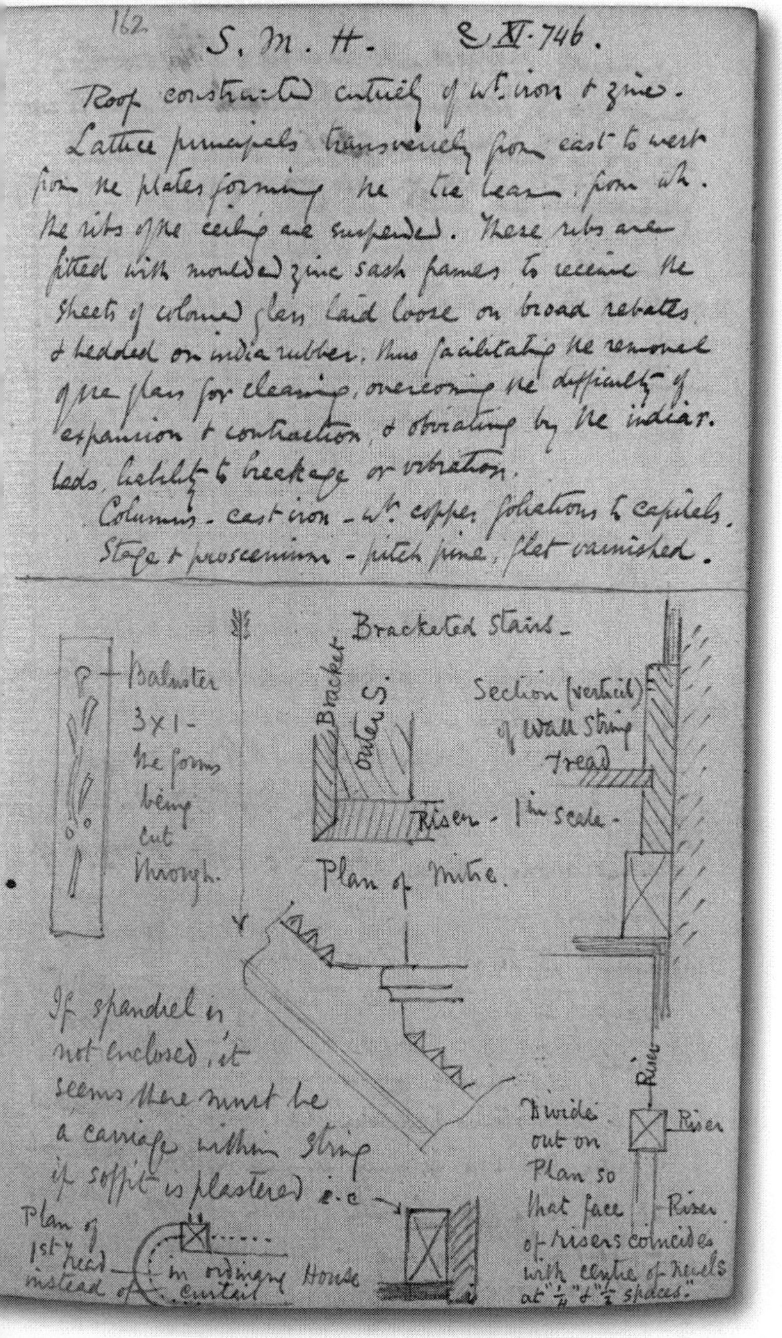

162 S. M. H. XI. 746.

Roof constructed entirely of wt. iron & zinc.
Lattice principals transversely from east to west from the plates forming the tie beam, from wh. the ribs of the ceiling are suspended. These ribs are fitted with moulded zinc sash frames to receive the sheets of coloured glass laid loose on broad rebates & bedded on india rubber, thus facilitating the removal of the glass for cleaning, overcoming the difficulty of expansion & contraction, & obviating by the india r. beds, liability to breakage or vibration.
Columns - cast iron - wt. copper foliations to capitals.
Stage & proscenium - pitch pine, flat varnished.

Cottages. prize design of 149 sent in to Yorksh. agric Society in 1861 – not to cost more than (?) 220£ the pair.

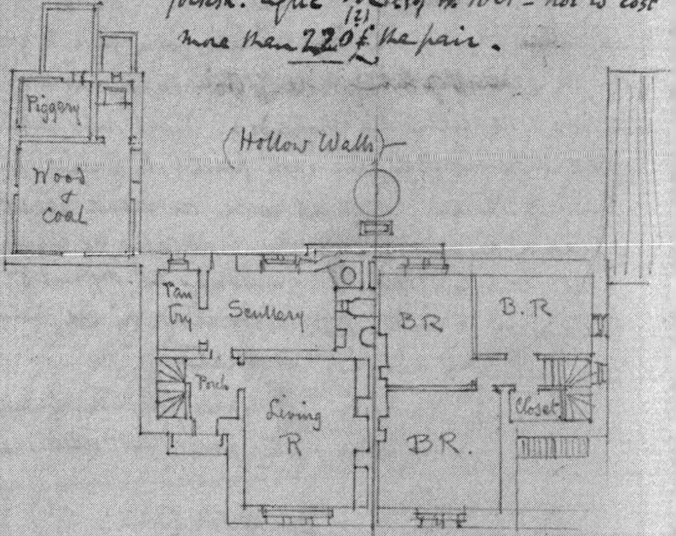

Dimensions for cottages wh experience teaches to be advisable –

Height of lower rooms 8ft.

Floor to ceiling of upper ditto 7.6.

Living room	area 150 ft.	c. contents 1200 ft.
Scullery	80	640
Parents B.R.	120	900
Boys	90	675
Girls	80	600

A downstairs bedroom has been recommended because though a labourer requires a third bedroom at one stage of his family's growth, he does not for any length of time – & it then may be used for a lodger or otherwise –

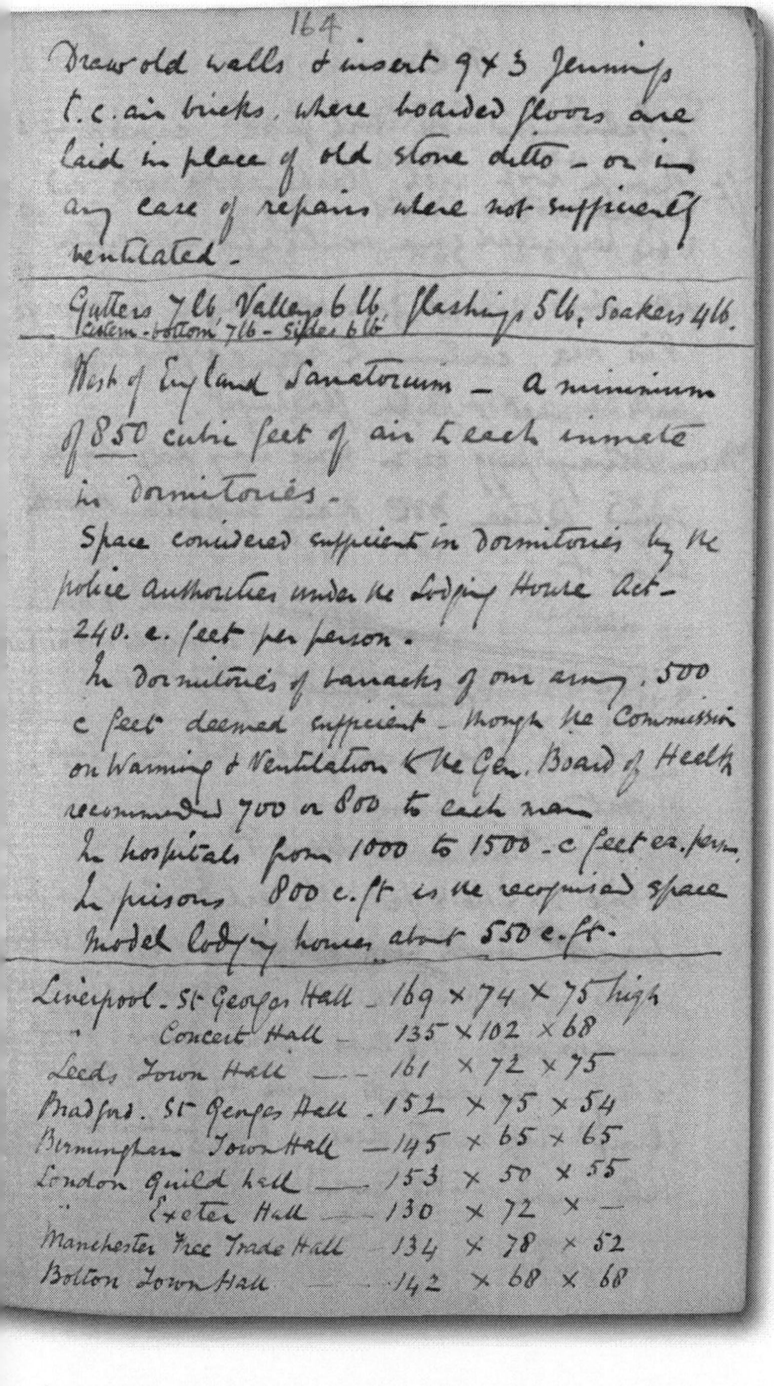

164

Drew old walls & insert 9 x 3 Jennings t.c. air bricks, where boarded floors are laid in place of old stone ditto – or in any case of repairs where not sufficiently ventilated –

Gutters 7 lb, Valleys 6 lb, flashings 5 lb, Soakers 4 lb.
cistern-bottom 7 lb – sides 6 lb

West of England Sanatorium – a minimum of 850 cubic feet of air to each inmate in dormitories –

Space considered sufficient in dormitories by the police authorities under the Lodging House Act – 240. c. feet per person.

In dormitories of barracks of our army, 500 c feet deemed sufficient – though the Commission on Warming & Ventilation & the Gen. Board of Health recommended 700 or 800 to each man

In hospitals from 1000 to 1500 – c feet ea. pers.

In prisons 800 c. ft is the recognised space

Model lodging houses about 550 c. ft.

Liverpool – St George's Hall	169	x 74	x 75 high
" Concert Hall	135	x 102	x 68
Leeds Town Hall	161	x 72	x 75
Bradford. St George's Hall	152	x 75	x 54
Birmingham Town Hall	145	x 65	x 65
London Guild hall	153	x 50	x 55
" Exeter Hall	130	x 72	x –
Manchester Free Trade Hall	134	x 78	x 52
Bolton Town Hall	142	x 68	x 68

W. C.

Galvanized iron soil pipe – carried up 6 ft. through roof with flashings & apron; end turned down.

A perforated zinc ventilator in ceiling, from which rises a zinc vent pipe No 14 gauge 8 in dia. continued to roof & 3 ft above (?) with bonnet & proper flashings.

Mem: Always pugg or in some way keep back sound between W.C & any important room below it.

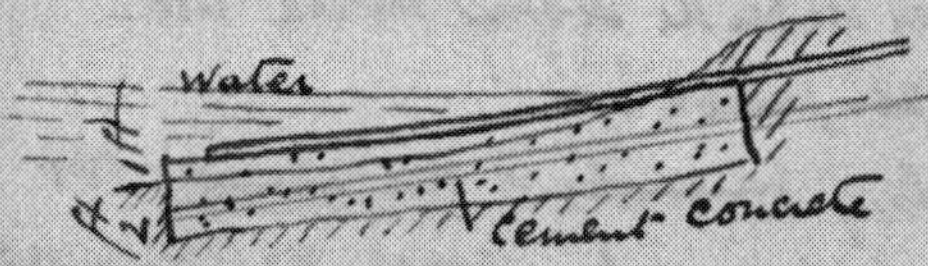

At end of drain a well constructed flap valve.

Handle to be in all cases outside flap of seat.

Sink in Butler's P.

Size 2/6 × 1/6 × 1/2. 1¼ deal, mitred, on fir bearers. lined with 8 lb cast lead, with soldered angles, copper nails &c. 4" Dye & Andrews's trap: 3 in waste pipe. 1¼ Cupb^d. fronts below, hung folding – 3 in brass butts. lock, &c. 1¼ top & champed flap – white deal – hung with 3 in brass butts – 4 in skirting around.

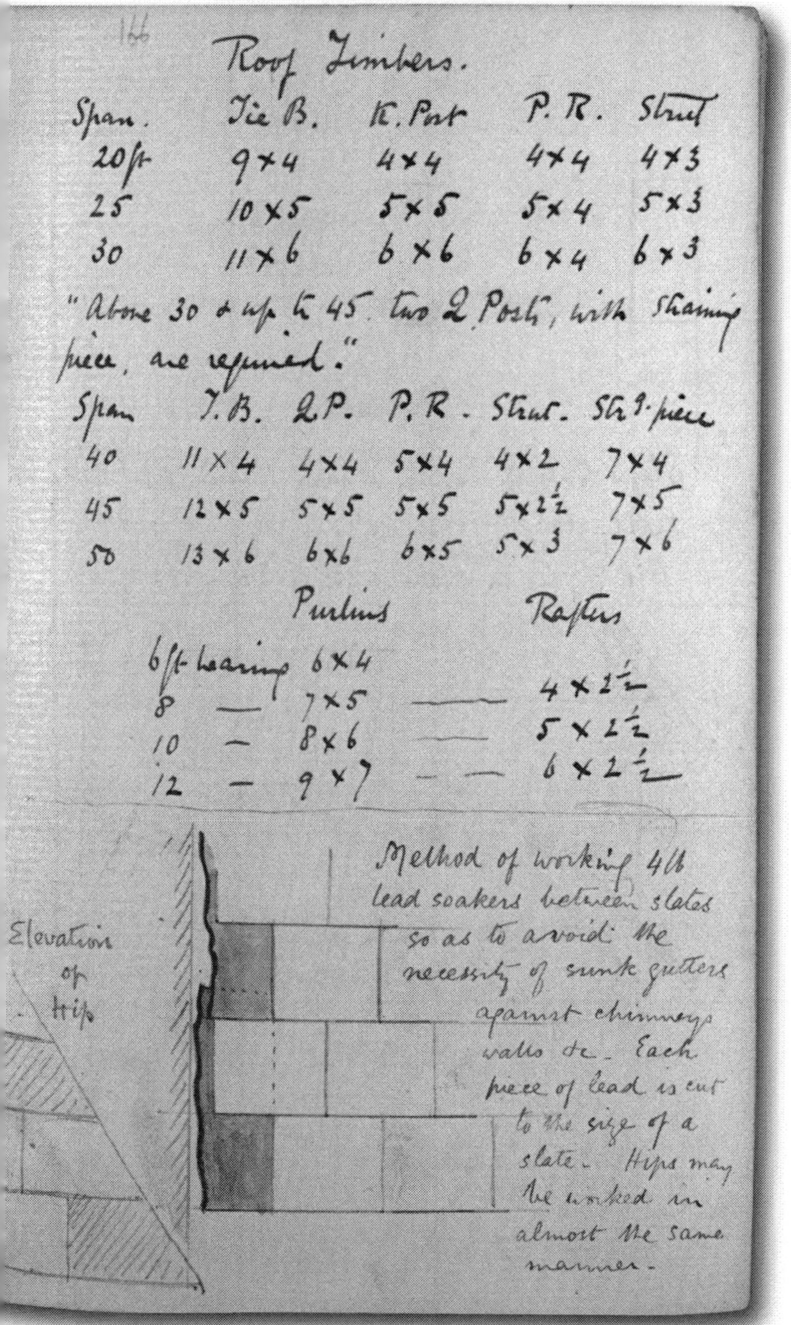

166

Roof Timbers.

Span.	Tie B.	K. Post	P. R.	Strut
20ft	9×4	4×4	4×4	4×3
25	10×5	5×5	5×4	5×3
30	11×6	6×6	6×4	6×3

"Above 30 & up to 45 two Q. Posts, with straining piece, are required."

Span	T. B.	Q. P.	P. R.	Strut.	Str'g-piece
40	11×4	4×4	5×4	4×2	7×4
45	12×5	5×5	5×5	5×2½	7×5
50	13×6	6×6	6×5	5×3	7×6

	Purlins	Rafters
6ft bearing	6×4	
8 —	7×5	4×2½
10 —	8×6	5×2½
12 —	9×7	6×2½

Elevation of Hip

Method of working 4lb lead soakers between slates so as to avoid the necessity of sunk gutters against chimneys walls &c. Each piece of lead is cut to the size of a slate. Hips may be worked in almost the same manner.

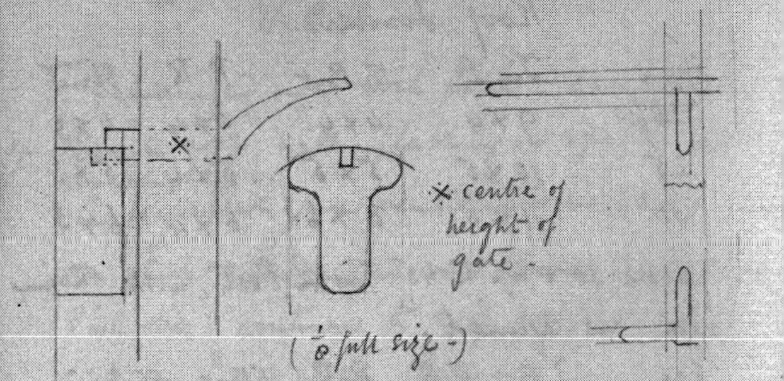

Steps to be of Portland Stone (hard "East Side")
neatly back jointed".
Air grates in stone wall @ 6" × 1/-

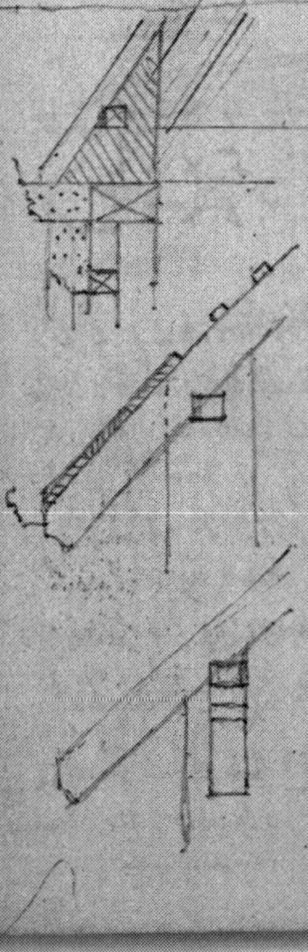

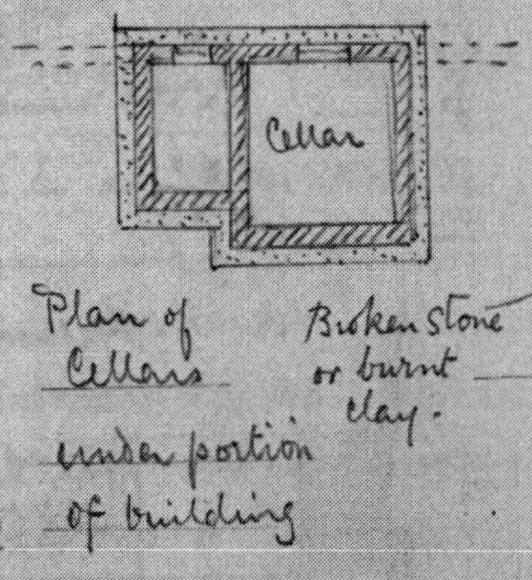

Plan of Cellars
under portion of building

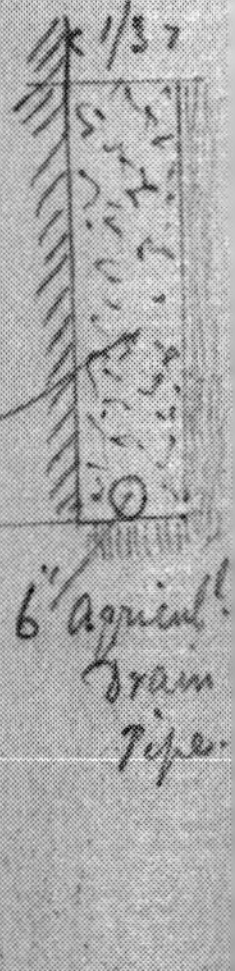

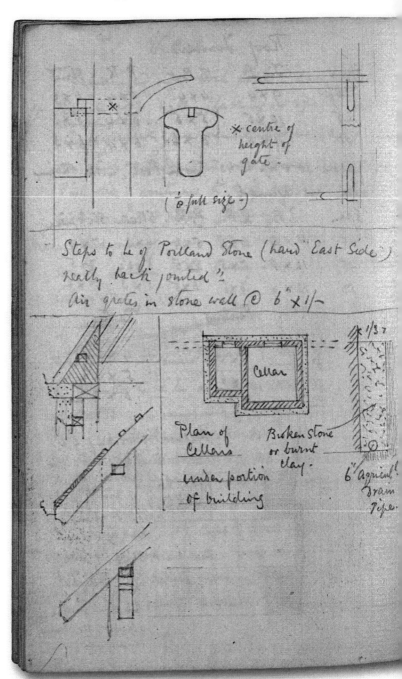

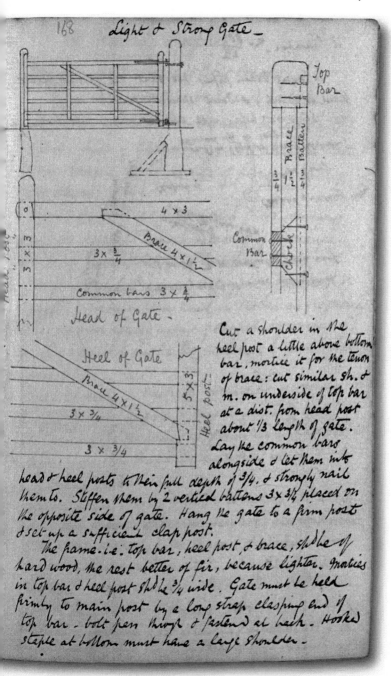

168 *Light & Strong Gate –*

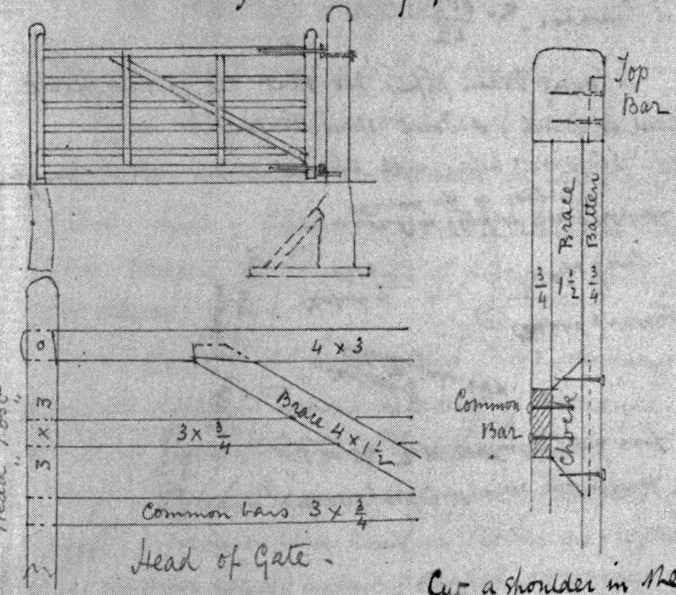

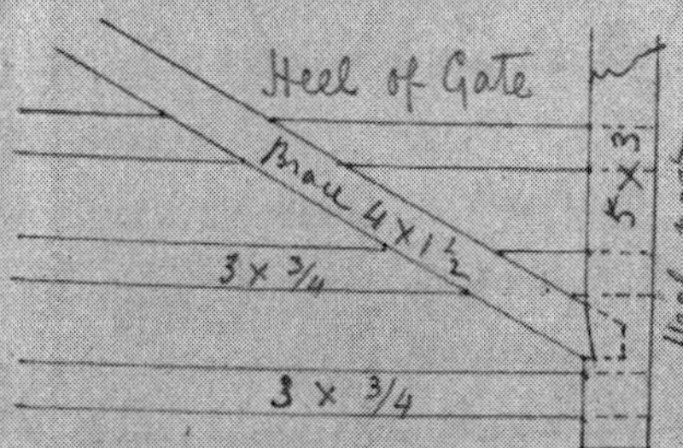

Cut a shoulder in the heel post a little above bottom bar, mortice it for the tenon of brace: cut similar sh. & m. on underside of top bar at a dist. from head post about 1/3 length of gate. Lay the common bars alongside & let them into head & heel posts to their full depth of 3/4. & strongly nail them to. Stiffen them by 2 vertical battens 3 x 3/4 placed on the opposite side of gate. Hang the gate to a firm post & set up a sufficient clap post.

The frame. i.e. top bar, heel post, & brace, sh^d be of hard wood, the rest better of fir, because lighter. Mortices in top bar & heel post sh^d be 3/4 wide. Gate must be held firmly to main post by a long strap clasping end of top bar – bolt pass through & fastened at back. Hook & staple at bottom must have a large shoulder –

A Plumber – R $\frac{887}{22}$

In laying drain pipes see that the ground below them is solid, & don't spare the cemt.

Stop rat holes with cement mixed with broken g

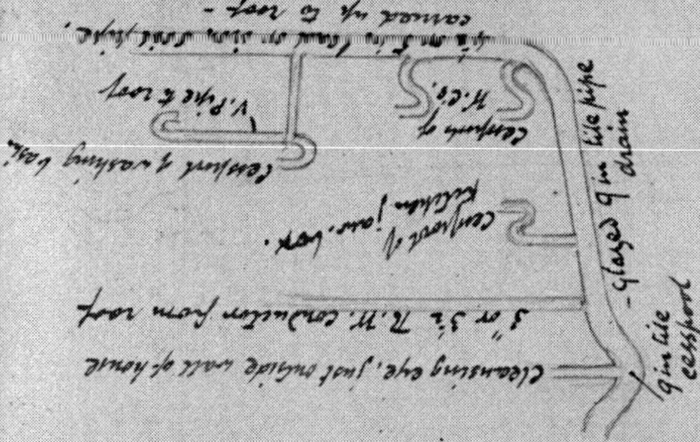

170

St Thomas's Hospital.

Footings – No 2 wire cut Galt Bricks

Walls specified to be built with best stocks

Piers, where reduced to small area by large w-ds space, built of Galt Bks in Port. Cemt. & Portland Stone bonder, the whole size of piers, at every 4 ft height.

Hoop iron bond at level of each floor, running round the building without necessity of severance.

Building faced with red Fareham bricks.

Floors of "Dennett" arching – the joists & sleepers, or concrete & paving, being laid on the top in the ordinary way. Waggon headed ceiling of chapel, & groining of aisles executed in same material – aisles having stone ribs.

Flues carried on back of main ribs of groining & to apex of roof (up piers of clerestory walls), provision being made for sweeping at points easy of access. Flues from low buildings are taken across & up with main building.

Flat roofs over low buildings & corridors, wh. in many parts form terraces of communication – are constructed of similar arching – the surface of arching being covered with concrete, laid to the required fall, & then covd. with asphalte – "Pilkington's Patent" – wh. consists in the introd. of layer of felt between 2 coats of asphalte. The lower coat is laid in Polinceau abt. ½" thick upper Seysell ½" thick, with flushing of same material – all executed by Mr Pilkington.

pp. 171 – 172

Paving &c in areas – Patent Victoria Stone – (granite chipp
& P. Cemt, in moulds) a capital paving, & considd less exp
than rubbed York.

Corridors paved with tiles 1ft sq. & 1" thick – red, buff, & blk.
of Ransome's material.

Ward wws – 3 divisions: lower part to open in usual way
& the upper sash drops to the depth of the transom

Windows of pavilions glazed with plate glass (with a
view to a more equal temperature; corridors glazed
with flatted crown.

(to save bed space
Warming – 3 open fireplaces in middle of each ward,
with vertical shafts, constructed with an outer case of
cast iron, & an inner smoke tube 15 in dia. Also
an auxiliary system of hot water.

Ventn the above mend space between the 2 tubes – also
at ceiling & floor level at ends of wards – all commun
with horizontal trunk in roof – which runs to shaft
in well hole of stairs, heated by smoke flue from boile
assisted by hot water coils. To replace the air thus
extracted, fresh air is introd. by means of zinc tubes
laid between the Dennett arching & the floor boards
communicating with the stoves & hot water coils (for
warming it in winter) – the whole admitting of regula
by valves.

In the upper story the iron casing of smoke flue is
discontinued & a brick casing built on the concrete floo
passing through roof & carrying external shaft. The 3 stove
(over each other) go into one flue – carried down to the
basement, & swept from below. Warming & V. carrie
out by Haden & Son Trowbridge.

172

Wards plastered with a setting coat of Parian on a backing of Portland Cement – (to be non-absorbent.)

Floors of ditto laid with wainscot tongued with hoop iron, the nail holes stopped with coloured putty, & prepared for waxing & polishing

Well holes of stairs occupied by lifts & V. shafts.

Intercepting lobbies, with windows on both sides, between W.C.s, Bath rooms, lavatories &c., & main buildings

Windows of wards carried close to ceiling

Entrance Hall forms sub-structure to Chapel –

Kitchen as nearly central as possible.

Difference in levels of foundns is obtained by stepping

Bed of Concrete 5ft thick, is laid over the whole surface of buildings exc. at ends of blocks towards river, where it reaches 22 ft thick.

Concrete – blue lias lime & clean Thames ballast – 6 to 1 below land water line – above, 8 to 1.

A drain was laid along the whole length of the hospital at the back of the river wall to a sump, & the excavations were all pumped dry before the concrete was put in.

Terrace wall towards river, & certain portions of low outbuildings in that direction, are built on piers in concrete (5ft sq. for t. wall) & arches in Port. Cemt. concrete (5 of ballast to 1 cemt.) turned from pier to pier (B Jan 27 & Feb 3 1871)

176
Celtic

Wrought Iron Hinge &
Closing Ring.
Bracket & Hart's Tongue Fern.

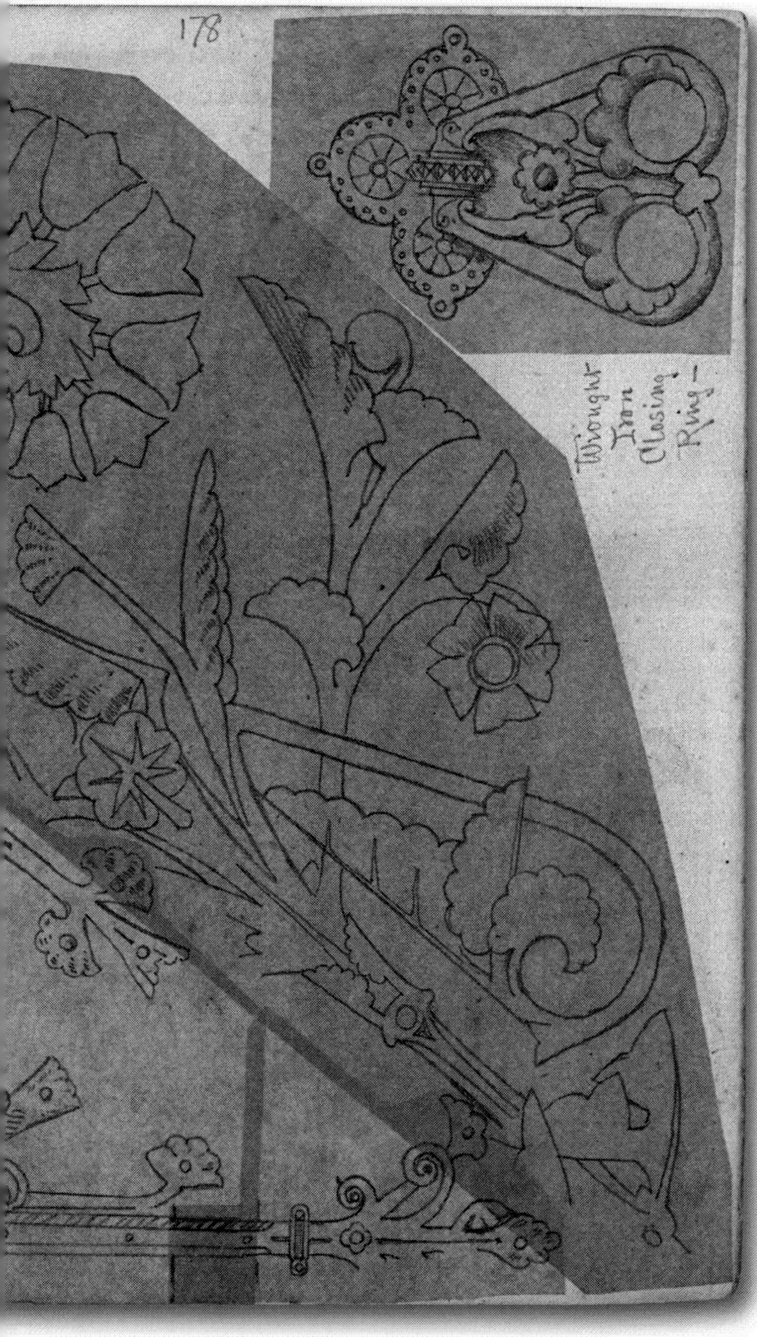
178
Wrought Iron Closing Ring –

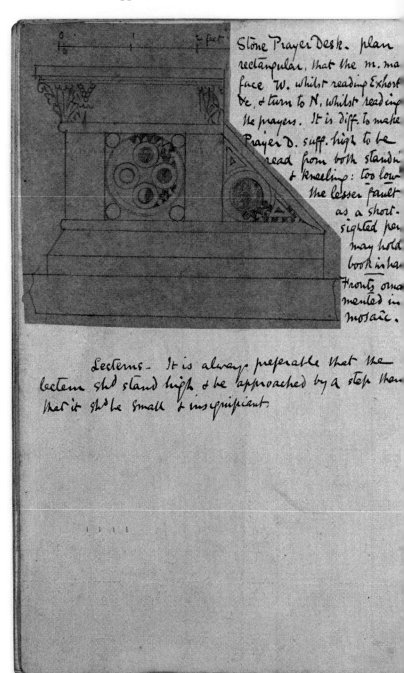

Stone Prayer Desk. plan
rectangular, that the m. ma
face W. whilst reading Exhort
&c, & turn to N. whilst reading
the prayers. It is diff. to make
Prayer D. suff. high to be
read from both standi
& kneeling: too low
the lesser fault
as a short-
sighted per
may hold
book in ha
Fronts orna
mented in
mosaic.

Lecterns – It is always preferable that the lectern shd stand high & be approached by a step than that it shd be small & insignificant.

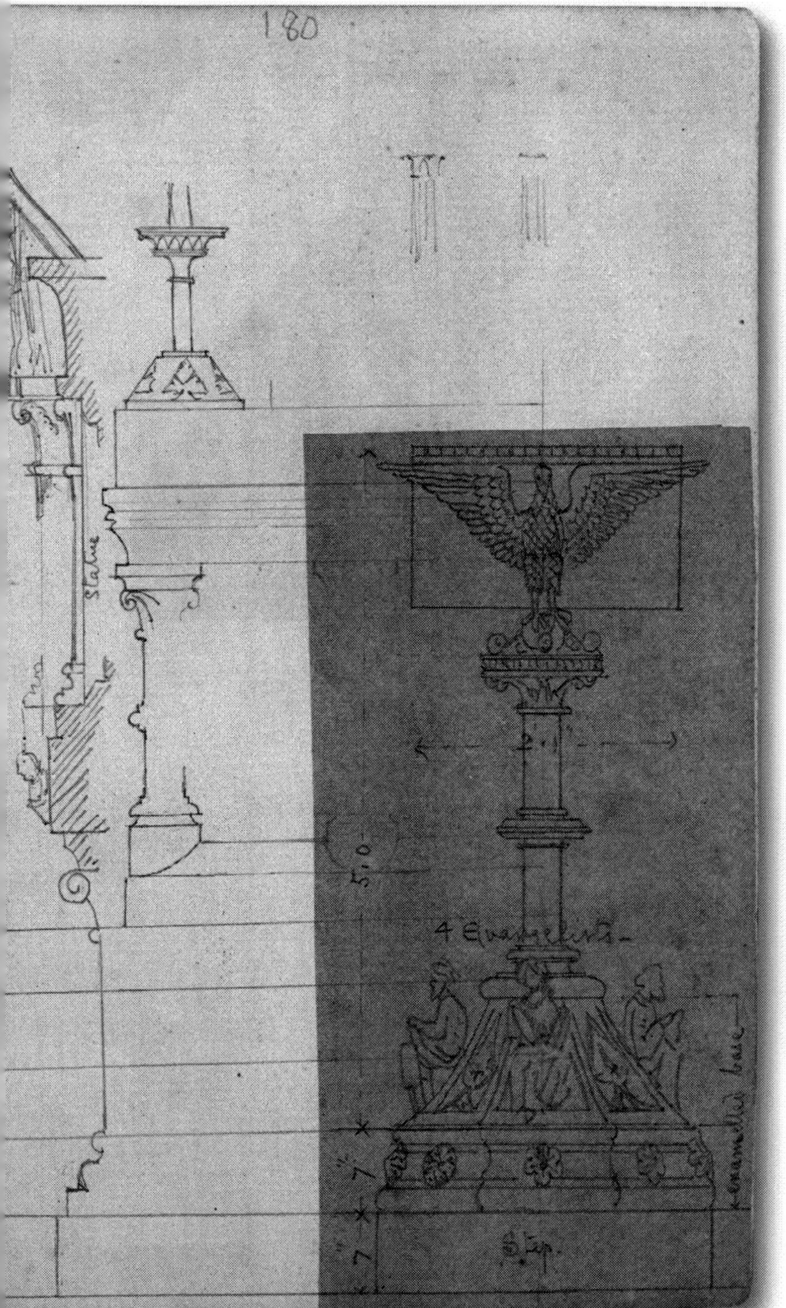
180
Statue
2.1
5.0
4 Evangelists
7½
7
Kenamelled base
Step.

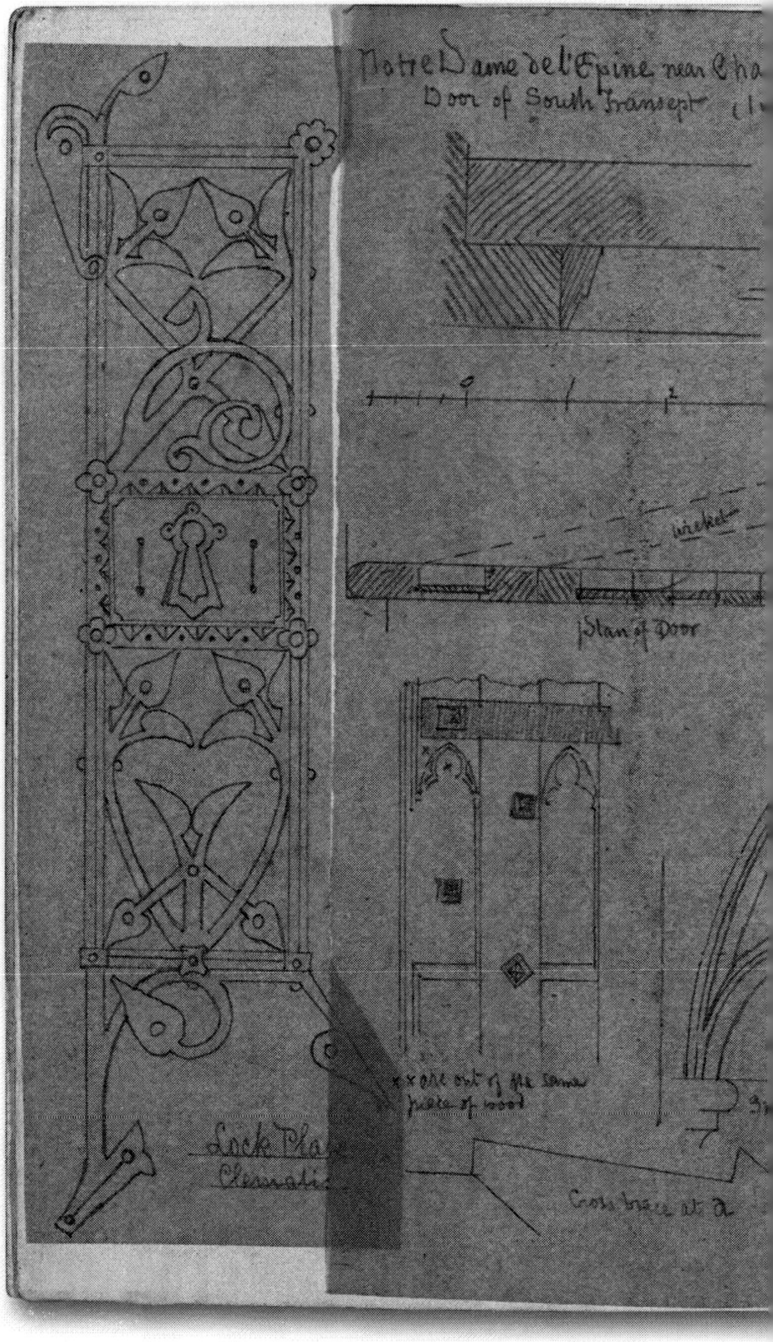
Notre Dame de l'Epine near Cha
Door of South Transept
wicket
Plan of Door
x x are out of the same piece of wood
Cross brace at a
Lock Pla
Clematis

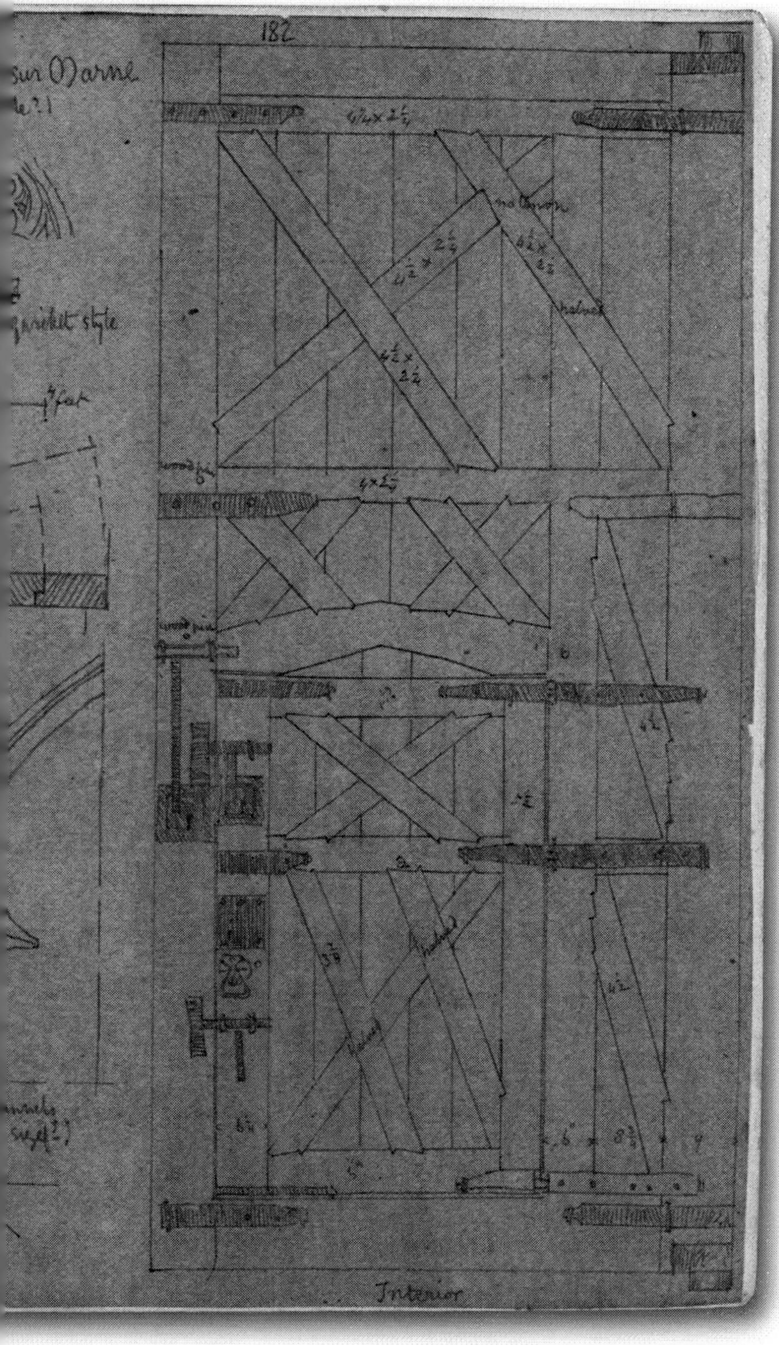

pp. 183 – 184

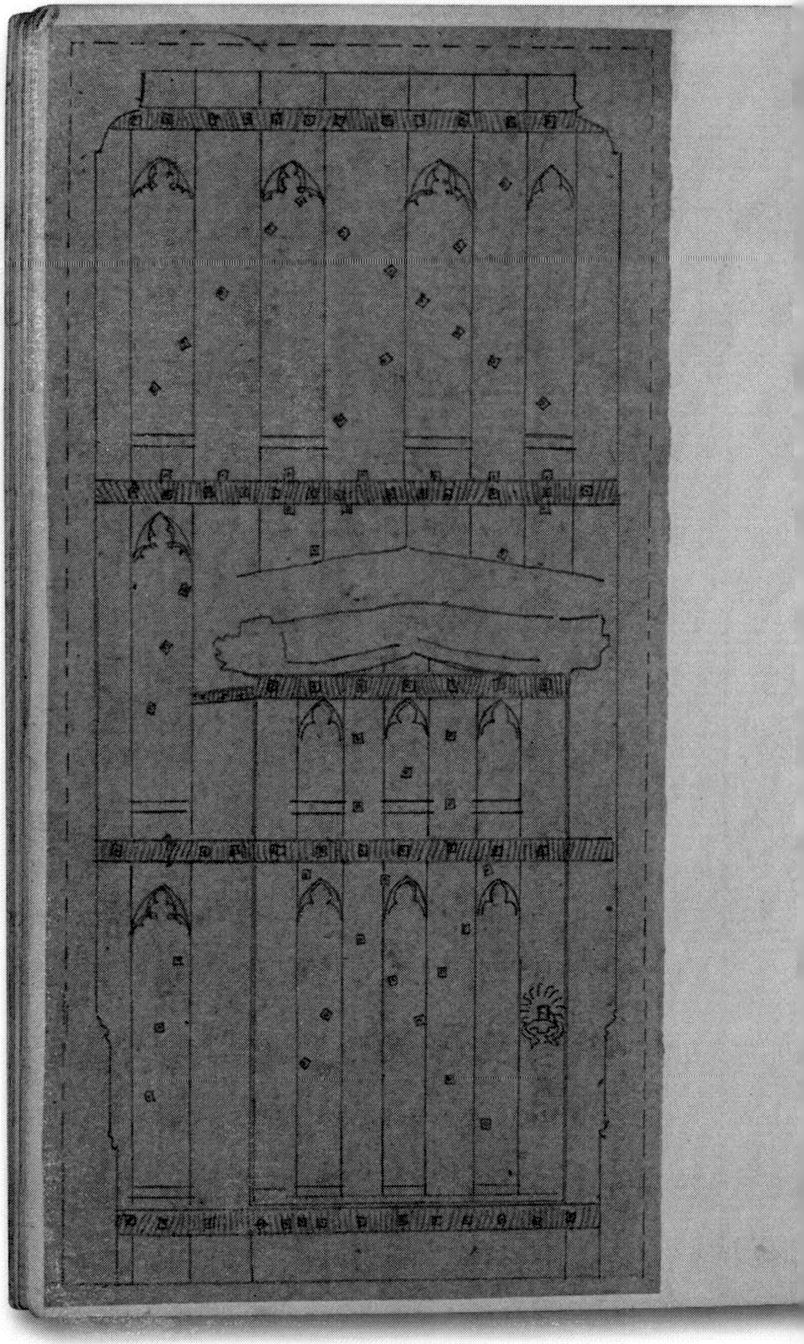

184

Circle
One of Shafts
Cusping

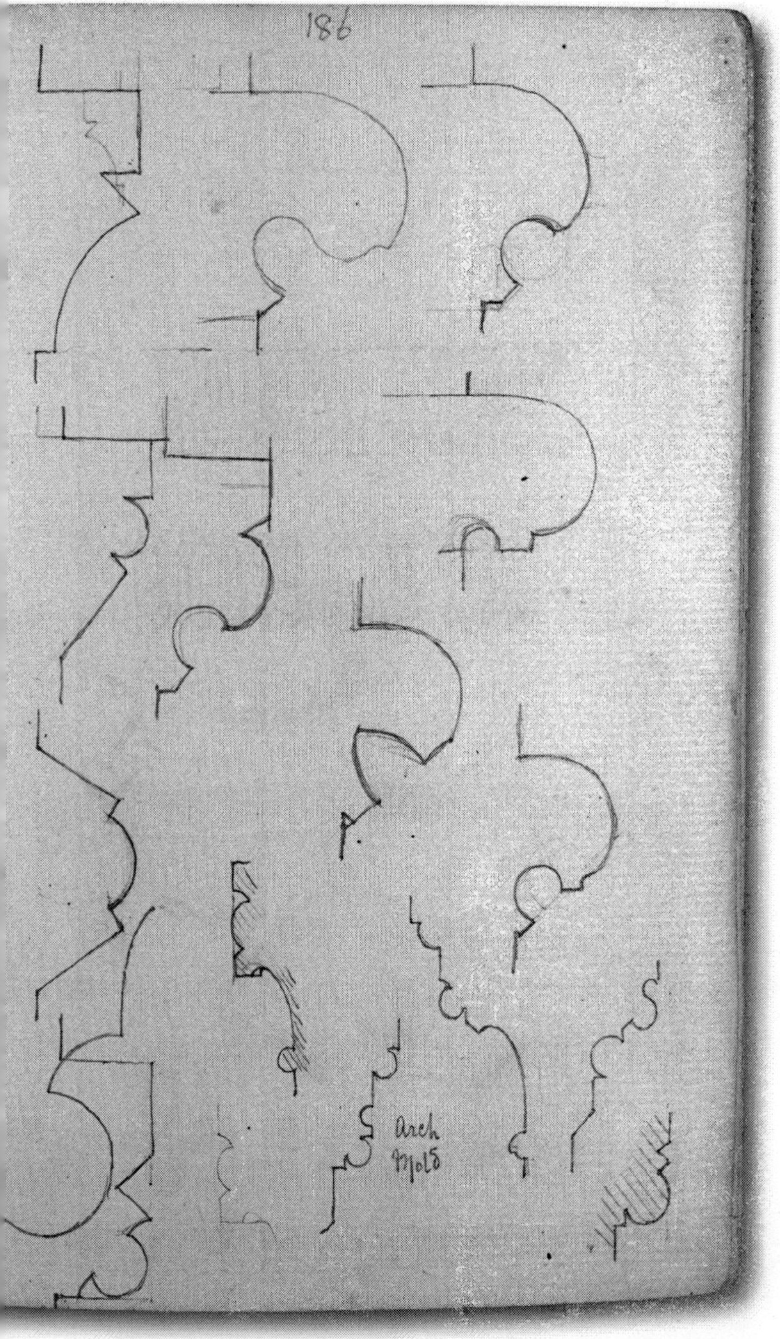
186
Arch
Mold

pp. 187 -- 188

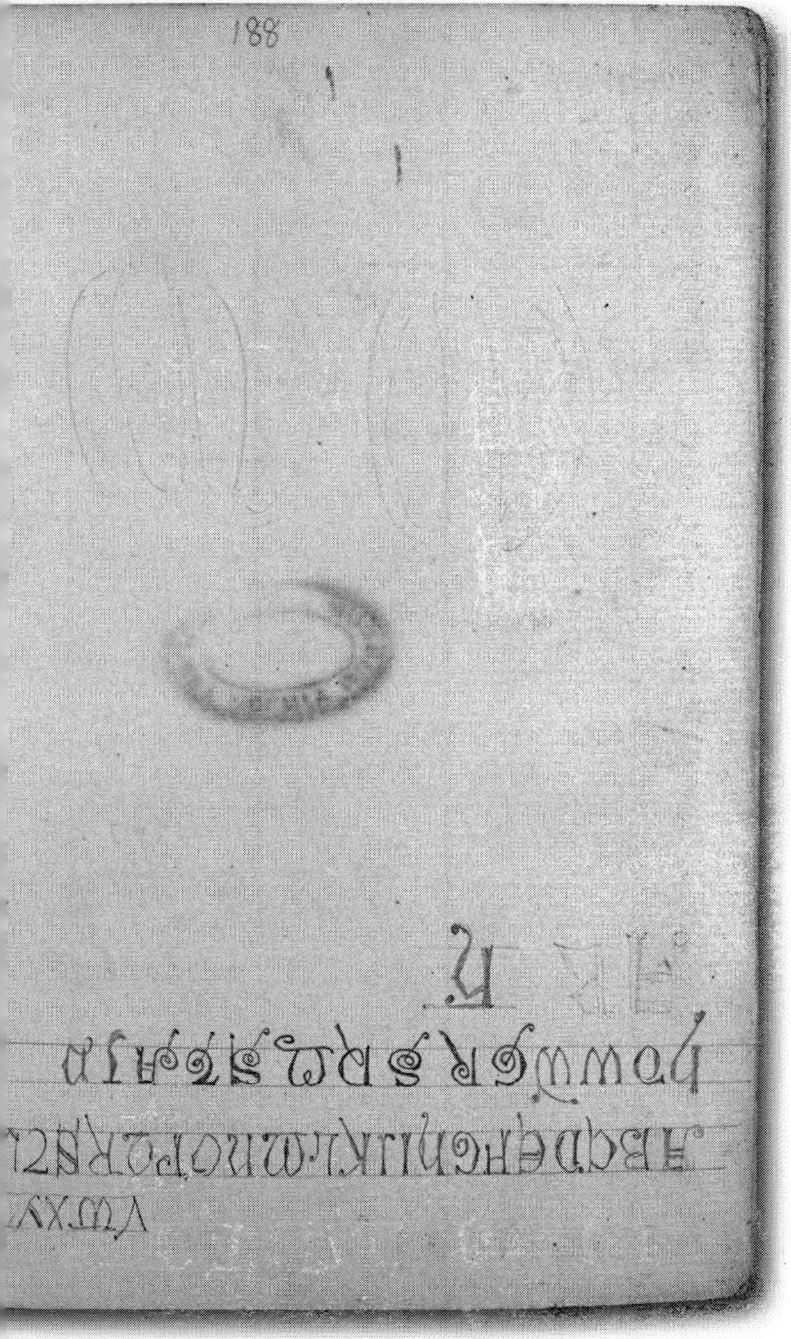

Indigo & Brown Madder — Slates -
Add Ind. Red - Dun Tiles
Ind Yell. & Crim. Lake — B. Stone
Pr. Blue & Ind Ink - Wood -
Ind Red, Indigo & {Bt Umber / Bt Sienna} (var) — Rubble & Rag -

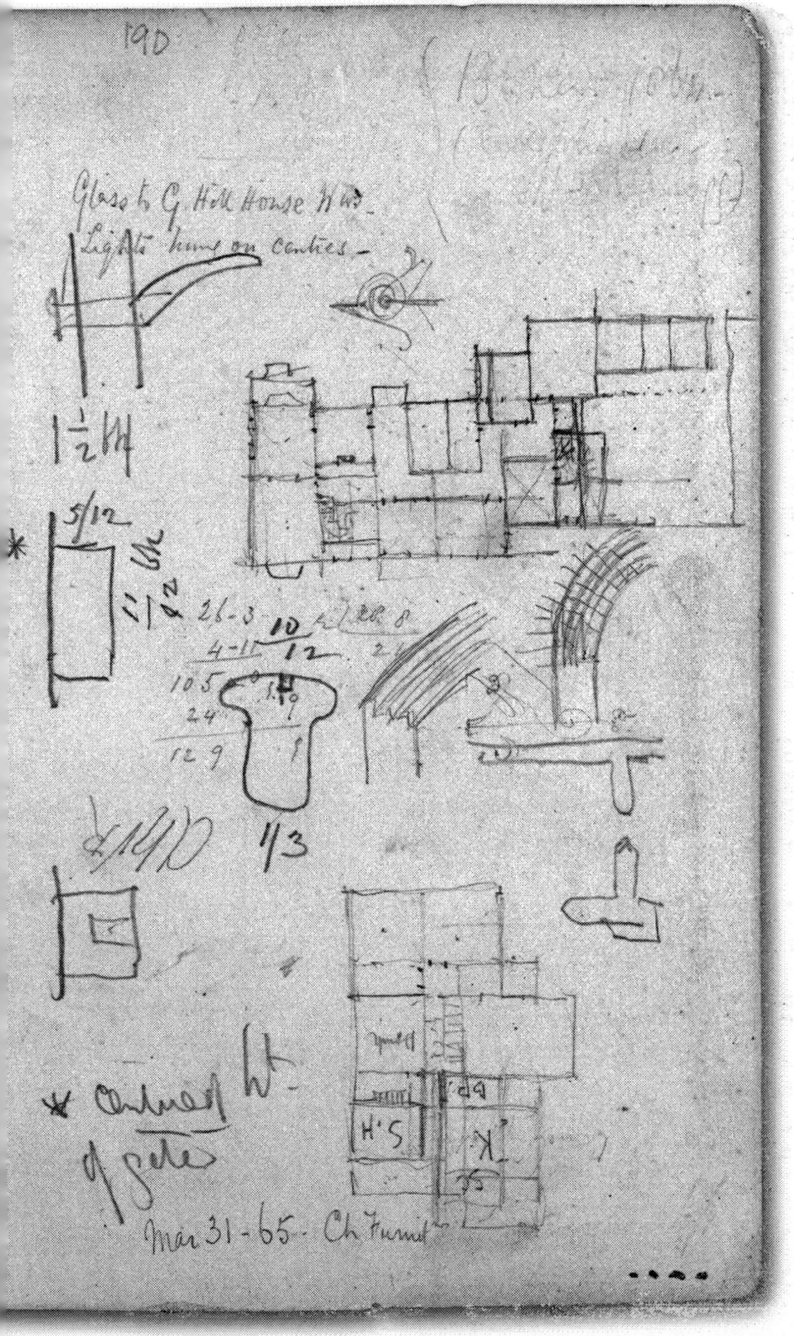
190
Glass to G. Hill House Wd.
Lights turne on centres
1 1/2 W
5/12
1/3
Mar 31 - 65 - Ch Furnit